JANE AUSTEN: *Emma* (Revi

U~~~~~~~~IES AT MEDWAY

BROWNING: *Men and Women' & Other Poems* J. R. Watson
CHAUCER: *The Canterbury Tales* J. J. Anderson
COLERIDGE: *'The Ancient Mariner' & Other Poems* Alun R. Jones & W. Tydeman
CONRAD:*'Heart of Darkness', 'Nostromo' & 'Under Western Eyes'* C. B. Cox
CONRAD: *The Secret Agent* Ian Watt
DICKENS: *Bleak House* A. E. Dyson
DICKENS: *'Hard Times', 'Great Expectations' & 'Our Mutual Friend"* Norman Page
DICKENS: *'Dombey and Son' & 'Little Dorrit'* Alan Shelston
DONNE: *Songs and Sonnets* Julian Lovelock
GEORGE ELIOT: *Middlemarch* Patrick Swinden
GEORGE ELIOT: *'The Mill on the Floss' & 'Silas Marner'* R. P. Draper
T.S. ELIOT: *Four Quartets*
T.S. ELIOT: *'Prufrock', 'Gerontion' & 'Ash Wednesday'* B. C. Southam
T.S. ELIOT: *The Waste Land* C. B. Cox & Arnold P. Hinchliffe
T.S. ELIOT: *Plays* Arnold P. Hinchliffe
HENRY FIELDING: *Tom Jones* Neil Compton
E.M. FORSTER: *A Passage to India* Malcolm Bradbury
WILLIAM GOLDING: *Novels 1954-64* Norman Page
HARDY: *The Tragic Novels* (Revised) R. P. Draper
HARDY: *Poems* James Gibson & Trevor Johnson
HARDY: *Three Pastoral Novels* R. P. Draper
GERARD MANLEY HOPKINS: *Poems* Margaret Bottrall
HENRY JAMES: *'Washington Square' & 'The Portrait of a Lady'* Alan Shelton
JONSON: *Volpone* Jonas A. Barish
JONSON: *'Every Man in his Humour' & 'The Alchemist'* R. V. Holdsworth
JAMES JOYCE: *'Dubliners' & 'A Portrait of the Artist as a Young Man'* Morris Beja
KEATS: *Odes* G. S. Fraser
KEATS: *Narrative Poems* John Spencer Hill
D.H. LAWRENCE: *Sons and Lovers* Gamini Salgado
D.H. LAWRENCE: *'The Rainbow' & 'Women in Love'* Colin Clarke
LOWRY: *Under the Volcano* Gordon Bowker
MARLOWE: *Doctor Faustus* John Jump
MARLOWE: *'Tamburlaine the Great', 'Edward II' & 'The Jew of Malta'* J. R. Brown
MARLOWE: *Poems* Arthur Pollard
MAUPASSANT: *In the Hall of Mirrors* T. Harris
MILTON: *Paradise Lost* A.E. Dyson & Julian Lovelock
O'CASEY: *'Juno and the Paycock', 'The Plough and the Stars' & 'The Shadow of a
  Gunman'* Ronald Ayling
EUGENE O'NEILL: *Three Plays* Normand Berlin
JOHN OSBORNE: *Look Back in Anger* John Russell Taylor
PINTER: *'The Birthday Party' & Other Plays* Michael Scott
POPE: *The Rape of the Lock* John Dixon Hunt
SHAKESPEARE: *A Midsummer Night's Dream* Antony Price
SHAKESPEARE: *Antony and Cleopatra* (Revised) John Russell Brown
SHAKESPEARE: *Coriolanus* B. A. Brockman

Issues in Contemporary Critical Theory

A CASEBOOK

EDITED BY

PETER BARRY

Published by
MACMILLAN PRESS LTD
Houndmills, Basingstoke, Hampshire RG21 6XS
and London
Companies and representatives
throughout the world

BWC

ISBN 0–333–39811–4 hardcover
ISBN 0–333–39812–2 paperback

A catalogue record for this book is available
from the British Library.

This book is printed on paper suitable for recycling and
made from fully managed and sustained forest sources.

10   9   8   7   6
05   04   03   02   01

Printed and bound in Great Britain by
Antony Rowe Ltd, Eastbourne

CONTENTS

GENERAL EDITOR'S PREFACE

The Casebook series, launched in 1968, has become a well-regarded library of critical studies. The central concern of the series remains the 'single-author' volume, but suggestions from the academic community have led to an extension of the original plan, to include occasional volumes on such general themes as literary 'schools' and genres.

Each volume in the central category deals either with one well-known and influential work by an individual author, or with closely related works by one writer. The main section consists of critical readings, mostly modern, collected from books and journals. A selection of reviews and comments by the author's contemporaries is also included, and sometimes comment from the author himself. The Editor's Introduction charts the reputation of the work or works from the first appearance to the present time.

Volumes in the 'general themes' category are variable in structure but follow the basic purpose of the series in presenting an integrated selection of readings, with an Introduction which explores the theme and discusses the literary and critical issues involved.

A single volume can represent no more than a small selection of critical opinions. Some critics are excluded for reasons of space, and it is hoped that readers will pursue the suggestions for further reading in the Select Bibliography. Other contributions are severed from their original context, to which some readers may wish to turn. Indeed, if they take a hint from the critics represented here, they certainly will.

A. E. DYSON

INTRODUCTION

During the past fifteen years or so important changes have taken place in literary studies. These changes are the product of a variety of pressures and influences – including marxism, feminism, linguistics and philosophy – which collectively have brought about a marked increase of interest in literary theory. Perhaps the word 'theory' gives the impression that criticism has entered a period of abstract internal debate of little interest to the teacher or student with no immediate professional stake in it. But this impression would be mistaken, for the questions now being asked are as far-reaching as those raised in the 1920s and 30s by T. S. Eliot, I. A. Richards, William Empson and F. R. Leavis: the pioneers whose work determined the direction taken by criticism until at least the 1960s. The consensus established by such figures (and represented here by the material in Part One) has now been profoundly shaken, the main areas of contention being indicated by the material in Part Two. Till recently, most of this new work had been broadly theoretical, and comparatively little had been done about converting large statements of intent into critical practice. For a time, indeed, it seemed that critical theory might replace literary criticism as the main activity in 'English' and related departments. But there is now evidence of a growing commitment to working again with literary texts in order to develop, not just a new theoretical framework, but a newly theoreticised practice of reading. Examples of this practice are to be found in Part Three.

Before discussing the specific items in the selection, it may be useful to sketch out, in a general way, the nature of the consensus which recent changes have effectively abolished. This consensus, as represented by the pieces in Part One, distinguished literature from autobiography (Eliot and Wimsatt), literary criticism from philosophy and sociology (Leavis), and the verbal essence of the text from constructs of the reader's such as plot, character and context (Knights and Wimsatt).

It should be emphasised, though, that conditions in Britain were somewhat different from those in the United States of America. In the former, sustained theoretical work virtually ended in the early 1930s, and from then on efforts were chiefly devoted to practical criticism. In the United States, the work of Eliot, Richards and Empson was an equally important influence, but it was built upon in a rather different way, resulting in a movement known as the New Criticism which laid greater stress than did English practical criticism upon working out a general theory of literary (especially poetic) meaning. The influence of the New Criticism extended from the early 1940s to the mid-1960s, and its highpoint was perhaps the publication of W. K. Wimsatt's *The Verbal Icon* in 1954. This book gave powerful formulations of the New Critical view of the poem as essentially a verbal complex of tensions, ironies, paradoxes and ambiguities, a textual network which could not be accounted for simply in terms of what an individual poet sat down with the intention of saying. Once the words were on the page they took on an autonomous existence, and to ignore this 'author-independent' dimension of the text was to be guilty of the 'intentional fallacy' (see Part One): as an autonomous verbal structure the poem did not communicate simple truths about life, and had to be understood as a 'verbal icon' whose main reference was to itself, rather than the world outside its textual borders.

This attitude towards literature has a long history and is often shared by writers themselves. T. S. Eliot, for instance, insisted upon the distinction between personal emotion and emotion as expressed in art; 'The emotion of art is impersonal', he wrote, '. . . the more perfect the artist, the more completely separate in him will be the man who suffers, and the mind which creates' (see Part One). American criticism, then, tended to present literature as a highly enigmatic form of utterance requiring expert exegesis and only fully comprehensible to a trained academic readership. In contrast, English practical criticism saw the literary work as part of a common culture, open to all (in theory, at least) and communicating truths and insights about common human experience, using, not a special tongue, but an intensified version of ordinary language.

Beneath these differences, though, English and American criticism shared a great deal, notably an acceptance of the tenets of Matthew Arnold's seminal essay, 'The Function of Criticism at the Present Time' (1864). Arnold saw the study of literature as a great civilising force, a substitute for religion in the post-religious age he saw approaching. Literary study should be 'disinterestedly intellectual' ('disinterested' is a key word in the essay) and should restrict itself to the 'free play of the mind' by 'keeping aloof from practice'. It should constitute a liberal and humane discipline whose object is to see without bias 'the object as in itself it really is'. In addition to this liberal ideal, English and American critics shared the belief that it was the critic's job to interpret the text, through which a human communication of some kind was taking place, whether its source was the author as such, or, in a more indirect way, an authorial persona the nature of which could only be deduced from the text. Thus, the two branches of Anglo-American criticism occupied adjacent plots within the same area of intellectual territory.

Why, then, was this consensus so dramatically broken at the end of the 1960s? One factor was the widespread 'student unrest' of the time which led to a general rejection of received academic practices within a highly politicised atmosphere. Fertile ground for curriculum change in Britain had already been prepared earlier in that decade with the founding of the new universities and the polytechnics to cater for the vastly expanded student body which resulted from acceptance of the principle of higher education for all qualified applicants. These institutions brought into being literature courses of a broader kind than had hitherto been seen; and as European literatures entered the curriculum, European critical traditions came with them, while inter-disciplinary courses gave currency to the methods of history, philosophy and linguistics. The momentum for change continued into the 1970s when former colleges of education began to teach 'diversified' (that is, non-teacher-training) degrees within structures much more flexible than those of the university single-subject tradition. So, by the early 1970s, texts from the major European movements in criticism were being translated and made widely available. These changes were not universally welcomed, of course, and their opponents attacked the new influences with anger and hostility. Supporters, naturally, replied in the same vein, and by the late 1970s civil war seemed to have broken out in English Departments. This came briefly to the notice of a wider public in Britain in 1981 when the newspapers reported the 'MacCabe affair' in which a young academic named Colin MacCabe, allegedly a structuralist, did not have his contract at Cambridge made permanent, and deep divisions were revealed between his opponents and his supporters. It became common to speak of the 'crisis' in English Studies, and though the polemical heat was dissipated within a year or so, the basic issues remain in contention. They are illustrated here by the material in Part Two.

One of the most acrimonious areas of debate in the late 1970s and early 80s concerned the question of whether or not there is really any need for literary theory. A vigorous English tradition has always maintained that there is not, and the material selected here to represent this point of view is a section from George Watson's book *The Discipline of English*. Watson argues that literary theory is usually reductive, tending to present oversimplified views of literary works in order to make them conform to general rules. Against this tendency he insists that our knowledge of literature is no less profound when we cannot spell it out in terms of general formulae. In opposition to this is set a lengthy extract from Jonathan Dollimore's essay 'Beyond Essentialist Humanism', a difficult piece, but one which well repays the effort of serious study, for it is a strongly argued exposition of an approach to literature which combines marxism and post-structuralism, and represents some of the most challenging work now being undertaken. He argues that explicit theory *is* needed because it is the only way to break the hold of a criticism so familiar that it has become 'naturalised' (that is, it has come to seem the natural and inevitable way of studying literature, so that no specific defence of it is required). He shows how this practice embodies a range of conservative assumptions and argues the need to 'deconstruct' these (that is, to destroy them by demonstrating their inherent inconsistencies and contradictions) – in particular, such ideas as 'human nature', 'literature' and 'the individual', in so far as these are seen as fixed entities which have an existence prior to or beyond the social functions and structures in which we encounter them.

A second and, obviously, related area of debate is the question of how the literary text relates to or portrays its author and the world beyond it. Is the text to be seen 'expressively' (as the expression of its author's views and feelings) or is it, as Roland Barthes argues here in the extract from 'The Death of the Author', merely 'a tissue of signs' to be read in such a way that 'at all its levels the author is absent'? Though this point of view was not new to Anglo-American criticism, it had never before been argued with such uncompromising rigour to the conclusion that in the absence of the author 'the claim to decipher a text becomes futile'. The discussion is taken up by Denis Donoghue who divides reading strategies into two types, epireading and graphireading. The former hears a voice in the text, the voice of the author, and believes that the text represents the voice of this absent speaker, enabling a communication between author and reader to take place through the medium of the text. Donoghue uses Derrida's word 'logocentrism' (meaning, roughly, that texts say one thing only, which is what their authors intended them to say) to describe this attitude. Graphireading, on the other hand, is the reading strategy which follows upon the 'death of the author': a written text is beyond its author's control, like a dog let off the leash in the park, and the result is an inexhaustible semantic profusion.

Another characteristic of the epireader is accepting the text as 'mimetic' or 'representational', seeing it as a window which presents us with the human world beyond its borders. Would it not be more accurate, recent theorists ask, to regard the text as, so to speak, a stained-glass window, meant to be looked *at* rather than through? Again, this is not a new idea in Anglo-American criticism, for L. C. Knights in the 1930s had argued a 'stained-glass' (or 'formalist') view of literature (see Part One). A. D. Nuttall, in his book *A New Mimesis*, argues against Knights and more recent proponents of this point of view. He coins the terms 'opaque' and 'transparent' criticism (roughly corresponding, respectively, to Donoghue's graphireading and epireading) for these two opposed approaches. The opaque critic does not look through and beyond the text but concentrates on matters of style, internal organisation and cross-references to other literary works, while the transparent critic accepts the text as a representation of the world beyond. Nuttall's own sympathies lie with transparent criticism, but readers may react impatiently to the discussion on the grounds that literature obviously has both a 'clear glass' and a 'stained glass' dimension, and cannot usefully be spoken of as entirely one or the other. It is worth reminding ourselves, though, that the 'opaque' critic recommends, not an absurdity, but a pervasive awareness of the mechanisms of the text, the ways in which it is constantly constructing, editing, ordering and juxtaposing its effects in order to determine the reader's response.

The third section in Part Two looks again at the question of language and literature, but from a rather different perspective. Essentially the issues concern the relevance to literary criticism of methods derived from linguistics. Debate on this matter has long been waged, and with considerable bitterness. Literary critics have suspected the linguists of aiming to turn criticism into a branch of applied linguistics, while linguists have accused the critics of relying upon intuitive methods which mystify the nature of literary effects and processes. Roger Fowler's essay is admirably comprehensive in its account of stylistics (that is, the application of linguistic methods to the literary text) and it includes a section of practical analysis which will make clear the difference between stylistics and Practical or New Criticism. For, while these latter schools also scrutinised literary language very minutely, they did so within the confines of an untechnical vocabulary, using terms such as 'imagery', 'irony', 'ambiguity', 'nuance', and 'connotation' which would be familiar to lay-people without a linguistic training. In contrast, stylistics uses a wide range of specialist terms and concepts taken from the science of linguistics – terms such as 'transitivity' or 'underlexicalisation' (both explained in Fowler's essay) – which have no currency outside the linguistic field.

The second piece in this section is by Stanley Fish, an American critic of great persuasive power who is, paradoxically, both a practitioner of stylistics (his own version of it, which he calls 'affective stylistics', sometimes regarded as a form of reader-response criticism) and an opponent of it. His essay illustrates and criticises the methods of mainstream stylistics. He argues that most stylisticians wrongly assume the neutrality and objectivity of the process of unearthing the linguistic data on which their conclusions are to be based. In practice, he claims, not all the linguistic data in a poem can be relevant to a given argument or interpretation; and, as there is no linguistic way of separating relevant from irrelevant data, it must follow that the act of selecting and laying out the data is a subjective interpretative act, not an objective descriptive one. Without a dimension which is neutrally objective and descriptive, the claims of stylistics to go even a little way beyond the impressionism of ordinary criticism are called seriously into question. Fish argues further that it is not a fixed standard of neutral objectivity which determines how interpretations are made, but the norms established by what he calls the 'interpretive community'. Nevertheless, by its practitioners, at least, it is now usually taken for granted that stylistics is a more 'objective' method than others, though it has to be said that critics of other persuasions continue to regard it with uneasy distrust.

The fourth section in Part Two is devoted to post-structuralism and deconstruction, both of which derive from structuralism, a movement which began in France in the 1950s in the work of Roland Barthes and the anthropologist Claude Lévi-Strauss. It has its roots in the thinking of the Swiss linguist Ferdinand de Saussure (1857–1913) and it regards the workings of language as described by Saussure as the key to all signifying systems, whether they be works of literature, tribal rituals, advertisements, fashions in clothing or anything else. Saussure emphasised the purely 'conventional' and 'relational' nature of the linguistic signs which constitute a language. Thus, the sense of a word such as 'hut' is maintained by convention only, since there is no inherent connection between the word and the object it signifies. The sense can also be described as 'relational', for the word depends for its meaning upon its position in a continuum of related terms – 'hovel', 'shed', 'hut', 'mansion', 'palace' – all of which would be subtly altered in meaning if any of the others were removed from the sequence. Saussure showed that 'differencing' networks like this are characteristic of languages, and he summed this up in his famous dictum: 'In a language there are only differences, without fixed terms.' This notion of meaning as conventional, relational and self-referential, rather than securely fixed to external reality, has greatly influenced all the new critical theories and is found in many different guises.

The structuralist critic examines literature in similar terms. Thus, no individual poem has significance in isolation – it can be understood only in terms of the relationship between itself and the structure of expectations (of period, of genre and of poetry itself) which exists in the reader's mind. Understanding this structure is more important than interpreting the individual poem, just as for the linguist the aim is not the interpretation of a given remark in (say) English, but the investigation of the structure known as 'English', which must have a prior existence in the speaker's mind, and within which alone the remark can make sense. Likewise, the structuralist insists that such mental constructs as 'literature' and 'poetry' are 'conventional' – they cannot give us an accurate representation of things outside, so that effectively what they tell us about is our own minds and how we perceive and structure reality. Thus, the structuralist looks at perceiving, not percepts, regards species (the Novel, for instance) as more important that specimens (*Middlemarch*, for instance), and always considers networks of interrelationships rather than individual items. Structuralism, then, is intellectualised and often abstract, playing down the concrete instance in favour of the broader generality, and necessarily relegating the close reading of individual texts to a relatively minor status. The challenge it represents to the familiar Anglo-American critical outlook is therefore easy to understand.

Post-structuralism shares all these characteristics, but it is more properly a denial of aspects of structuralism than a development from it. It, too, goes back to Saussure, but it accuses the structuralists of not following through the implications of his work. Post-structuralists accept Saussure's views about the impossibility of fixed and intrinsic meanings, but they deny that a system which consists solely of interrelationships can produce a reliable system of signification. The prime theorist of post-structuralism is the French philosopher Jacques Derrida, who agrees that words can only be defined by their differences from each other, but shows that all the words in the system relate to each other in an anarchic and unquantifiable way (partly because of the pervasiveness of metaphorical roots and interconnections) rather than through neat pairings of binary opposites, or sequences of near synonyms of the kind envisaged by Saussure. Thus, meaning recedes further and further away from us the more we enquire into it; it is endlessly *deferred* and endlessly *differed*: two words Derrida combines to give the coinage *différance*. The play of *différance* through every level of the text means that we constantly encounter *aporias* (cul-de-sacs) where our search for meaning is blocked, leaving us with a tissue of gaps, slippages, discontinuities and lacunae before which a critic is as helpless as any other reader. Deconstruction is the kind of reading which results: its aim is to trace and expose the self-contradictions and discontinuities which result from the play of *différance* and ultimately defeat the possibility of coherent communication.

The pieces in section 4 of Part Two are, first, a basic exposition of Derrida's thought by Jonathan Culler, who is one of the best-known exponents of post-structuralist theory. The second piece is a critique of aspects of Derrida's thought and influence by Nicolas Tredell, who is sceptical about deconstruction's claims that it is both intellectually and politically radical. The issues debated by these contributors are of crucial importance, since Derrida, in effect, argues the inefficacy of language itself as a communicative medium. If he is right, the effect of his work on literary criticism would be to terminate it altogether.

The final section of Part Two concerns reader-response criticism – an approach to the text which originated in Germany in the late 1960s – and devotes its main attention, not to the words on the page, but to the interaction between those words and the reader, regarding the literary work as a joint construct. We might imagine the literary work as a building which is erected by the reader using plans supplied by the author; but these plans do not programme the reader's response in an automatic way, and are sometimes more like an outline sketch than a detailed blue-print, leaving a good deal to be supplied from the reader's own resources. The complex processes which take place in the reader's mind are described in the densely-written and thought-provoking piece by Wolfgang Iser. He shows that when we think about a novel the entity to which we devote our attention is not fixed and determinate like print but a shifting and dynamic complex produced by the various reading processes which he describes. These include: the 'concretisation' of the text (the reader's filling out of the authorial sketches); the foreshortening in the memory of passages previously read; the gradual building up of the 'virtual dimension' of the text (the part which comes into existence with the reading and is not actually on the printed page); the interaction among anticipated events, 'present' events and events held in the mind retrospectively; the phenomenon of 'advance retrospection' which occurs on second reading when we know in advance what happens next and interpret previous events in that light; the grouping together of incidents in the mind which results in a 'configurative meaning' (or thematic viewpoint) being imposed upon the text; and, finally, the 'alien associations' which we subsequently perceive and which lead us to modify or develop our previously constructed configurative meaning.

The great strength of Iser's work is to emphasise that reading is creative and is not just a passive taking in by the reader of the author's words. Iser's descriptions of the reading process are especially useful to students and teachers of literature, for we do not just read novels privately but go on to discuss them in tutorials and seminars during which the very mechanisms described by Iser can be seen in action constructing a *Little Dorrit* or a *Great Gatsby* which is quite distinct from the words printed on the pages in front of us.

The second piece in this concluding section of Part Two is a trenchant criticism by Terry Eagleton of reader-response work, which also contains useful exposition. He points out, in effect, that while reader-response criticism, like post-structuralism, is very much aware of the gaps and indeterminacies in the text, it envisages these as being smoothly filled in by the reader to produce a reliable structure with stable and completed meanings. Post-structuralism, by contrast, sees these gaps as disruptive of stable meaning, resulting in textual disorder and conceptual challenge. For Eagleton, the reader-response scenario always envisages a calm and successful outcome to the reader's encounter with the text, with never any question of the building being left uncompleted, or the architect's authority being challenged. Art is thereby seen as a collaboration rather than a transgression, and the social or political power of literature on the Iserian model must therefore, in Eagleton's view, be limited.

Though Part Three is predominantly practical, it is also intended as a supplement to the overall picture provided in Part Two. Separate subsections are not given in Part Two to marxist, feminist and psychoanalytic criticism, on the grounds that each derives from a vast body of non-literary theory which could not usefully be extracted from for a volume such as the present one. Marxist criticism, however, is seen in a recent and highly sophisticated form in Jonathan Dollimore's piece in the first section of Part Two, and feminist criticism is given substantial representation in Part Three in the work of Rachel Brownstein, Penny Boumelha and Lisa Jardine.

Feminist criticism derives from a series of twentieth-century founding texts – Virginia Woolf's *A Room of One's Own* (1929), Simone de Beauvoir's *The Second Sex* (1949) and Kate Millett's *Sexual Politics* (1970) – which in turn build upon a tradition of feminist writings from the nineteenth century. In the early part of the present phase of feminist criticism, during the late 1960s and early 70s, the major effort was devoted to showing how literature perpetuated the oppressive 'patriarchal' mechanisms which feminists had identified in society: sexism, the double standard of sexual morality, stereotyping in representations of women, and so on. The works examined were 'androtexts' (books by men), and Kate Millett's reading of D. H. Lawrence in *Sexual Politics* was an influential model. This merged into a second stage in which 'gynotexts' (books by women) became the centre of attention, the object being to describe and analyse the special qualities of women's style (an investigation sometimes called 'gender stylistics') and women's ways of perceiving and 'constructing' the world. The writers studied were those already of 'canonical' status, that is, figures such as Jane Austen, the Brontës and George Eliot who were already regarded, within the 'phallocratic' (male-dominated) culture as part of the central literary tradition. This in turn merged into a third stage which has two major variants. The first of these rejected the phallocratic map of the canon and began to redraw it so as to include female writers hitherto regarded as minor figures or else entirely forgotten. The second variant is more complex and eclectic; it draws upon a wide range of modern literary theory (marxist, psychoanalytic and post-structuralist, for instance) and upon documentary evidence in order to examine the ways in which femininity is 'socially constructed and conditioned'. The writers included here represent this second variant of the most recent stage of feminist critical writing.

This is followed by a brief extract from the work of the Soviet critic Mikhail Bakhtin (1895–1975) whose major writings were produced in the 1930s but only effectively published and promulgated in the 1960s and 70s. Bakhtin admires the way the literary text is never 'univocal' (single-voiced) but generates a riotous plurality of meanings. He sees this as being especially so of the novel, which for him is characterised by its 'heteroglossia' (the word means 'different tongues') whereby the text provides us with a dialogue or carnival of many different voices, some ironic, some humorous, some self-mocking or self-parodying. Within this textual carnival there can be no place for the reasoned, authoritative, single voice to silence all others and impose a fixed and reliable version of the events depicted, for the text is by nature anarchic rather than authoritarian. All this has been favourably received within the climate of opinion created by structuralism and post-structuralism, and Bakhtin is a critic whose influence is growing. Even from the extract printed here it will be seen that he is able, in a remarkable way, to combine the virtues of the graphireader and the epireader, the opaque and the transparent critic.

The extract from the work of Robert Scholes has a double purpose in the context of the present collection. Firstly, it gives a summary of another aspect of the thinking of Roland Barthes, showing him as 'narratologist', working out the rules which underlie all narratives. This exemplifies the traditional concern of the structuralist with the system (narrative as such in this case) rather than the individual item (in this case a given story). Secondly, Scholes gives an example of how the structuralist would use the system to 'decode' an actual story, the specimen used being James Joyce's 'Eveline' which is widely available and not reprinted here.

By contrast, the following piece, by the French critic Lucette Finas, is an example of post-structuralist practical criticism. She analyses a short story called 'The Brigands' by Villiers de l'Isle Adam (1839–89), which will probably be less familiar to most readers and is therefore reprinted here immediately after her essay. The unfamiliarity of the subject material is more an advantage than otherwise for it means that we approach the essay with fewer preconceptions than would normally be the case. One of the most evident qualities of the piece is that it is itself structured with an aesthetic or artistic purpose. As Roland Barthes said in his introduction to her collection *Le Bruit d'Iris*, Finas's writing 'accepts itself as a *text*'. The critic sees no dichotomy between critical and creative writing, and her aim (as she has said of her work) is to 'exploit' the text rather than just to explicate it. For Barthes she demonstrates an 'excess in reading' which results from slowing down the tempo of the text so that it is 'read slowly, in eccentric waves' bringing about an effect like intoxication. For Denis Donoghue, more soberly, her work shows us 'what a Derridean criticism would look like, diligently pursued' (*Ferocious Alphabets*, p. 187).

Two contrasting pieces of poetry criticism follow: in the first, H. G. Widdowson applies the methods of stylistics to Philip Larkin's poem 'Mr Bleaney's Room' (which he quotes in full); in the second, a reading of George Herbert's 'Prayer (1)', Bernard Sharratt exemplifies the deconstructionist method of interrogating a text up to and beyond the point where its communicative efficacy breaks down. The lively intensity of this piece seems, like Finas's approach, to result in an intoxicating excess of reading, and again the critic is highly conscious of the aesthetic status of his own work, constructing an elaborate fictional context for his reading whereby, under a name not his own which amalgamates those of two novelists ('Lawrence Fielding'), he 'reviews' the work of an imaginary critic whose name ('John Joseph Andrews') is like that of a character in a novel – all this set in the future in the pages of an invented critical journal called *New Crisis Quarterly*.

The piece which follows this, by the French post-structuralist Jacques Lacan, represents psychoanalytic criticism: an approach which, in its early stages, had been content to demonstrate the presence of classic Freudian complexes (such as the Oedipal conflict or the death wish) in the authors of literary works or in the characters depicted within them. Typical examples would be Ernest Jones's reading of *Hamlet* as an Oedipal drama (*A Psychoanalytic Study of Hamlet*, 1922) and Marie Bonaparte's analysis of the tales of Edgar Allen Poe in terms of sexual repression and the mother fixation (*The Life and Works of Edgar Allen Poe*, English translation 1949), both these having the approval of Freud himself. In effect, such work amounted to little more than quarrying literature for evidence favourable to Freudian theory and it quickly acquired a bad reputation for reducing fiction and drama to ready-made psychological formulae.

A more sophisticated phase ensued in which attention moved from author and character to reader and text. Lacan argued that, since the unconscious is structured like a language, an analysis of the linguistic structure of a text, conducted according to psychological principles, would reveal things about the unconscious and about basic psychic drives. His work has proved particularly attractive to feminist critics, who see it as relatively free from the 'androcentric' bias of classic Freudianism. In the piece included here Lacan is seen, in characteristic guise, revising and rewriting Freud. He modifies the simple Freudian-Jonesian view of Hamlet as an Oedipal son, for though Oedipus also figures in Lacan's account of *Hamlet* he does so within the context of a far wider-ranging account of the structures and significance of desire, mourning, curtailment, secrecy, guilt, retribution and punishment. Whereas Freud and Jones stressed the similarities between *Hamlet* and Sophocles's play *Oedipus Rex*, Lacan stresses the differences; and just as the individual life, as Freud says, acts out the Oedipal drama but in a distorted or modified form, so *Hamlet* provides only a partial enactment of Freud's Oedipal theory. Of course, the brief extract does not do justice to the subtleties of Lacan's lengthy reading of the play, nor can it give even a glimpse of the complexities of his theoretical system; but it does show that psychological criticism can enrich rather than impoverish our view of a text, even one as exhaustively analysed as *Hamlet*.

A word, finally, about how this book might be used. The selections are intended to provide material for discussion and debate on all the issues raised. No attempt is made to reconcile, or adjudicate between, the different viewpoints represented. It is essentially a workbook for those who, though committed to the reading and discussion of chosen literary texts, also recognise the fact that close reading cannot take place in a theoretical vacuum. Guidance for further reading is given in the bibliography, which is divided into sections roughly corresponding to the viewpoints and critical genres presented in our selection.

PART ONE

Early Modern Viewpoints: The Critical Background to Contemporary Debates

T. S. Eliot   (1919)

'The Impersonality of Poetry'

. . . What happens [to the poet in the act of poetic composition] is a continual surrender of himself as he is at the moment to something which is more valuable. The progress of an artist is a continual self-sacrifice, a continual extinction of personality. . . . the mind of the mature poet differs from that of the immature one . . . by being a more finely perfectly medium in which special, or very varied, feelings are at liberty to enter into new combinations. . . . The mind of the poet . . . may partly or exclusively operate upon the experience of the man himself; but, the more perfect the artist, the more completely separate in him will be the man who suffers, and the mind which creates; the more perfectly will the mind digest and transmute the passions which are its material. . . . My meaning is, that the poet has, not a 'personality' to express, but a particular medium, which is only a medium and not a personality, in which impressions and experiences combine in peculiar and unexpected ways. Impressions and experiences which are important for the man may take no place in the poetry, and those which become important in the poetry may play quite a negligible part in the man, the personality. . . . It is not in his personal emotions, the emotions provoked by particular events in his life, that the poet is in any way remarkable or interesting. His particular emotions may be simple, or crude, or flat. The emotion in his poetry will be a very complex thing, but not with the complexity of the emotions of people who have very complex or unusual emotions in life. . . . The business of the poet is not to find new emotions, but to use the ordinary ones and, in working them up into poetry, to express feelings which are not in actual emotions at all. . . . There are many people who appreciate the expression of sincere emotion in verse, and there is a smaller number of people who can appreciate technical excellence. But very few know when there is an expression of *significant* emotion, emotion which has its life in the poem and not in the history of the poet. The emotion of art is impersonal. And the poet cannot reach this impersonality without surrendering himself wholly to the work to be done. . . .

SOURCE: extracts from 'Tradition and the Individual Talent' (1919); reprinted in *Selected Essays* (London, 1932; 3rd edition 1951), excerpted from pp. 17–22.

L. C. Knights   (1933)

'Literature as Complex Language rather than *Plot*, *Character* and
Theme'

. . . In the mass of Shakespeare criticism there is not a hint that
'character' – like 'plot', 'rhythm', 'construction' and all our other
critical counters – is merely an abstraction from the total response in
the mind of the reader or spectator, brought into being by written or
spoken words; that the critic therefore – however far he may
ultimately range – begins with the words of which a play is composed.
This applies equally to the novel or any other form of art that uses
language as its medium. 'A Note on Fiction' by Mr C. H. Rickword in
The Calendar of Modern Letters expresses the point admirably with
regard to the novel: 'The form of a novel only exists as a balance of
response on the part of the reader. Hence schematic plot is a
construction of the reader's that corresponds to an aspect of the
response and stands in merely diagrammatic relation to the source.
Only as precipitates from the memory are plot or character tangible;
yet only in solution have either any emotive valency.'[1]

A Shakespeare play is a dramatic poem. It uses action, gesture,
formal grouping and symbols, and it relies upon the general
conventions governing Elizabethan plays. But, we cannot too often
remind ourselves, its end is to communicate a rich and controlled
experience by means of words – words used in a way to which, without
some training, we are no longer accustomed to respond. To stress in
the conventional way character or plot or any of the other
abstractions that can be made, is to impoverish the total response. 'It
is in the total situation rather than in the wrigglings of individual
emotion that the tragedy lies.'[2] 'We should not look for perfect
verisimilitude to life', says Mr Wilson Knight, 'but rather see each
play as an expanded metaphor, by means of which the original vision
has been projected into forms roughly correspondent with actuality,
conforming thereto with greater or less exactitude according to the
demands of its nature. . . . The persons, ultimately, are not human at
all, but purely symbols of a poetic vision.'[3] . . .

Since everyone who has written about Shakespeare probably
imagines that he has 'treated him primarily as a poet', some
explanation is called for. How should we read Shakespeare?

We start with so many lines of verse on a printed page which we read as we should read any other poem. We have to elucidate the meaning (using Dr Richards's fourfold definition[4]) and to unravel ambiguities; we have to estimate the kind and quality of the imagery and determine the precise degree of evocation of particular figures; we have to allow full weight to each word, exploring its 'tentacular roots', and to determine how it controls and is controlled by the rhythmic movement of the passage in which it occurs. In short, we have to decide exactly why the lines 'are so and not otherwise'.

As we read other factors come into play. The lines have a cumulative effect. 'Plot', aspects of 'character' and recurrent 'themes' – all 'precipitates from the memory' – help to determine our reaction at a given point. There is a constant reference backwards and forwards. But the work of detailed analysis continues to the last line of the last act. If the razor-edge of sensibility is blunted at any point we cannot claim to have read what Shakespeare wrote, however often our eyes may have travelled over the page. A play of Shakespeare's is a precise particular experience, a poem – and precision and particularity are exactly what is lacking in the greater part of Shakespeare criticism, criticism that deals with *Hamlet* or *Othello* in terms of abstractions that have nothing to do with the unique arrangement of words that constitutes these plays. . . .

SOURCE: extracts from *How Many Children Had Lady Macbeth?: An Essay in the Theory and Practice of Shakespeare Criticism* (Cambridge, 1933); reprinted in *'Hamlet' and Other Essays* (Cambridge, 1979), pp. 273–4 & 285–6.

NOTES

[Reorganised and renumbered from the original – Ed.]

1. [Ed.] Rickword edited the *Calendar*, a forerunner of Leavis's *Scrutiny*, in the 1920s. His point is that plot and character are retrospective constructs in the reader's mind, rather than part of the text itself: or, in the terms of a later critic, Wolfgang Iser, they are part of the 'configurative meaning' which is produced when 'we reduce the polysemantic possibilities [of a text] to a single interpretation'. See section 5 of Part Two, below.

2. M. C. Bradbrook, *Elizabethan Stage Conditions* (1932), p. 102.

3. G. Wilson Knight, *The Wheel of Fire* (1930), p. 16.

4. [Ed.] The critic I. A. Richards defined meaning as comprising Sense, Feeling, Tone and Intention, these being, respectively, the thing to be communicated, the writer's attitude towards it, the writer's attitude towards the audience, and the effect the writer wishes to communicate.

F. R. Leavis   (1937)

'The Distinction between Literary Criticism and Philosophy'

[Leavis is here replying to an essay by the Czech-American critic René
Wellek, who had argued the need for literary critics to spell out their
principles of interpretation in a way which would meet philosophical
criteria – Ed.] . . . Literary criticism and philosophy seem to me to be
quite distinct and different kinds of discipline – at least, I think they
ought to be. . . . I should not find it easy to define the difference
satisfactorily, but Dr Wellek knows what it is and could give at least
as good an account of it as I could. Philosophy, we say, is 'abstract'
(thus Dr Wellek asks me to defend my position 'more abstractly'),
and poety 'concrete'. Words in poetry invite us, not to 'think about'
and judge but to 'feel into' or 'become' – to realise a complex
experience that is given in the words. They demand, not merely a
fuller-bodied response, but a completer responsiveness – a kind of
responsiveness that is incompatible with the judicial, one-eye-on-the-
standard approach suggested by Dr Wellek's phrase: 'your "norm"
with which you measure every poet.' The critic – the reader of poetry
– is indeed concerned with evaluation, but to figure him as measuring
with a norm which he brings up to the object and applies from the
outside is to misrepresent the process. The critic's aim is, first, to
realise as sensitively and completely as possible this or that which
claims his attention; and a certain valuing is implicit in the
realising. . . . It would be reasonable to fear – to fear blunting of edge,
blurring of focus and muddled misdirection of attention:
consequences of queering one discipline with the habits of another.
The business of the literary critic is to attain a peculiar completeness
of response and to observe a peculiarly strict relevance in developing
his response into commentary; he must be on his guard against
abstracting improperly from what is in front of him and against any
premature or irrelevant generalising – of it or from it. His first concern
is to enter into possession of the given poem (let us say) in its concrete
fulness, and his constant concern is never to lose his completeness of
possession, but rather to increase it. . . .

From this consistency and this coherence (in so far as I have
achieved them) it should, of course, be possible to elicit principles and
abstractly formulable norms. . . . I think I have gone as far in
explicitness as I could profitably attempt to go, and that I do not see

what would be gained by the kind of explicitness [Wellek] demands. . . . If, as I did, I avoided such generalities, it was not out of timidity; it was because they seemed too clumsy to be of any use. I thought I had provided something better. My whole effort was to work in terms of concrete judgements and particular analyses: 'This – doesn't it? – bears such a relation to that; this kind of thing – don't you find it so? – wears better than that,' etc. . . .

SOURCE: extracts from 'Literary Criticism and Philosophy: A Reply', *Scrutiny* (June 1937), vol. 6, excerpted from pp. 60–3.

W. K. Wimsatt & Monroe C. Beardsley   (1946)

'Authorial Intention and the Distinction between Internal (textual) and External (biographical) Evidence'

. . . The meaning of a poem may certainly be a personal one, in the sense that a poem expresses a personality or state of soul rather than a physical object like an apple. But even a short lyric poem is dramatic, the response of a speaker (no matter how abstractly conceived) to a situation (no matter how universalised). We ought to impute the thoughts and attitudes of the poem immediately to the dramatic *speaker*, and if to the author at all, only by an act of biographical inference. . . .

There is a difference between internal and external evidence for the meaning of a poem. And the paradox is only verbal and superficial that what is (1) internal is also public: it is discovered through the semantics and syntax of a poem, through our habitual knowledge of the language, through grammars, dictionaries and all the literature which is the source of dictionaries, in general through all that makes a language and culture; while what is (2) external is private or idiosyncratic; not a part of the work as a linguistic fact: it consists of revelations (in journals, for example, or letters or reported conversations) about how or why the poet wrote the poem – to what lady, while sitting on what lawn, or at the death of what friend or brother. There is (3) an intermediate kind of evidence about the character of the author or about private or semi-private meanings attached to words or topics by an author or by a coterie of which he is a member. The meaning of words is the history of words, and the biography of an author, his use of a word and the associations which the word had for *him*, are part of the word's history and meaning. But the three types of evidence, especially (2) and (3), shade into one another so subtly that it is not always easy to draw a line between examples, and hence arises the difficulty for criticism. The use of biographical evidence need not involve intentionalism, because while it may be evidence of what the author intended, it may also be evidence of the meaning of his words and the dramatic character of his utterance. On the other hand, it may not be all this. And a critic who is concerned with evidence of type (1) and moderately with that of type (3) will in the long run produce a different sort of comment from that of the critic who is concerned (2) and with (3) where it shades into (2). . . .

SOURCE: extract from 'The Intentional Fallacy' (1946); reproduced in Wimsatt's *The Verbal Icon: Studies in the Meaning of Poetry* (Lexington and London, 1954, 1967), pp. 5 & 10–11.

F. R. Leavis   (1953)

'The Separation between a Poem and its Social Context'

[Leavis is here replying to an essay by the critic F. W. Bateson, who had argued the relevance of 'social context' to the interpretation of poetry – Ed.] . . . He starts from the commonplace observation that a poem is in some way related to the world in which it was written. He arrives by a jump (at least, his arrival there is not by any steps of sober reasoning) at the assumption that the way to achieve the correct reading of a poem – of, say, Marvell's or Pope's – is to put it back in its 'total context' in that world. No idea of such an undertaking troubles the reader whose attention is really and intelligently focussed upon the poem, and if the undertaking were proposed to him he would see its absurdity at once. He would see that it was gratuitous, and worse; and at the same time he would see that any achievement corresponding to it is impossible – that the aim, in fact, is illusory. What *is* this 'complex of religious, political and economic factors that can be called the social context', and the reconstruction of which enables us (according to Mr Bateson) to achieve the 'correct reading', 'the object as in itself it really is, since it is the product of progressive corrections at each stage of the contextual series'. How does one set to work to arrive at this final inclusive context, the establishment of which puts the poem back in 'its original historical setting', so that 'the human experience in it begins to be realised and re-enacted by the reader'? Mr Bateson doesn't tell us, and doesn't begin to consider the problem. He merely follows up those plainly false assertions about the passage of Marvell and Pope with some random notes from his historical reading.

That is all he *could* do. And all he could do more would be to go on doing that more voluminously and industriously. For the total 'social context' that he postulates is an illusion. And so it would have been, even if he had started by reading the poem. But he would then – at least, if he had really *read* the poem, and kept himself focussed upon that – have seen that in the poem, whatever minor difficulties of convention and language it might present, he had something determinate – something indubitably *there*. But 'context', as something determinate, is, and can be, nothing but his postulate; the wider he goes in his ambition to construct it from his readings in the period, the more is it *his* construction (in so far as he produces anything more than a mass of heterogeneous information alleged to be relevant).

It will not, I think, be supposed that I should like to insulate literature for study, in some pure realm of 'literary values' (whatever *they* might be). But on the one hand it is plain to me that no poem we have any chance of being able to read as a poem requires anything approaching the inordinate apparatus of 'contextual' aids to interpretation that Mr Bateson sees himself deploying. On the other hand it is equally plain to me that it is to creative literature, read *as* creative literature, that we must look for our main insights into those characteristics of the 'social context' (to adopt for a moment Mr Bateson's insidious adjective) that matter most to the critic – to the reader of poetry.

I do indeed (as I have explained in some detail elsewhere) think that the study of literature should be associated with extra-literary studies. But to make literary criticism *dependent* on the extra-literary studies (or to aim at doing so, for it can't be done) in the way Mr Bateson proposes is to stultify the former and deprive the latter of the special profit they might have for the literary student. To suggest that their *purpose* should be to reconstruct a postulated 'social context' that once enclosed the poem and gave it its meaning is to set the student after something that no study of history, social, economic, political, intellectual, religious, can yield. The poem, as I've said, is a determinate thing; it is *there*; but there is nothing to correspond – nothing answering to Mr Bateson's 'social context' that can be set over against the poem, or induced to re-establish itself round it as a kind of framework or completion, and there never *was* anything. The student who sets out in quest of such a 'context' may read historical works of various kinds and he may assemble a number of general considerations such as Mr Bateson offers us as explaining why Marvell has been 'forced to say what he cannot have wanted to say', but he will find that the kind of 'context' that expands indeterminately as he gets from his authorities what *can* be got contains curiously little significance – if significance is what, for a critic, illuminates a poem. And he may go on and on – indeterminately.

SOURCE: extract from 'The Responsible Critic', *Scrutiny* (1953), vol. 19, pp. 173–4.

PART TWO

Major Issues in
Contemporary Debates

1. IS THEORY NECESSARY? – EMPIRICISM *v.* THEORETICISM

George Watson   'On General Theories of Literature' (1978)

. . . Many ages of criticism, and none more than the present, are avid for a general theory of literature. It is hard to see why. A theory that explained the totality of literature, or even some vast area within it such as tragedy, would plainly diminish its interest. A general theory is reductive: convenient as it may be, it contracts the object to be studied in its subtle complexity. Much recent critical theory, from Northrop Frye to the *Nouvelle Critique*, has failed to take account of this. It is not just that these grandiose theories have failed to work, at least in the absolute sense once hoped for them. It is rather that one may be glad they did fail. It is good to know that the literature of Western man is not reducible to these fribbles.

Another weakness of critical theory in its grandiose forms is its claim to be fundamental. It is nothing of the kind. When a general observation is true, its truth is parasitic on the particular instances it claims to describe. A theory of tragedy depends on knowing tragedies; never, if it is worth a farthing, on anything else. Any generalisation, to be worth anything, needs to represent a summary of particular instances; and any contrary instance weakens or destroys it. Critical theory *cannot* be the foundation of literary knowledge: who ever heard of a foundation that was up in the air? The foundations of literary knowledge are the poems, plays and novels that are there to be known. And what one knows about *Hamlet* or *Phèdre* must always surpass in importance what one knows about the concept of tragedy. The particular takes precedence, and in a double sense: it comes first in the sense that one acquires it first; and it is the stronger of the two. Theory is its slave.

A literary understanding can easily grow deformed if it fails to take account of this. In matters of evidence, one can best look for analogies in courts of law, where the principle is already well understood. A witness who does not claim to understand the total significance of what he saw is more likely to be trustworthy than one who does. And some bad literary criticism is like the testimony of a witness who thinks he understands the affair: 'I saw the whole thing.' Those who believe they understand the whole nature of tragedy or comedy, for just this reason, are likely to be poor readers of tragedies or comedies; just as those who believe that all human history illustrates the hand of God or the class war are unlikely to prove attentive and accurate readers of such social fiction as Dickens or Balzac or Trollope. It is disabling to suppose one knows all the answers before one begins to read. Wordsworth's *Prelude* is the more convincing as autobiography because it abounds with phrases like 'I cannot say. . .' or 'I cannot paint. . .'. Wordsworth *knows* he does not understand the total meaning of his own past life. A critic, in the same way, who remains uncertain about the total significance of works of literature, or less than confident that such meanings can be altogether expressed, need not be charged with prevarication or culpable ignorance. His caution may be well based.

This argument about literary knowledge needs to be pressed further. At the furthest extremes of the question, there are two kinds of knowledge: that which is described or describable in words, and that which is not. In schools of literature the second kind has been gravely underrated, precisely because they are schools. In any highly verbal community such as a classroom, there is a powerful tendency to suppose that any formula is better than the absence of a formula. The critical mind, with its intermittent cravings for abstraction, has rarely excelled at silence. Critics are articulate if they are anything. But silence, or a monosyllable, or a pointed finger, can at times suggest a more advanced state of knowledge than any formula or verbal definition.

Consider the following instance. As a native speaker of English who learned French at school and in travel, I plainly know English better than French. Not just because I speak it more readily and more accurately, but because I can reply with great assurance when asked by a foreigner: 'Can I say this in English?. . .'. I know what is impossible in English as well as what is possible. On the other hand, I know the grammatical rules of French better than those of English, in the sense of being able to state them; and I need to know them better, in that sense, since I cannot speak French without recalling them to mind. For just this reason, I might prove a better teacher of the French language than of English. And yet it seems lunatic to deny that I know English better than French.

A knowledge of rules and definitions, then, is not evidence of relative knowledge but of relative ignorance. True, if I did not know the rules of French grammar, I should know French even less. But then if I were to live in France, and forget them, I might know French even better. A knowledge of the rules is never a symptom of knowledge in the most intimate sense. Those who demand verbal definitions of literary terms like 'tragedy', 'irony' and 'realism' need to be reminded of this – especially if they claim or assume that to lack definitions is to be ignorant of tragedy or irony or realism. And those who imagine they are capable of defining tragedy are showing their ignorance of tragedies in two ways: their definition is itself ignorant, in that it fails to include all the cases and exclude the rest; and it is also a symptom of ignorance in a more general and damaging sense. No one who had really studied the plays of Aeschylus, Shakespeare, Racine, Ibsen and Pinter beyond the earliest stage would have felt the need for it.

Another instance may count here in a manner at once related and yet distinct. Most of us, most of the time, can tell at a glance the difference between an old man and a young one, and with fair accuracy we can estimate the intermediate stages as well. But few, and with reason, trouble to list the indicators of age: greying and diminishing hair, a stooping figure, a withered skin and the rest. Recognising age, then, though commonly instantaneous, is evidently a perception of some complexity; and no one would want to insist that all the characteristics of age – hair, stoop, skin, and the rest – should be simultaneously present; still less to answer questions about how many are required, or which matters most. There can be no precise answers to those questions that are also true answers; and the more precise, the less true they would be. That will seem a surprising conclusion to those who confuse truth with precision, and the first among many salutary surprises.

On the other hand, it is possible to know about old age in another sense, and one more like that in which an Englishman knows French. A gerontologist knows about age in that way, even to the point of quantifying blood-pressures. Much of the insistence laid upon criticism in recent times, in effect, has been a demand to move from the first kind of knowledge to the second. The sheer prestige of mathematics and the sciences would make that probable. Even a craving for quantification is not unknown in literary studies: it is already partly satisfied in the statistical study of vocabulary. The arts in universities have long felt themselves something of a country mouse, with science as the rich city cousin. The arts cost less, for one thing. They are sometimes in a mood of wishing to cost more, on the principle that what costs more is likely to be more appreciated. They can be bitterly conscious of achieving less than the sciences that is audible and visible. They need no laboratories, only a library. It is natural they should seek at times to pace their rivals, if not outpace them, by entering the same race.

But that race is not for the arts. Those who study literature may need assurance here, but it is an assurance that can reasonably be given. There is a powerful inclination to assume that anything that is not formulaic, like the definitions that govern the terminology of chemistry, or quantifiable, as in statistics, can only be a matter of personal choice. 'Intuition' is the next danger signal in the argument: it is often argued that all subjects are faced with a stark choice of imitating the physical sciences or proceeding intuitively. But what good reason has ever been given for supposing anything of the sort? What grounds are there for assuming that intellectual progress is always of one kind or the other? Distinguishing old men from young, for instance, is plainly neither one nor the other. Most of us do it neither scientifically nor intuitively. And yet we do it efficiently.

Even the arts man's assumption that the physical sciences are necessarily and always exact is a rash assumption. The inspired hunch counts in the laboratory as well as in the library; astronomers are often content to deal in approximate figures in calculating the distances between heavenly bodies; and physicists since Heisenberg have known something called the Uncertainty Principle that governs particles of matter. Our view of the sciences needs enlarging. They do not move assuredly from one established truth to the next, and their history is often one of creative error. 'We cannot identify science with truth', as Karl Popper once remarked,

for we think that both Newton's and Einstein's theories belong to science; but they cannot both be true, and they may well both be false. ('Conversation with Karl Popper', in *Modern British Philosophy*, ed. B. Magee [1971] p. 78)

A view of the arts may need enlarging, too, if it is thought that the art historian works on a painting, or a critic on a poem, by any process so unitary that it could be summed up by the word 'intuition'. To intuit means to guess more or less justly without evidence, or at least without sufficient evidence. But the critic *has* evidence, after all, and it need not be insufficient. That evidence is the poem itself, and the historical knowledge that interprets it. If he cannot define or quantify it, that is not a reason for denying that his procedure is cognitive – a matter of knowledge. The critic knows literature in a way in which men know what they have experience of. We *know* the ways in which old men look different from young ones, whether we can define those ways or not; and we know them neither by rule nor by intuition, but by experience.

The disagreement of experts, what is more, is often more apparent than real. Eliot and Lewis almost certainly agreed about more aspects of *Paradise Lost* than they could ever have found to disagree about. They emphasised their disagreements, and rightly, because that is how a subject progresses. In a negotiation between statesmen or diplomats, in a similar way, disagreements are rightly given longer attention than those matters where agreement has already been reached or has never been needed. Industrial disputes are much the same. And intellectual disagreements, including those between literary critics, are like negotiations in diplomacy or in the field of labour relations.

But disagreement can be less than real in a subtler sense. Again and again in aesthetic questions and in moral ones, men underrate the extent to which the factual elements in highly complex judgements have shifted the nature of the question itself. They suppose they think differently from their grandparents when the difference is in the nature of the question as well as in the answer given. Sexual morality, for instance, is often said to be more permissive today than half a century ago, and perhaps is; but then factual elements like contraception and family inheritance have shifted the nature of the question itself. If the social arrangements that existed before the First World War could be miraculously reproduced, the case for sexual regulation would look much stronger than it does. When experts disagree or appear to do so, as Johnson and A. C. Bradley disagree about what matters most in Shakespearean tragedy, some of that seeming disagreement can be resolved by considering how different were the questions they supposed themselves to be answering. They had different texts of Shakespeare; they knew radically different performances in the theatre; and above all, Bradley knew the Victorian novel and the questions about human motive it posed, and Johnson did not. Even when taken together, that does not account for all the differences, or even most of them. But it does diminish them. . . .

. . . It would be hard to think of a critical essay, however distinguished, that put an end to a question for ever and ever, or even for long. Literary judgements rarely partake of the simplicity that enables them to be totally understood by a great body of individuals; in that respect they are more like moral and political judgements than arithmetical. Johnson's contrast in *Rasselas* is well taken:

We differ from ourselves just as we differ from each other when we see only part of the question, as in the multifarious relations of politicks and morality.

But when we perceive the whole at once, as in numerical computations, all agree in one judgement, and none ever varies his opinion. (ch. 28)

SOURCE: extracts from ch. 3, 'Why Literary Judgements are Objective', in *The Discipline of English* (London and Basingstoke, 1978), pp. 42–7, 48.

Jonathan Dollimore   Beyond Essentialist Humanism   (1984)

1. Origins of the Transcendent Subject

Anti-humanism and its declared objective – the decentring of man – is probably the most controversial aspect of Marxist, structuralist and post-structuralist theory. . . . Anti-humanism, like materialist criticism more generally, challenges the idea that 'man' possesses some given, unalterable essence which is what makes 'him' human, which is the source and *essential* determinant of 'his' culture and its priority over conditions of existence.

. . . It is the Enlightenment rather than the Renaissance which marks the emergence of essentialist humanism[1] as we now know it; at that time concern shifts from the metaphysically derivative soul to what Robert Paul Wolff* has termed 'individual centres of consciousness' (*The Poverty of Liberalism*, p. 142) which are said to be self-determining, free and rational by nature. Those forms of individualism (eg. 'abstract individualism') premised on essentialism tend, obviously, to distinguish the individual from society and give absolute priority to the former. In effect the individual is understood in terms of a pre-social essence, nature, or identity and on that basis s/he is invested with a quasi-spiritual autonomy. The individual becomes the origin and focus of meaning – an individuated essence which precedes and – in idealist philosophy – transcends history and society.

Reflecting here its religious antecedents, idealist philosophy marks off the domain of the spiritual as superior to, and the ultimate counter-image of, actual, historical, social, existence. It is not only that (as Nietzsche contended) the entire counterfeit of transcendence and of the hereafter has grown up on the basis of an impoverished life, but that transcendence comes to constitute an ideological

* See the listing in Note 6, concluding Dollimore's study, below, for publication details of the authorities quoted and discussed in his argument [Ed.].

mystification of the conditions of impoverishment from which it grew: impoverishment shifts from being its cause to its necessary condition, that required to pressure one's true (spiritual) identity into its true transcendent realisation. As Robbe-Grillet puts it, in the humanist tragic sense of life 'interiority always leads to transcendence . . . the pseudo-necessity of tragedy to a metaphysical beyond;' but at the same time it 'closes the door to any realist future' since the corollary of that beyond is a static, paralysed present ('Nature, Humanism and Tragedy', pp. 81, 84). The truth that people do not live by bread alone may then be appropriated ideologically to become the 'truth' that spiritual nourishment is an adequate substitute for bread and possibly even preferable to it (Marcuse, *Negations*, pp. 109–22). But most importantly, the '*revolutionary force of the ideal, which in its very unreality keeps alive the best desires of men amidst a bad reality*' (*Negations*, p. 102, my italics) is lost, displaced by ideals of renunciation and acquiescence. Rebellious desire is either abdicated entirely or tamed in service to the cultural reification of 'man', the human condition, the human spirit and so on.

Marcuse, writing in 1936, was trying to explain the transition from liberalism to authoritarianism which Europe was witnessing. We may be unable to accept some of Marcuse's conclusions but the task he set himself then seems as urgent as ever. In one thing he was surely right: the essentialism of western philosophy, especially that of the idealist tradition, could be used to sanction that process whereby 'the soul was able to become a useful factor in the technique of mass domination when, in the epoch of authoritarian states, all available forces had to be mobilised against a real transformation of social existence' (*Negations* p. 114). The attacks upon idealist culture by Brecht, Walter Benjamin and Theodore Adorno were made from similar positions. In their very different ways these three writers engage with the materialist conception of subjectivity, one which, in so far as it retains the concept of essence, construes it not as that which is eternally fixed but as social potential materialising within limiting historical conditions. Conditions will themselves change – in part under the pressure of actualised potential – thus enabling new potentialities to unfold.

Arguably, to accept with Marx that Feuerbach was wrong 'to resolve the essence of religion into the essence of *man*', since 'the real nature of man is the totality of social relations' (*Selected Writings*, p. 83), should be to dispense altogether with 'essence', 'nature' and 'man' as concepts implicated irredeemably in the metaphysic of determining origin. Such at least is the implication of cultural materialism and that most famous of its formulations by Marx: 'The mode of production of material life conditions the social, political and intellectual life process in general' (*Selected Works*, p. 182). Consequently it is social being that determines consciousness, not the reverse. . . .

In recent years the critique of essentialism has become even more searching partly in an attempt to explain its extraordinary recuperative power. Thus for Althusser humanism is characterised by two complementary and indissociable postulates: '(i) that there is a universal essence of man; (ii) that this essence is the attribute of "*each single individual*" who is its real subject' (*For Marx*, p. 228; the italicised phrase is a direct reference to Marx's sixth thesis on Feuerbach). Humanism gives rise to the concept of 'man' which, says Althusser, must be abolished: 'It is impossible to *know* anything about men except on the absolute precondition that the philosophical (theoretical) myth of man is reduced to ashes' (p. 229). Against humanism Althusser contends that 'The human subject is decentred, constituted by a structure which has no "centre" either, except in the imaginary misrecognition of the "ego", that is to say in the ideological formations where it finds recognition' (*Lenin and Philosophy*, p. 201). . . . I cannot provide here a detailed history of essentialist humanism in all its post-Enlightenment complexity, but propose instead to indicate, through some important textual landmarks, its centrality for the development of English studies. . . .

2. Essence and Universal; Enlightenment Transitions

Put very schematically, western metaphysics has typically had recourse to three indissociable categories: the universal (or absolute), essence, and teleology. If universals and essences designate, respectively, what ultimately and essentially exists, then teleology designates metaphysical destiny – for the universe as a whole and its essences in particular.

In Descartes we can see a crucial stage in the history of metaphysics, one whereby essence takes on a new importance in the schema: the metaphysically derivative soul gives way to the autonomous, individuated essence, the self-affirming consciousness. (But just as the individuated essence typically presupposed its counterpart and origin, the universal form, so the subject of essentialist humanism comes to presuppose a universal human nature/condition). For Descartes the self was a pure, non-physical substance whose 'whole essence or nature . . . is to think'; he also equated mind, soul, understanding and reason (*Works* I. 101 and 152). Therefore he clearly retained an *a priori* and thoroughly metaphysical account of consciousness, one which was in important respects challenged, in others assimilated, by empiricists like Locke. But by elucidating in terms of empiricist epistemology a conception of the person which, however modified, contained an irreducibly metaphysical component, these empiricists were embarking upon a philosophical programme inherently problematic.

The trouble with Locke's definition of a person is that it still makes it a contingent rather than a necessary truth that people are of human form: 'It being the same consciousness that makes a man be himself to himself, personal identity depends on that only' (*Essay Concerning Human Understanding*, II. 27. 10). But if Locke is here still working with Cartesian assumptions, his empiricist epistemology nevertheless leads him to the radical supposition that the mind is 'as we say, white Paper, void of all Characters, without any *ideas*'. He then asks 'how comes it to be furnished? . . . Whence has it all the *materials* of Reason and Knowledge? To this I answer, in one word, From *experience*. In that, all our Knowledge is founded' (II. i. 2). Elsewhere Locke asserts that of all men 'nine parts of ten are what they are, good or evil, useful or not, by their education' (*Some Thoughts Concerning Education*, p. 114).

Hume for his part conducts a devastating critique of essentialism, getting rid of *substance* (an age-old metaphysical category which in this context was the supposed basis of the self) and arguing instead that 'mankind . . . are nothing but a bundle or collection of different perceptions which succeed each other with an inconceivable rapidity and are in perpetual flux and movement'. There is not, he adds, 'any single power of the soul which remains unalterably the same', and regarding 'the mind . . . there is properly no *simplicity* in it at one time nor *identity* in different' (*Treatise*, I. iv. 6). And yet, contrary to what the foregoing might lead us to expect, Hume gives one of the most explicit statements of what Robert Solomon calls the 'transcendental pretence':[2] 'human nature remains still the same in its principles and operations . . . Mankind are so much the same, in all times and places, that history informs us of nothing new or strange in this particular. Its chief use is only to discover the constant and universal principles of human nature by showing men in all varieties of circumstances and situations' (*Enquiry*, section VIII, part 1). In effect, and crucially, 'man' as a universal remains, notwithstanding a radical transition from being given *a priori* to being given contingently, in 'nature'.

There is yet another inconsistency, more important than any so far noted: Hume's 'universal principles of human nature' are not, even in his terms, universal after all, for he suspects 'negroes . . . to be *naturally* inferior to whites. There never was a civilised nation of any other complexion than white'. And the reason? 'Nature . . . made an original distinction betwixt these breeds [ie. black and white]. Not to mention our colonies, there are NEGRO slaves dispersed all over EUROPE of which none ever discovered any symptom of ingenuity' (*Essays, Moral Political and Literary*, I. 252).

In the period between Locke and Hume we witness the emergence of a conception of man which rejected explicitly metaphysical categories only to re-import mutations of them in the guise of 'nature'. *Pace* Hume, 'history informs us' that nature has been as powerful a metaphysical entity as any, God included.

In contrast to the emerging British empiricism, the tradition of philosophical idealism recast essentialism in an explicitly metaphysical form. Immanuel Kant said of Rousseau that he was 'the first to discover beneath the varying forms human nature assumes, the deeply concealed essence of man' (Solomon, p. 54). Rousseau's essence was, of course, an innate goodness or potentiality existing in contradistinction to the corruption of society. But Kant legitimated essentialism in the context of transcendental idealism, a revolutionary philosophy which posited the phenomenal world as determined by the structure of the human mind itself, by the formal categories of consciousness: 'Hitherto it has been assumed that all our knowledge must conform to objects' says Kant, only then to present the truth as precisely the reverse of this: 'objects must conform to our knowledge' (*Critique of Pure Reason*, p. 22). Man as a rational being is part of the noumenal world possessed of an autonomous will serving its own law; he is an end in himself just as objects in the noumenal world are things in themselves. The enormous differences between the two philosophical traditions represented by Hume and Kant respectively could hardly be exaggerated yet on two things at least they agree: first (like Descartes) they begin with the individual taken in abstraction from any socio-political context; second, Kant concurs with Hume on the (human) condition of blacks: 'Mr Hume challenges anyone to cite a simple example in which a negro has shown talents . . . So fundamental is the difference between these two races of men [black and white] and it appears to be as great in regard to mental capacities as in colour' (*Observations on the Feeling of the Beautiful and Sublime*, pp. 100–11; quoted in Richard Popkin, *The High Road to Pyrrhonism*, pp. 259–60). This second point on which Hume and Kant agree is in part consequence of the first; the abstraction in abstract individualism (i.e. its metaphysics) is the means whereby the historically specific has been universalised as the naturally given.

3. Discrimination and Subjectivity

The example of racism is included here not as a gratuitous slur but rather as a reminder that the issues involved have not been, and still are not, limited to the realm of contemplative philosophy. As Popkin points out, the Enlightenment was the watershed of modern racial theories (*The High Road to Pyrrhonism*, especially chapters 4 and 14). Essentialist theories of human nature, though not intrinsically racist, have contributed powerfully to the ideological conditions which made racism possible. Similarly, when an ideological legitimation of slavery proved necessary (because of growing opposition to it) such theories helped provide that too. (See Ashley Montagu, *Man's Most Dangerous Myth*, pp. 21ff.)

The following is an instance of essentialist legitimation from our own century:

History has shown, and daily shows anew, that man can be trained to be nothing that he is not genuinely, and from the beginning, in the depths of his being; against this law, neither precept, warning, punishment nor any other environmental influence avails. Realism in the study of man does not lie in attributing evil tendencies to him, but in recognising that all that man can do emerges in the last resort from himself, from his innate qualities.

Here essence and teleology are explicitly affirmed while 'history' becomes the surrogate absolute. If we are used to finding this kind of utterance in our own cultural history it comes as something of a shock to realise that these were the words of Alfred Bäumler, a leading Nazi 'philosopher' writing on race.[3] In part (that is, taking into account the historical context) they substantiate the claim of Marcuse that since Descartes essentialism has 'followed a course leading from autonomy to heteronomy, from the proclamations of the free, rational individual to his surrender to the powers of the authoritarian state' (*Negations*, pp. 44–5). This in turn underscores the importance of Derrida's contention that the critique of ethnocentrism, together with the emergence of ethnology and the corresponding decentring of European culture, are 'historically contemporaneous with the destruction of the history of metaphysics' (*Writing and Difference*, p. 282). Metaphysics can be finally displaced only when the twin concepts of centred structure and determining origin are abandoned (pp. 278–9).

Derrida writes also of the importance of passing beyond 'Man and humanism, the name of man being the name of that being who, throughout the history of metaphysics or of ontotheology – in other words throughout his entire history – has dreamed of full presence, the reassuring foundation, the origin and the end of play' (*Writing and Difference*, p. 292). If this echoes Levi-Strauss' pronouncement that 'the ultimate goal of the human sciences' is 'not to constitute, but to dissolve man' (*The Savage Mind*, p. 247), or Foucault's equally notorious 'man is an invention of recent date', one likely soon to 'be erased, like a face drawn in sand at the edge of the sea' (*The Order of Things*, p. 387) – pronouncements upon which some in the humanist tradition had become fixated in horror – then it is worth interjecting that the anti-humanism of Foucault's variety at least does not involve the elimination of individuality, only of 'man'. In fact, it is those discourses centred around 'man' and human nature which, historically, have regulated and repressed *actual* diversity and *actual* human difference. To speak of the uniqueness of an individual may mean either that s/he is contingently unlike anyone else actually known *or* that s/he approximates more closely to a normative paradigm, spiritual or natural, than anyone else who has ever, or will, or can, exist. The materialist view of the subject would at least render the former possible by rejecting the premises of the latter; in that sense, far from eliminating individuality, it realises it (interestingly, Lawrence's conception of individuality seems to be closer to the latter – Part 5, below).

In a sense Barthes is right to attack the petit-bourgeois for being 'unable to imagine the Other . . . because the Other is a scandal which threatens his essence' (*Mythologies*, p. 151), but we should remember that the experience of this kind of threat has by no means been limited to the petit-bourgeois, and the forms of discrimination which it has invited have operated in terms of several basic categories of identity, including race, sexuality and class.

The crucial point is surely this: essentialism, rooted as it is in the concept of centred structure and determining origin, constitutes a residual metaphysic within secularist thought which, though it has not entailed has certainly made possible the classic ideological effect: a specific cultural identity is universalised or naturalised; more specifically, in reaction to social change this residual metaphysic is activated in defence of one cultural formation, one conception of what it is to be truly human, to the corresponding exclusion of others.

4. Formative Literary Influences: Pope to Eliot

Although in both the empiricist and the idealist traditions of philosophy universal and essence are never ultimately dissociated, the emphasis falls differently; sometimes it will be on the universal – man's, but also each individual's, underlying nature; sometimes it will be on the individual essence – that which instantiates or incorporates the universal. We find both positions in English literary criticism – not surprisingly since both the empiricist and the idealist traditions feed into it and, in different ways, underpin one of its central tenets: great literature penetrates beyond the historically and culturally specific to a realm of universal truth whose counterpart is an essentially unchanging human condition.

Pope, in The Design of his *Essay on Man* declares that 'The Science of Human Nature is, like all other sciences, reduced to a *few clear points*' (his italics); appropriate to this he offers 'a general Map of MAN', one concerned with '*fountains*' rather than '*rivers*'. Universal man not only constitutes people as one, over and above the inequalities which apparently divide them, but renders those inequalities quite *inessential*:

> Condition, circumstance is not the thing;
> Bliss is the same in subject or in king,
>
> Heav'n breathes thro' ev'ry member of the whole
> One common blessing, as one common soul.   (Epistle IV)

Having cited this passage, it has to be conceded that the ideological use of essentialism though not less powerful in recent times, is rarely so blatant! Samuel Johnson, following Hume, found 'such a Uniformity in the Life of Man . . . that there is scarce any Possibility of Good or Ill, but is common to Human Kind' (*Rambler*, 60). And Shakespeare, says Johnson, depicts human nature in its universal forms, appropriately disregarding the 'Particular manners' of any one of its diverse cultural manifestations; his characters 'are the genuine progeny of common humanity, such as the world will always supply and observation will always find'; they exemplify 'those general passions and principles by which all minds are agitated and the whole system of life is continued in motion'. And all this is so because the poet correctly 'overlooks the casual distinction of country and condition, as a painter, satisfied with the figure, neglects the drapery' (*Preface to Shakespeare*, in *Selected Writings*, pp. 264–7).

Kantian metaphysics, together with that of Fichte and Schelling, finds its way into Romantic criticism through Coleridge who, searching for 'a truth self-grounded, unconditional and known by its own light' finds it in 'the SUM or I AM, which I shall hereafter indiscriminately express by the words spirit, self, and self-consciousness' (*Biographia Literaria*, pp. 150–1; the conflation of spirit, self and self-consciousness is of course exactly what is at issue). Coleridge's celebrated account of the Primary Imagination (derived from Schelling) is a classic statement of essentialism, but note how it manages to harness the absolute and the teleological as well: 'The primary imagination I hold to be the living power and prime agent of all human perception, and as a repetition in the finite mind of the eternal act of creation in the infinite I AM' (p. 167). Elsewhere, and drawing now on a 'native' tradition, Coleridge speaks of Shakespeare's ability to concentrate upon 'our common nature', an ability which makes him 'the pioneer of true philosophy'. A play like *Lear* is, says Coleridge, representative of 'men in all countries and of all times'; we find in it that 'which in all ages has been, and ever will be, close and native to the heart of man' (*Essays and Lectures on Shakespeare*, pp. 56–7, 126); note how in these two extracts the plural 'men' and the singular 'man' signify one and the same, also how 'heart of man' carries inconspicuously the sense of man as both universal and individuated essence.[4] . . .

Believing their society to be in decline or dangerously off course, many literary critics in the English tradition have seen as even more imperative than usual their task of reaffirming the universal values associated with man's essential nature. Seminal for this school has been Matthew Arnold's affirmation of Culture. Once again absolute and essence are conflated to become the teleological motor of man: 'Religion says: *The Kingdom of God is within you*; and culture, in like manner, places human perfection in an *internal* condition, in the growth and predominance of our humanity proper' (*Culture and Anarchy*, p. 8). Arnold speaks often of this given 'human nature' which it is the function of culture to bring into full flower 'by means of its spiritual standard of perfection' (p. 13). In Arnold's writing we see how important was essentialist humanism in reconstituting criticism as a surrogate theology. Eventually though Arnold's optimistic humanism would be displaced by a more explicit theology, and one avowedly tragic in its implications. . . .

The early Eliot goes even further; alienation from the urban landscape is so extreme that consciousness itself fragments: 'The thousand sordid images / Of which your soul was constituted' (*Preludes*). But the unity of the subject is dispersed only to be reconstituted as a disembodied centre of consciousness instantiated by its own suffering, a vulnerability so profoundly redemptive as to enable the subject finally to suffer into truth, moved by 'some infinitely gentle / Infinitely suffering thing'. The subject in Eliot's later verse finds its way back to a 'point of intersection of the timeless / With time', and there achieves a mystical sense of unity not dissimilar to, yet now so much more tentative than, Wordsworth's 'central peace subsisting at the heart of endless agitation'. Others in this tradition have been less successful yet managed nevertheless to vindicate the transcendent subject. It is sustained now by two surrogate universals – the absurdity of the human condition and (once again) consciousness as the grid of a determining absence, the latter now so powerfully conditioning experience and knowledge as to function as a kind of inverted Kantian category of consciousness. Despite this, or maybe because of it, a writer like Beckett (in the words of Edward Bond) 'is said to have made liberal – even capitalist – culture possible. He is said to have shown that however you degrade people an unquenchable spark of humanity remains in them' (*Guardian*, 3.11.80, p. 12). Texts like *Waiting for Godot* do indeed sustain those surrogate universals though only by collapsing them almost entirely into the subject where they survive as the forms not of Unchanging Truth but of an etiolated, suffering stasis.

5. Lawrence, Leavis and Individualism

D. H. Lawrence is a writer-critic seminal in a movement in many ways opposed to both modernism as represented by Hulme and Eliot, and existentialism. Yet he shared with the former at least a dislike of humanism or, more precisely, of democratic humanitarian philosophy. In his essay on Whitman and democracy Lawrence identifies and attacks 'the great ideal of Humanity' (*Selected Essays*, p. 80), an ideal based on a fetishing of 'Average Man' (p. 75). Interestingly Lawrence also attacks the essentialist corollary of humanist ideology proper; he summarises it as follows: 'the Whole is inherent in every fragment . . . every human consciousness has the same intrinsic value . . . because each is an essential part of the Great Consciousness. This is the One Identity which identifies us all' (p. 81). But Lawrence's alternative to this remains within the essentialist problematic. It is an alternative rooted in an uncompromising individualism; for Lawrence 'the Whitman One Identity, the *En Masse*, is a horrible nullification of true identity and being' (p. 85). More generally, when Lawrence asserts that 'once you . . . postulate Universals, you have departed from the creative reality' (p. 88) he articulates an idea which will give impetus to a powerful subsequent movement in literary criticism, one which fetishises the concrete and finds perhaps its most celebrated statement in Leavis's interpretation of Lawrence. It is a movement which is strenuously anti-metaphysical in its polemics, yet which cannot eradicate metaphysics from its own vision. Consider, for example, Lawrence's belief in the creative reality of individuality: 'A man's self is a law unto itself'; the living self is 'an unscrutable, unfindable, vivid quick;' it is not, insists Lawrence, *spirit*. On the contrary, (and he insists on this too), it is simply there, simply given. We must, he adds, allow 'the soul's own deep desires to come direct, spontaneous into consciousness . . . from the central Mystery into indefinable *presence* . . . The central mystery is no generalised abstraction. It is each man's primal original soul or self, within him' (pp. 89–90). The *transcendent* universal is repudiated only to be collapsed back into its *immanent* counterpart. And teleology is just a few lines further on: 'The living self has one purpose only: to come into its own fullness of being' (p. 91; cf. the reference in *Kangaroo* to the 'absolute . *. the central self, the *isolate, absolute self*', p. 309).

Obviously, there is a sense in which Lawrence's individualism could be positive, in for example his conception of another individual in terms of '*present otherness*' (p. 92). At first this looks like commitment to otherness. Yet, because uniqueness is conceived still as the instantiation of a universal – the 'actual man present before us is an inscrutable and incarnate Mystery' (p. 90) – it works to guard against rather than to comprehend difference. What is foregrounded is not the identity of the other so much as the integrity of the self, the precondition of perceiving this other 'who is himself' being that 'I am my own pure self' (p. 92). Otherness becomes a projection of the self, a foil against which subjective integrity is confirmed. Behind this is a more general concern with 'homogeneous, spontaneous coherence' as against the 'disintegrated amorphousness' which according to Lawrence characterised American life (p. 94; cf. Yeats: 'We Irish, born into that ancient Sect / But thrown upon this filthy modern tide / And by its formless spawning fury wrecked', *Collected Poems*, p. 376).

The 1917–18 essay on Whitman makes explicit the defensive, potentially reactionary nature of Lawrence's individualism; here is an even more urgent affirmation of the soul's integrity: 'the soul wishes to keep clean and whole. The soul's deepest will is to preserve its own integrity, against the mind and the whole mass of disintegrating forces' (p. 274). The unspoken discourse running through this passage is that of power, something which becomes explicit in *Aaron's Rod*: 'yield to the deep power-soul in the individual man, and obey implicitly . . . men must submit to the greater soul in a man . . . and women must submit to the positive power-soul in man, for their being' (p. 347).

Lawrence's fear of the supposedly disintegrative forces in the modern world, especially their effects upon selfhood, is taken up by his most celebrated critic, F. R. Leavis and, more generally, the movement Leavis inspired. He writes of 'the vital intelligence,

unthwarted by emotional disorders and divisions in the psyche'
which links Lawrence with Blake; there is, says Leavis, no profound
emotional disorder in Lawrence, no major disharmony; intelligence is
the servant of 'the whole integrated psyche . . . not thwarted or
disabled by inner contradictions' (*D. H. Lawrence: Novelist*, pp. 12,
27–8; in fact, the work of recent writers – for example Paul Delany and
Kate Millett[5] – suggests rather the opposite). Leavis also finds in
Lawrence the familiar universal/essence conjunction: 'the intuition of
the oneness of life' which 'expresses itself in an intensity of
preoccupation with the individual' (p. 105). This intensity is
'religious' because it moves 'to something transcending the
individual' (p. 115), or, reversing the direction of the spiritual
metaphor, to a 'depth that involves an impersonal wholeness'
(p. 124). What follows is predictable enough: in Lawrence class (for
example) is important 'but attention focusses on the *essential humanity*'
(p.88).

Lawrence takes pride of place in the Great Tradition, about which
I can only afford the space to remark that what it excludes is the most
significant thing about it. Indeed, what is so striking now is just how
much not only the Hulme–Eliot but also the Lawrence–Leavis
inspired movements wanted to actively exclude and deny; 'tradition',
'essential humanity', 'spontaneous fullness of being', far from being
affirmations of 'life' seem now more like a fear of it – in particular a
fear of contamination by difference and otherness, a fear of
disintegration through democracy and change. . . .

6. The Decentred Subject

When Lawrence elaborates his philosophy of individualism he
reminds us of the derivation of 'individual': that which is not divided,
not divisible (*Selected Essays*, p. 86). Materialist analysis tends to avoid
the term for just those reasons which led Lawrence to embrace it,
preferring instead 'subject'. Because informed by contradictory social
and ideological processes, the subject is never an indivisible unity,
never an autonomous, self-determining centre of consciousness.

The main historical antecedents of this process of decentring have
often been cited: Copernicus displaced man and his planet from their
privileged place at the centre of the universe; Darwin showed that the
human species is not the *telos* or goal of that universe; Marx displaced
man from the centre of history while Freud displaced consciousness as
the source of individual autonomy. Foucault adds the decentring
effected by the Nietzschean genealogy (an addition which would
appropriately challenge the suspiciously sequential coherence of the

foregoing 'history' of decentring!): 'What is found at the historical beginning of things is not the inviolable identity of their origin; it is the dissension of other things. It is disparity' (*Language, Counter-Memory, Practice*, p. 142).

Foucault identifies an 'epistemological mutation' of history not yet complete because of the deep resistance to it, a resistance, that is, to 'conceiving of difference, to describing separations and dispersions, to dissociating the reassuring form of the identical' (*Archaeology of Knowledge*, pp. 11–12). He summarises his own task as one of freeing thought from its subjection to transcendence and analysing it 'in the discontinuity that no teleology would reduce in advance; to map it in a dispersion that no pre-established horizon would embrace; to allow it to be deployed in an anonymity on which no transcendental constitution would impose the form of the subject; to open it up to a temporality that would not promise the return of any dawn. My aim was to cleanse it of all transcendental narcissism' (p. 203). Transcendental narcissism validates itself in terms of teleology, the subject, the pre-established horizon; against this Foucault's history charts discontinuity, anonymity, dispersion.

Barthes offers a similar emphasis. To speak positively of the decentred subject is never just to acknowledge his or her contradictions: 'It is a diffraction which is intended, a dispersion of energy in which there remains neither a central core nor a structure of meaning: I am not contradictory, I am dispersed' (*Roland Barthes*, p. 143); 'today the subject apprehends himself *elsewhere*' (p. 168). This entails not only a non-centred conception of identity but, correspondingly, a non-centred form of political awareness: 'According to Freud . . . one touch of difference leads to racism. But a great deal of difference leads away from it, irremediably. To equalise, democratise, homogenise – all such efforts will never manage to expel "the tiniest difference", seed of racial intolerance. For that one must pluralise, refine, continuously' (p. 69). Sexual transgression is affirmed while recognising that it tends to carry within itself a limiting inversion of the normative regime being transgressed (pp. 64–5, 133). The more radical alternative to sexual liberation through transgression is a release of sexuality from meaning. Then there would be for example not homosexuality but '*homosexualities*' 'whose plural will baffle any constituted, centred discourse' (p. 69).

This dimension of post-structuralist theory arouses justifiable suspicion for seeming to advance subjective decentring simply in terms of the *idea* of an anarchic refusal adequate unto itself, thereby recuperating anti-humanism in terms of the idealism it rejects and rendering the subject so completely dispersed as to be incapable of acting as any agent, least of all an agent of change. Equally though, this criticism itself runs the risk of disallowing the positive sense of the ideal cited earlier – that which in virtue of its present unreality affirms known potentialities from within existing, stultifying, social realities. Ideologically ratified, those 'realities' become not merely an obstacle to the realisation of potential, to the possibility of social change, but work to make both potential and change literally unthinkable. This is why, quite simply, a vision of decentred subjectivity, like any other vision of liberation, cannot be divorced from a critique of existing social realities and their forms of ideological legitimation. It is here that we might, finally, invoke an earlier emphasis in Barthes's work. In *Mythologies* he reminded us that the myth of the human condition 'consists in placing Nature at the bottom of History'; to thus eternalise the nature of man is to render the destiny of people apparently unalterable. Hence the necessity to reverse the terms, to find history behind nature and thereby reveal nature itself as an ideological construct preempting change (*Mythologies*, p. 101).

Perhaps this remains the most important objective in the decentring of man, one which helps make possible an alternative conception of the relations between history, society and subjectivity, and invites that '*affirmation* which *then determines the noncentre otherwise than as loss of the centre*' (Derrida, *Writing and Difference*, p. 292, his italics). It is a radical alternative which, in the context of materialist analysis, helps vindicate certain objectives: not essence but potential, not the human condition but cultural difference, not destiny but collectively identified goals.[6]

SOURCE: extracts from ch. 16, 'Beyond Essentialist Humanism', in *Radical Tragedy* (Brighton, 1984), pp. 250–2, 253–60, 261, 264–7, 269–71.

NOTES

[Reorganised and renumbered from the original – Ed.]

1. [Ed.] The essentialist humanism called into question in this essay is the belief that there exists a fixed and unchanging 'human nature' which is independent of social and cultural factors. The 'transcendent subject' is the notion of a unique, personal consciousness which transcends sociocultural factors and constitutes the essence of each individual. The essay traces the development of these ideas in Western philosophy, argues that they have frequently been the vehicle of social, political, and racial ideologies, and ends with a discussion of their effects in a number of important literary and critical works.

2. The transcendental pretence is defined by Robert C. Solomon as the ideological conviction that 'the white middle classes of European descent

were the representatives of all humanity, and as human nature is one, so its history must be as well. This transcendental pretence was – and still is – the premise of our thinking about history, "humanity" and human nature' (*History and Human Nature*, p. *xii*).

3. Alfred Bäumler, quoted in Ashley Montagu, *Man's Most Dangerous Myth*, p. 14.

4. M. H. Abrams and, more recently, Jonathan Culler, have pointed to the determinism implicit in the concepts of Romanticism, especially that of organic form which according to Coleridge is 'innate. It shapes as it develops itself from within'. This, as Abrams points out, was merely to substitute for the determinism of mechanistic philosophy its organic – and of course, essentialist – counterpart (see Abrams, *The Mirror and the Lamp*, p. 173; Culler, *The Pursuit of Signs*, ch. 8).

5. Kate Millett, *Sexual Politics*; Paul Delany, *D. H. Lawrence's Nightmare*.

6. [Ed.] Publication details for editions of works referred to in this essay are as follows:

Althusser, Louis, *For Marx* and *Lenin and Philosophy* (New Left Books, 1977).

Arnold, Matthew, *Culture and Anarchy* (Smith, Elder, 1981).

Barthes, Roland, *Mythologies* (Paladin, 1973) and *Roland Barthes by Roland Barthes* (Macmillan, 1977).

Coleridge, S. T., *Biographia Literaria*, ed. George Watson (Dent, 1965).

Derrida, Jacques, *Writing and Difference* (Routledge, 1978) and *Positions* (Athlone Press, 1981).

Descartes, René, *The Philosophical Works* (Cambridge University Press, 1931).

Foucault, Michel, *The Order of Things; An Archaeology of the Human Sciences* (Tavistock Press, 1970), *The Archaeology of Knowledge* (Tavistock Press, 1974) and *Language, Counter-Memory, Practice* (Cornell University Press, 1977).

Hume, David, *A Treatise of Human Nature*, ed. L. A. Selby-Bigge (Oxford, 1978).

Kant, Immanuel, *Critique of Pure Reason*, trans. Norman Kemp-Smith (Macmillan, 1968).

Lawrence, D. H., *Selected Essays* (Penguin, 1950).

Leavis, F. R., *D. H. Lawrence: Novelist* (Chatto & Windus, 1955).

Levi-Strauss, Claude, *The Savage Mind* (Weidenfeld & Nicholson, 1966).

Locke, John, *Some Thoughts Concerning Education* in *Educational Writings*, ed. James L. Axtell (Cambridge University Press, 1968) and *An Essay Concerning Human Understanding*, ed. P. H. Nidditch (Oxford University Press, 1975).

Marcuse, Herbert, *Negations: Essays in Critical Theory* (Penguin, 1968).

Marx, Karl, *Selected Writings in Sociology and Social Philosophy* (Penguin, 1963).

Montagu, Ashley, *Man's Most Dangerous Myth: The Fallacy of Race* (Oxford University Press, 1974).

Popkin, Richard, H., *The High Road to Pyrrhonism* (San Diego, 1980).

Solomon, Robert C., *History and Human Nature* (Harvester Press, 1980).

Wolff, Robert Paul, *The Poverty of Liberalism* (Beacon Press, 1968).

2. WHAT DOES THE LITERARY WORK REPRESENT?

Roland Barthes   The Death of the
Author   (1968)

. . . The removal of the Author (one could talk here with Brecht of a
veritable 'distancing', the Author diminishing like a figurine at the far
end of the literary stage), is not merely an historical fact or an act of
writing; it utterly transforms the modern text (or – which is the same
thing – the text is henceforth made and read in such a way that at all
its levels the author is absent). The temporality is different. The
Author, when believed in, is always conceived of as the past of his own
book: book and author stand automatically on a single line divided
into a *before* and an *after*. The Author is thought to *nourish* the book,
which is to say that he exists before it, thinks, suffers, lives for it, is in
the same relation of antecedence to his work as a father to his child. In
complete contrast, the modern scriptor is born simultaneously with
the text, is in no way equipped with a being, preceding or exceeding
the writing, is not the subject with the book as predicate; there is no
other time than that of the enunciation and every text is eternally
written *here and now*. The fact is (or, it follows) that *writing* can no
longer designate an operation of recording, notation, representation,
'depiction' (as the Classics would say); rather, it designates exactly
what linguists, referring to Oxford philosophy, call a performative, a
rare verbal form (exclusively given in the first person and in the
present tense) in which the enunciation has no other content
(contains no other proposition) than the act by which it is uttered –
something like the *I declare* of kings or the *I sing* of very ancient poets.
Having buried the Author, the modern scriptor can thus no longer
believe, as according to the pathetic view of his predecessors, that this
hand is too slow for his thought or passion and that consequently,
making a law of necessity, he must emphasise this delay and
indefinitely 'polish' his form. For him, on the contrary, the hand, cut
off from any voice, borne by a pure gesture of inscription (and not of
expression), traces a field without origin – or which, at least, has no

other origin than language itself, language which ceaselessly calls into question all origins.

We know now that a text is not a line of words releasing a single 'theological' meaning (the 'message' of the Author-God) but a multi-dimensional space in which a variety of writings, none of them original, blend and clash. The text is a tissue of quotations drawn from the innumerable centres of culture. . . . The writer can only imitate a gesture that is always anterior, never original. His only power is to mix writings, to counter the ones with the others, in such a way as never to rest on any one of them. Did he wish to *express himself*, he ought at least to know that the inner 'thing' he thinks to 'translate' is itself only a ready-formed dictionary, its words only explainable through other words, and so on indefinitely; something experienced in exemplary fashion by the young Thomas de Quincey, he who was so good at Greek that in order to translate absolutely modern ideas and images into that dead language, he had, so Baudelaire tells us (in *Paradis Artificiels*), 'created for himself an unfailing dictionary, vastly more extensive and complex than those resulting from the ordinary patience of purely literary themes'. Succeeding the Author, the scriptor no longer bears within him passions, humours, feelings, impressions, but rather this immense dictionary from which he draws a writing that can know no halt: life never does more than imitate the book, and the book itself is only a tissue of signs, an imitation that is lost, infinitely deferred.

Once the Author is removed, the claim to decipher a text becomes quite futile. To give a text an Author is to impose a limit on that text, to furnish it with a final signified, to close the writing. Such a conception suits criticism very well, the latter then allotting itself the important task of discovering the Author (or its hypostases: society, history, psyché, liberty) beneath the work: when the Author has been found, the text is 'explained' – victory to the critic. Hence there is no surprise in the fact that, historically, the reign of the Author has also been that of the Critic, nor again in the fact that criticism (be it new) is today undermined along with the Author. In the multiplicity of writing, everything is to be *disentangled*, nothing *deciphered*; the structure can be followed, 'run' (like the thread of a stocking) at every point and at every level, but there is nothing beneath: the space of writing is to be ranged over, not pierced; writing ceaselessly posits meaning ceaselessly to evaporate it, carrying out a systematic exemption of meaning. In precisely this way literature (it would be better from now on to say *writing*), by refusing to assign a 'secret', an ultimate meaning, to the text (and to the world as text), liberates what may be called an anti-theological activity, an activity that is truly . .

revolutionary since to refuse to fix meaning is, in the end, to refuse God and his hypostases – reason, science, law. . . .

SOURCE: extracts from 'The Death of the Author', *Mantéia*, V (1968), reprinted in *Roland Barthes: Image-Music-Text*, essays selected and translated by Stephen Heath (London, 1977), excerpted from pp. 145–7.

Denis Donoghue   'Epireading and Graphireading' (1981)

. . . So what is epireading? A stance, an attitude, a prejudice in favour of such assumptions as the following:

(i) Freud, *Civilization and its Discontents*, ch. 3: 'Writing was in its origin the voice of an absent person, and the dwelling-house was a substitute for the mother's womb, the first lodging, for which in all likelihood man still longs, and in which he was safe and felt at ease.'

(ii) Epireading is predicated upon the desire to hear; to hear the absent person; to hear oneself in that person. Imagination finds a place at this point, unintimidated by current rhetoric which almost disavows it. In 'The Plain Sense of Things' Wallace Stevens writes:

> Yet the absence of the imagination had
> Itself to be imagined

If so, the imagination must be introduced at the point of seeming defeat, of destitution, beginning again.

(iii) As for the charge of nostalgia and a yearning for origin: the illusion of presence, created by voice in the act by which we suppose we hear it, is no worse than the illusion of absence, created by print.

(iv) So the epireader moves swiftly from print and language to speech and voice and the absent person. Prolific in narrative, the epireader construes reading as translation. Words may be translated, not without the change we feel as loss, into other words, because they are continuous, though not identical. And the use of words may be translated into corresponding acts and gestures: these are understood as symbolic acts. If you want to go further, you search for principles of action among the actions disclosed. Meanwhile: Hopkins loved words because he loved, or prayed to love, the God he construed as Word.

(v) There is a kind of poem you write to someone, knowing that you could as well pick up the telephone and speak to him/her directly.

The poem is not the same as the telephone call, but it has the same relation to the call that other poems have to paper and print. Frank O'Hara called the attitude Personism: 'The poem is at last between two persons instead of two pages.'

(vi) Virginia Woolf in *How It Strikes a Contemporary*: '[Scott and Wordsworth] know the relations of human beings towards each other and towards the universe. Neither of them probably has a word to say about the matter outright, but everything depends on it. . . . To believe that your impressions hold good for others is to be released from the cramp and confinement of personality.' Conversation, too, is a good cure for the cramp.

(vii) From 'Litany' from John Ashbery's *As We Know*:

> The talk leads nowhere but is
> Inside its space.

(viii) The best text I know on Epireading is Shakespeare, Sonnet 23, the ryming couplet:

> O learn to read what silent love hath writ.
> To hear with eyes belongs to love's fine wit.   . . .

. . . So what is graphireading? A stance, an attitude, a prejudice in favour of such assumptions as the following:

(i) No reconciliation between logocentrism and deconstruction.

(ii) Print is cool, unsentimental, unyearning; it is the space in which we can best be intelligent, uncluttered if not free.

(iii) The best sense is visual rather than auditory. With sight, you keep the object at a distance, and determine the best distance at which you keep it. In his Introduction to Finas's *Le Bruit d'Iris*, Barthes refers to the classic admonition that an object must be seen, to be truly seen, from an exactly judged point of view: not too close, not too far away. There is a precise point from which it is truly seen. Barthes refers to the admonition, but only to say that he, like Finas, rejects the privilege of the point of view; he insists on seeing the object from many different points, and giving each just as much privilege as Pascal gave his exact, classical point. The 'point of view' turns the one who stations himself there into an autocrat.

(iv) The enemy is the bourgeois state; its arrangements are consolation prizes for a besotted populace; its language is a programme for making unofficial thinking impossible.

(v) Interpretation is a bourgeois procedure because it offers its adept the satisfaction of discovery; this is the intellectual's version of acquiring goods, property, possessions. The single, true inter-pretation is an autocrat's dream of power.

(vi) The author is not the hero. Epireading turns literature into a sentimental tragedy, the most bourgeois form of literature, short of the realistic novel.

(vii) Graphireading eludes the sighs of time by recourse to the disinterestedness of space; silences the whine induced by tepid reflection upon mortality.

(viii) 'The signifer is what represents the subject for another signifier. . . . Only the relationship of one signifier to another signifier engenders the relationship of signifier to signified' (Lacan).

(ix) Put under the greatest possible stress such words as these: self, subject, author, imagination, story, history and reference.

(x) Graphireading wants to retrieve words from their public life (as negotiated by writer and reader) and restore them to their virtuality. Interpretation is regarded as sinister because it proposes to hold the words in common; that is, in a bourgeois system of commodity and exchange.

(xi) Do whatever you like with words, so long as you do not give them the privilege of being spoken. Thus Derrida's omnivorous attention to words (puns, ambiguities, phonetic quirks) is predicated upon their not being spoken: immobilised, rather. His play with etymologies gives words an impersonal mobility and range, but absolutely no personal or vocal reverberation.

(xii) Deconstruction: 'the eclipse of voice by text' (Geoffrey Hartman).

(xiii) Abandon the self to language: give up all psychological categories; replace them by linguistic functions.

(xiv) After reading Paul de Man's *Allegories of Reading*: Enforce a preference for *A* rather than *B*; that is

> Allegory rather than Symbol;
> Fancy rather than Imagination;
>
> Metonymy rather than Metaphor;
> Grammar rather than Rhetoric;

since the figures of *A* do not aspire to unity of experience, or claim that such a blessing may be had by recourse to an idealist relation between man and nature, self and landscape. The figures of *B* have accepted a distance in relation to their origin: they do not yearn. . . .

SOURCE: extracts from *Ferocious Alphabets* (London and Boston, Mass., 1981), pp. 146–8 & 199–201.

A. D. Nuttall 'Opaque and Transparent Criticism' (1983)

. . . There are two languages of criticism, the first 'opaque', external, formalist, operating outside the mechanisms of art and taking those mechanisms as its object, the second 'transparent', internal, realist, operating within the 'world' presented in the work. The first language throws upon the screen of critical consciousness all the formal devices of a work in such a way that the eye is arrested by them. Formal characters, in order that they should be the more visible, are deliberately made opaque. In the second language, formal devices are, like windows, transparent. We shall refer to the first mode, shortly, as the Opaque language and the second as the Transparent language. 'Opaque' and 'Transparent' are morally neutral terms. The initial capitals mark these words as technical terms.

The following sentences are all in the Opaque language:

1 In the opening of *King Lear* folk-tale elements proper to narrative are infiltrated by a finer-grained dramatic mode.

2 In Brueghel's *Fall of Icarus*, as the eye travels from the top of the picture, the shapes become increasingly curved; the bottom third of the painting is a sort of rollicking march of swooping, overlapping loops.

3 In *Portrait of a Lady* James applies to human figures language normally reserved for artefacts; Isabel Archer is 'written in a foreign tongue'; Daniel Touchett presents 'a fine, ivory surface'; Henrietta Stackpole 'has no misprints'.

4 In *Hamlet* Shakespeare contrives that the delay should be unintelligible, because the principal figure functions not as an explanatory device but as a source of intellectual frustration.

These sentences on the other hand, are in the Transparent language:

1 Cordelia cannot bear to have her love for her father made the subject of a partly mercenary game.

2   The ploughman may
   Have heard the splash, the forsaken cry,
   But for him it was not an important failure; the sun shone

As it had to on the white legs disappearing into the green
Water; and the expensive delicate ship that must have seen
Something amazing, a boy falling out of the sky,
Had somewhere to get to and sailed calmly on.
                    (W. H. Auden, 'Musée des Beaux Arts')

3 Isabel Archer is innocent, but in a quite a different way from
  Henrietta Stackpole.

4 Hamlet delays because, once he has cut himself off from the psychic
  support of human society, the central structure of his original
  motivation decays.

It is highly likely that to many readers of this book the first list will
automatically look like 'real criticism' and the second like 'self-
indulgent pseudo-criticism'. Yet sentences of the second type have
always figured in critical writing.

Each sentence in the first list makes explicit reference to the artifice
of the work; it takes as its province the artist's distinctive disposition
of forms, the mechanisms of representation, evocation, enchantment.
There is a mild presumption that to move from such formal scrutiny
into a freer discussion of that which is represented would be to leave
criticism altogether. Each sentence from the second set, on the other
hand, passes shamelessly into the world mimetically proposed in the
work of art, and discusses elements of that world as though they were
people or physical objects. Cordelia is considered, not as a sequence of
harsh yet appealing chords cutting across the sombre confusion
created by the Lear figure, but as a young woman in great distress. In
the Opaque group explanation is generally sought in terms of what
happens in other works of art, or elsewhere in the present work. In the
Transparent group no tabu exists against explaining fictitious
behaviour by analogy with real-life equivalents.

Latent in the Opaque approach is a severe separation of critic and
reader (or spectator). The critic knows how the conjuror does the
tricks, or how the tricks fool the audience, and is thereby excluded, by
his very knowingness, from the innocent delight of those who marvel
and applaud. Such criticism can never submit to mimetic
enchantment because to do so would be to forfeit critical
understanding of the means employed. The Transparent party, on
the other hand, is less afraid of submission, feeling the enchantment
need involve no submersion of critical faculties, but that on the
contrary without such a willingness to enter the proffered dream a
great many factors essential to a just appreciation may be artificially

excluded from discussion. After all its members are not in any fundamental sense fooled by the conjuror. They know perfectly well that all is done by artificial means. But at the same time they can perceive the magic as magic. They know that Ophelia is not a real woman but are willing to think of her as a possible woman. They note that Shakespeare implicitly asks them to do this, but they do more than note the request; they comply with it. They are much less aware than the Opaque party of restrictions on what they are allowed to discuss. For example, they are free to explore all the formal features which in Opaque criticism expand to fill the picture. A statement like 'The ideas of women presented in this novel are inadequate', although it refers externally to the artifice of the work, is thoroughly Transparent in its acceptance of mimetic reference. Adverse criticism of the values implied by texts is normally thus. Without a prior submission to the sovereign force of mimesis, no injustice could ever have been perceived. The Opaque critic, on the other hand, can be displeased by a work, but can never dissent from it. An Opaque critic would censor all the statements in the second group; a Transparent critic would pass all the statements in the first. The Transparent critic can and will do all the things done by the Opaque critic but is willing to do other things as well.

The main thrust of the case against Transparent criticism is that it confounds art and reality. Such was the case put in L. C. Knights's celebrated essay, 'How many children had Lady Macbeth?' Knights damned Bradleyan character-critics for speculating about Hamlet as if he were a real person; 'Hamlet' is not a real man at all, but a string of poetic expressions, a constellation of images. With human beings we may legitimately indulge in inference and supposition; we may say, 'She must have lived in India' or 'He must have been very religious at one time'; but with dramatic characters such inference is manifestly absurd; we cannot guess at Lady Macbeth's previous life for the simple reason that she has no previous life; her being begins and ends with what Shakespeare sets down for her to say.

It is strange that so coarse a piece of reasoning should have passed for a great stroke of destructive theory. Knights's singular presumption that humane inference is inapplicable to drama is simply mistaken. When a character sits up and yawns we infer that he has been sleeping. When another character gives a certain sort of start we infer that he is guilty (readers of *Macbeth*, especially, should be aware of this). If no inferences whatever are allowed, certain negative conclusions, on the other hand, can be drawn about Hamlet. For example he has no legs. For Shakespeare never mentions them – or may we infer (*infer?*) one leg from a down-gyved stocking? This may be thought merely silly, but a large part of Knights's case really does depend on the absolute exclusion of inference. Moreover, in a curious manner, Knights's criticism suggests that he really was more than half-willing to draw the conclusion that Hamlet is not a man. Here too one is drawn to offer a consciously philistine reply: 'Hamlet is a funny name for a sequence of images – sounds more like a person, a sort of Danish prince.' A dramatist faced with an entire audience who austerely repressed all inferences and bayed for image-patterns might well despair. Of course Bradley never supposed for a moment that Hamlet was a real man. Knights's ill-made shaft misses both Shakespeare and Bradley, and falls on stony ground. But the stony ground, it must be confessed, received it with joy.

What remains strong in Knights's attack is his intuition that Bradleyan critics occasionally carried their unverifiable surmises to ludicrous lengths. I cannot agree that the question about Lady Macbeth's children is as absurd as Knights would have had us believe, but certain of Maurice Morgann's observations on the military career of Falstaff . . . are truly foolish. But the simple test of verifiability will not serve to distinguish an absurd from a reasonable surmise. All our inferences and suppositions with regard to fictitious persons are in terms of probability, not fact. The objection to Morgann's speculations is not that Falstaff has no previous life but that Shakespeare does not give us enough clues to render Morgann's more detailed inferences probable. Knights's logical universe (like Todorov's later) was Puritan. There are facts and there are images. He is a logical Calvinist, forbidding all intercourse with the hypothetical, the merely probable.

The Transparent critic, who wonders why Cordelia cannot answer more warmly and thinks of other daughters, some of whom have lived outside the pages of books, is charged with confusing art and reality, but the charge is simply false. Where is the confusion? When Balzac sent for Dr Bianchon (a character in one of his books) to come to his bedside, he really did confuse art and reality. If he had merely asked 'What would Bianchon have said about a case like this?' no eyebrow would have been raised. The question is perfectly rational.

A whole generation was taught by Herbert Read to repress its natural engagement with mimetic painting. Delighted gazers at Edvard Munch's *House under Trees* (1905) had allowed their eyes to linger on the group of women in the foreground, so close to one another, so enigmatic, and then to be drawn into the further space, the pale wall and the trees, wintry yet with a bloom of spring in their soft extremities, and then beyond again to someone else's house, darker in the distance. Herbert Read, on the other hand, taught them, perfectly correctly, that Munch 'sacrificed tone to line' and that his lines enclosed definite, powerful planes.[1] The error was to suppose that such formal analysis somehow prohibited the other way of looking and this error was repeated again and again. It became fashionable to laugh at Walter Pater's rhapsodic musings on the *Mona Lisa*[2] and John Addington Symond's prose poem on Lorenzo de' Medici.[3]

An early consequence of this severe separation of technical ('critical') appreciation and ordinary 'entranced' appreciation is an impoverishment of criticism itself. If the critic never enters the dream he remains ignorant about too much of the work. The final result may be a kind of literary teaching which crushes literary enjoyment, the natural *coitus* of reader and work endlessly *interruptus*. The student who begins to talk excitedly about Becky Sharp will suddenly find himself isolated in the seminar. Another cooler student who is careful to speak of 'the Becky Sharp motif' tactfully assumes the central role in the discussion and covers the first student's confusion.

There is one other characteristic of the Opaque set of criticisms which should be noticed. They can never quite attain to pure formalism. Language has accepted (one suspects by Darwinian principle) the convenience of referring to characters in books by their fictitious names. We may remorselessly prefix such allusions with formal specifiers – 'the character, Hamlet', 'the motif, Becky Sharp' and so on – but there is something ponderously redundant about such scrupulousness. Language permits the bare use of the name because context renders the meaning sufficiently unambiguous. As we have seen, old-fashioned readers are in no way confused by this way of discussing fictional persons. Meanwhile the mere use of the proper name, 'Becky Sharp', however we fence it about with formal impediments, propels us into the world mimetically proposed, sets our thought in terms of people rather than artistic conventions. It is very hard indeed to describe a novel without referring to the things which are described as happening in it. It is similarly hard to describe a picture without occasionally looking through the arrangement of colour as if it were a window and allowing ourselves to notice, as it might be, the face, the raised hand, the distant tower.

SOUCE: extract from *A New Mimesis: Shakespeare and the Representation of Reality* (London, 1983), pp. 80–4.

NOTES

[Reorganised and renumbered from the original – Ed.]

1. Herbert Reed, *Art Now* (1933; 2nd edn London, 1960), pp. 62–3.

2. Walter Pater, *Studies in the History of the Renaissance* (1873; reprinted London, 1961), pp. 172–3.

3. J. A. Symonds, *The Life of Michelangelo Buonarroti* (London, 1893), vol. 2, p. 32.

3. IS LITERATURE LANGUAGE? – THE CLAIMS OF STYLISTICS

Stanley Fish   What is Stylistics and Why are they Saying such Terrible Things about It?   (1973)

The first of the questions in my title – what is stylistics – has already been answered by the practitioners of the art. Stylistics was born of a reaction to the subjectivity and imprecision of literary studies. For the appreciative raptures of the impressionistic critic, stylisticians purport to substitute precise and rigorous linguistic descriptions and to proceed from these descriptions to interpretations for which they can claim a measure of objectivity. Stylistics, in short, is an attempt to put criticism on a scientific basis. Answering my second question – why are they saying such terrible things about it? – will be the business of this essay. . . .

My first example is taken from the work of Louis Milic, author of *A Quantitative Approach to the Style of Jonathan Swift* and other statistical and computer studies. In an article written for *The Computer and Literary Style*, Milic attempts to isolate the distinctive features of Swift's style.[1] He is particularly interested in the Swiftian habit of piling up words in series and in Swift's preference for certain kinds of connectives. His method is to compare Swift, in these and other respects, with Macaulay, Addison, Gibbon and Johnson, and the results of his researches are presented in the form of tables: 'Word-Class Frequency Distribution of All the Whole Samples of Swift, with Computed Arithmetic Mean', 'Percentage of Initial Connectives in 2000-Sentence Samples of Addison, Johnson, Macaulay and Swift', 'Total Introductory Connectives and Total Introductory Determiners as Percentages of All Introductory Elements', 'Frequency of Occurrences of the Most Common Single Three-Word Pattern as a Percentage of Total Patterns', 'Total Number of Different Patterns per Sample'. It will not be my concern here to scrutinise the data-gathering methods of Milic or the other stylisticians (although some of them are challengeable even on their own terms), for my interest is primarily in what is done with the data after they have been gathered. This is also Milic's interest, and in the final paragraphs of his essay he poses the major question: 'What interpretive inferences can be drawn from the material?' (p. 104). The answer comes in two parts and illustrates the two basic manoeuvres executed by the stylisticians. The first is circular: 'The low frequency of initial determiners, taken together with the high frequency of initial connectives, makes [Swift] a writer who likes transitions and made much of connectives' (p. 104). As the reader will no doubt have noticed, the two halves of this sentence present the same information in slightly different terms, even though its rhetoric suggests that something has been explained. Here is an example of what makes some people impatient with stylistics and its baggage. The machinery of categorisation and classification merely provides momentary pigeonholes for the constituents of a text, constituents which are then retrieved and reassembled into exactly the form they previously had. There is, in short, no gain in understanding; the procedure has been executed, but it hasn't gotten you anywhere. Stylisticians, however, are *determined* to get somewhere, and exactly where they are determined to get is indicated by Milic's next sentence: '[Swift's] use of series argues [that is, is a sign of or means] a fertile and well stocked mind.' Here the procedure is not circular but arbitrary. The data are scrutinised and an interpretation is *asserted* for them, asserted rather than proven because there is nothing in the machinery Milic cranks up to authorise the leap (from the data to a specification of their value) he makes. What does authorise it is an unexamined and highly suspect assumption that one can read directly from the description of a text (however derived) to the shape or quality of its author's mind, in this case from the sheer quantity of verbal terms to the largeness of the intelligence that produced them.

The counter-argument to this assumption is not that it cannot be done (Milic, after all, has done it), but that it can be done all too easily, and in any direction one likes. One might conclude, for example, that Swift's use of series argues . . . an unwillingness to finish his sentences; or that Swift's use of series argues an anal-retentive personality; or that Swift's use of series argues a nominalist rather than a realist philosophy and is therefore evidence of a mind insufficiently stocked with abstract ideas. These conclusions are neither more nor less defensible than the conclusion Milic reaches, or reaches for (it is the enterprise and not any one of its results that should be challenged), and their availability points to a serious defect in the procedures of stylistics, the absence of any constraint on the way in which one moves from description to interpretation, with the result that any interpretation one puts forward is arbitrary. . . .

Milic affords a particularly good perspective on what stylisticians do because his assumptions, along with their difficulties, are displayed so nakedly. A sentence like 'Swift's use of series argues a fertile and well stocked mind' does not come along very often. More typically, a stylistician will interpose a formidable apparatus between his descriptive and interpretive acts, thus obscuring the absence of any connection between them. For Richard Ohmann, that apparatus is transformational grammar and in 'Generative Grammars and the Concept of Literary Style' he uses it to distinguish between the prose of Faulkner and Hemingway.[2] Ohmann does this by demonstrating that Faulkner's style is no longer recognisable when 'the effects of three generalised transformations' – the relative clause transformation, the conjunction transformation and the comparative transformation – are reversed. 'Denatured' of these transformations, a passage from 'The Bear', Ohmann says, retains 'virtually no traces of . . . Faulkner's style' (p. 142). When the same denaturing is performed on Hemingway, however, 'the reduced passage still sounds very much like Hemingway. Nothing has been changed that seems crucial' (p. 144). From this, Ohmann declares, follow two conclusions: (1) Faulkner 'leans heavily upon a very small amount of grammatical apparatus' (p. 143), and (2) the 'stylistic difference . . . between the Faulkner and Hemingway passages can be largely explained on the basis of [the] . . . apparatus' (p. 145). To the first of these I would reply that it depends on what is meant by 'leans heavily upon.' Is this a statement about the apparatus or about the actual predilection of the author? (The confusion between the two is a hallmark of stylistic criticism). To the second conclusion I would object strenuously, if by 'explained' Ohmann means anything more than made formalisable. That is, I am perfectly willing to admit that transformational grammar provides a better means of fingerprinting an author than would a measurement like the percentage of nouns or the mean length of sentences; for since the transformation model is able to deal not only with constituents but with their relationships, it can make distinctions at a structural, as opposed to a merely statistical, level. I am not willing, however, to give those distinctions an independent value, that is, to attach a fixed significance to the devices of the fingerprinting mechanism, any more than I would be willing to read from a man's actual fingerprint to his character or personality.

But this, as it turns out, is exactly what Ohmann wants to do. 'The move from formal description of styles to . . . interpretation', he asserts, 'should be the ultimate goal of stylistics', and in the case of Faulkner, 'it seems reasonable to suppose that a writer whose style is so largely based on just three semantically related transformations demonstrates in that style a certain conceptual orientation, a preferred way of organising experience' (p. 143). But Faulkner's style can be said to be 'based on' these three transformations only in the sense that the submission of a Faulkner text to the transformational apparatus yields a description in which they dominate. In order to make anything more out of this, that is, in order to turn the description into a statement about Faulkner's conceptual orientation, Ohmann would have to do what Noam Chomsky so pointedly refrains from doing, assign a semantic value to the devices of his descriptive mechanism, so that rather than being neutral between the processes of production and reception, they are made directly to reflect them. In the course of this and other essays, Ohmann does just that, finding, for example, that Lawrence's heavy use of deletion transformations is responsible for the 'driving insistence one feels in reading' him,[3] and that Conrad's structures of chaining reflect his tendency to 'link one thing with another associatively',[4] and that Dylan Thomas's breaking of selectional rules serves his 'vision of things' of 'the world as process, as interacting forces and repeating cycle';[5] in short, 'that these syntactic preferences *correlate* with habits of meaning'.[6]

The distance between all of this and 'Swift's use of series argues a fertile and well stocked mind' is a matter only of methodological sophistication, not of substance, for both critics operate with the same assumptions and nominate the same goal: the establishing of an inventory in which formal items will be linked in a fixed relationship to semantic and psychological values. Like Milic, Ohmann admits that at this point his interpretive conclusions are speculative and tentative; but again, like Milic, he believes that it is only a matter of time before he can proceed more securely on the basis of a firm correlation between syntax and 'conceptual orientation', and the possibility of specifying such correlations, he declares, 'is one of the main justifications for studying style.' If this is so, then the enterprise is in trouble, not because it will fail, but because it will, in every case, succeed. Ohmann will always be able to assert (although not to prove) a plausible connection between the 'conceptual orientation' he discerns in an author and the formal patterns his descriptive apparatus yields. But since there is no warrant for that connection in the grammar he appropriates, there is no constraint on the manner in which he makes it, and therefore his interpretations will be as arbitrary and unverifiable as those of the most impressionistic of critics. . . .

It is possible, I suppose, to salvage the game, at least temporarily, by making it more sophisticated, by contextualising it. One could simply write a rule that allows for the different valuings of the same pattern by taking into account the features which surround it in context. But this would only lead to the bringing forward of further counterexamples, and the continual and regressive rewriting of the rule. Eventually a point would be reached where a separate rule was required for each and every occurrence; and at that point the assumption that formal features *possess* meaning would no longer be tenable, and the enterprise of the stylisticians – at least as they conceive it – will have been abandoned. . . .

[In the section here omitted Fish considers cases where linguistic analysis seems to ignore all the information available to the reader from context, experience, and other sources which, he argues, is used to decode textual details. He continues. . .]

This goes to the heart of my quarrel with the stylisticians: in their rush to establish an inventory of fixed significances, they bypass the activity in the course of which significances are, if only momentarily, fixed. I have said before that their procedures are arbitrary, and that they acknowledge no constraint on their interpretations of the data. The shape of the reader's experience is the constraint they decline to acknowledge. Were they to make that shape the focus of their analyses, it would lead them to the value conferred by its events. Instead they proceed in accordance with the rule laid down by Martin Joos. 'Text signals its own structure', treating the deposit of an activity as if it were the activity itself, as if meanings arose independently of human transactions. As a result, they are left with patterns and statistics that have been cut off from their animating source, banks of data that are unattached to anything but their own formal categories, and are therefore, quite literally, meaningless.

In this connection it is useful to turn to a distinction, made by John Searle, between institutional facts – facts rooted in a recognition of human purposes, needs, and goals – and brute facts – facts that are merely quantifiable. 'Imagine,' says Searle,

a group of highly trained observers describing a . . . football game in statements only of brute facts. What could they say by way of description? Well, within certain areas a good deal could be said, and using statistical techniques certain 'laws' could even be formulated . . . we can imagine that after a time our observers would discover the law of periodic clustering: at regular intervals organisms in like coloured shirts cluster together in roughly circular fashion . . . Furthermore, at equally regular intervals, circular clustering is followed by linear clustering . . . and linear clustering is followed by the phenomenon of linear interpenetration . . . But no matter how much data of this sort we imagine our observers to collect and no matter how many inductive generalisations we imagine them to make from the data, they still have not described football. What is missing from their description? What is missed are . . . concepts such as touchdown, offside, game, points, first down, time out, etc. . . . The missing statements are precisely what describes the phenomenon on the field *as a game of football.* The other descriptions, the description of the brute facts can [only] be explained in terms of the institutional facts.[8]

In my argument the institutional facts are the events that are constitutive of the specifically human activity of reading, while the brute facts are the observable formal patterns that can be discerned in the traces or residue of that activity. The stylisticians are thus in the position of trying to do what Searle says cannot be done: explain the brute facts without reference to the institutional facts which give them value. They would specify the meaning of the moves in the game without taking into account the game itself. . . .

Does this mean a return to the dreaded impressionism? Quite the reverse. The demand for precision will be even greater because the object of analysis is a process whose shape is continually changing. In order to describe that shape, it will be necessary to make use of all the information that formal characterisations of language can provide, although that information will be viewed from a different perspective. Rather than regarding it as directly translatable into what a word or a pattern *means*, it will be used more exactly to specify what a reader, as he comes upon the word or pattern, is *doing*, what assumptions he is making, what conclusions he is reaching, what expectations he is forming, what attitudes he is entertaining, what acts he is being moved to perform. When Milic observes that in Swift's prose connectives are often redundant and even contradictory – concessives cheek by jowl with causals – we can proceed from what he tells us to an account of what happens when a reader is alternately invited to anticipate a conclusion and asked to qualify it before it appears. When Ohmann declares that the syntactical deviance of Dylan Thomas's 'A Winter's Tale' 'breaks down categorical boundaries and converts juxtaposition into action', the boundaries, if they exist, take the form of a reader's expectations and their breaking down is an action *he* performs, thereby fashioning for himself the 'vision of things' which the critic would attribute to the language. . . .

SOURCE: extracts from 'What is Stylistics and Why are they Saying such Terrible Things about It?' in Seymour Chatman (ed.), *Approaches to Poetics* (New York, 1973); reprinted in Fish's *Is There a Text in This Class?* (Cambridge, Mass., 1980), pp. 69–70, 71–3, 73–6, 77–8, 84–5, 91–2.

NOTES

[Reorganised and renumbered from the original – Ed.]

1. Louis Milic, article in Jacob Leed (ed.), *The Computer and Literary Style* (Columbus, Ohio, 1966).
2. Richard Ohmann, 'Generative Grammars and the Concept of Literary Style,' in Glen A. Love & Michael Payne (eds), *Contemporary Essays on Style* (Urbana, Ill., 1969).
3. Ibid., p. 148.   4. Ibid., p. 154.   5. Ibid., p. 156.
6. Ibid., p. 154.   7. Ibid., p. 143.
8. John Searle, *Speech Acts: An Essay in the Philosophy of Language* (Cambridge, 1969), p. 52.

Roger Fowler   Studying Literature as Language   (1984)

For the past twenty-five years or so, there has been a running dispute between literary critics and linguists on the question of whether it is appropriate to apply linguistic methods – that is to say, methods derived from the discipline of linguistics – to the study of literature. There has been almost universal confidence among the linguists that this activity is entirely justified; and almost universal resistance by the critics, who have regarded the exercise with almost moral indignation. In this unyielding dispute, the claims and denials on both sides have been voiced with great force and passion. Here is Roman Jakobson putting the linguist's case, in 1958:

Poetics deals with problems of verbal structure, just as the analysis of painting is concerned with pictorial structure. Since linguistics is the global science of verbal structure, poetics may be regarded as an integral part of linguistics.[1]

But the critics will not have this. In a long, bitter controversy between the late F. W. Bateson and myself in 1967, the counter-argument against linguistics was based essentially on an allegation of unfitness. Linguistics is a science, claims Bateson, but literature has what he calls an 'ineradicable subjective core' which is inaccessible to science. Again, linguistic processing is only a preliminary to literary response, so the linguist is incapable of taking us far enough in an account of literary form and experience.

Finally, here is a dismissive opposition formulated by David Lodge, which is really saying that never the twain shall meet:

> One still feels obliged to assert that the discipline of linguistics will never *replace* literary criticism, or radically change the bases of its claims to be a useful and meaningful form of human inquiry. It is the essential characteristic of modern linguistics that it claims to be a science. It is the essential characteristic of literature that it concerns values. And values are not amenable to scientific method.[2]

The opposition between science and values is at the heart of the refusal to agree; it manifests itself in different specific forms in many distinct arguments among protagonists for the two cases. What I would like you to note in this contribution by Lodge is the way in which the key terms, 'science' and 'values', are felt to be self-explanatory and conclusive. Lodge, like most of the debaters on both sides, requires us to take the central terms on trust, to accept them in their commonsense meanings with their ordinary values presupposed. In effect, Lodge is perceiving the two disciplines in terms of stereotypes, rather than analysing carefully the terms and concepts involved in the comparison. I do not say that Lodge is especially culpable, merely that this statement of his is characteristic of this habit, in the debate, of relying on undefined and stereotypical terms. Both sides are guilty of this.

I realised a long time ago that I must stop adding fuel to this dispute; since the confrontation was conducted in conditions of quite inadequate theorisation, it was impossible to participate in it as a reasoned debate. Without getting involved in the controversy again, I would like to merely mention some common failures of theorisation which render it impossible to deal sensibly with a question so naively formulated as 'Can linguistics be applied to literature?'

1. A major difficulty, on both sides, is a completely uncritical understanding of what is meant by 'linguistics'. The literary critics make no allowance for the fact that there exist different linguistic theories with quite distinct characteristics. While it might be true of linguistic model 'A' that it can or cannot carry out some particular function of criticism, the same might not be true of model 'B' which has a different scope or different manner of proceeding. If the critics are not well enough informed to discriminate between models, the linguists do not acknowledge the distinctions; a linguist will work on literature in terms of the theory s/he happens to uphold as the 'correct' theory. Such is the competitiveness of the schools of

linguistics that a devotee of one theory will not acknowledge that a rival might have some advantages for the task in hand.

2. A second persistent fallacy about linguistics, again represented on both sides, concerns the analytic *modus operandi* of linguistic method. It will be clear from what I have just said that different models have quite diverse aims, and procedures towards those aims. One model may have the purpose of accounting for the structure of particular texts; another may focus on sociolinguistic variation; another may be concerned to increase our knowledge about linguistic universals; and so on.

But there is a common misconception that linguistics – any linguistics – is a kind of automatic analyising device which, fed a text, will output a description without human intervention. (The critics of course regard this as a soullessly destructive process, a cruelty to poems, but that is simply an emotional over-reaction based on a misconception.) Now whatever differences there are between contemporary linguistic theories, I think they would all agree with Chomsky's insistence that linguistics is *not* a discovery procedure. Linguistic analysis works only in relation to what speakers know already, or what linguists hypothesise in advance. So the whole range of objections to linguistics on the grounds that it is merely a mechanical procedure can be dismissed; linguistic analysis is a flexible, directed operation completely under the control of its users, who can direct it towards any goals which are within the scope of the model being used. Complete human control is possible if you carefully theorise the nature of your objective, and the nature of the object you are studying.

Which leads me to mention a second set of deficiencies in the way linguistic criticism is theorised, and then to the more positive part of my argument.

Even if critics and linguists positively acknowledge that language is of fundamental importance to the structure of the literary text, there is no guarantee that they will present language in a realistic and illuminating way. There are three representations of language that I regard as particularly unhelpful, and I will briefly instance them by reference to the work of scholars whose commitment to language is undoubted and substantial.

1. The first problematic attitude is that which regards language in literature as an *object*. This position is implicit throughout the work of Roman Jakobson.[3] Jakobson's 'poetic function' claims that the important thing about literature is the way in which structure is organised to foreground the substantive elements of text – in particular, phonology and syntax. The patterns of parallelism and

equivalence which he finds in his poems, at these levels of language, bulk out the formal structure, e.g. metrical and stanzaic structure, so that the text is re-presented as if its main mode of existence were perceptible physical form. The cost of this imaginary process is minimisation of what we might call communicative and interpersonal – in a word, *pragmatic* – functions of the text. As I shall show in a moment, it is exactly these pragmatic dimensions which give the richest significance for critical studies. It is a pity that this 'objective' theory of language in literature should have been given currency by such a brilliant and influential linguist as Jakobson.

2. A second unhelpful attitude to language is that which treats it as a *medium* through which literature is transmitted. Here I quote David Lodge again: 'The novelist's medium is language: whatever he does, *qua* novelist, he does in and through language.'[4] Presumably language as a medium is analogous to paint, bronze or celluloid for other arts. But the metaphor easily comes to mean '*only* a medium': the real thing is the novel (or poem, etc.) which is conveyed 'in and through' the medium. Thus the substance of literature is shifted into some obscure, undefined, sphere of existence which is somehow beyond language. But for linguistics, literature *is* language, to be theorised just like any other discourse; it makes no sense to degrade the language to a mere medium, since the meanings, themes, larger structures of a text, 'literary' or not, are uniquely constructed by the text in its interrelation with social and other contexts.

This position is difficult for literary critics to swallow, because it appears to remove the claimed special status (and value) of literature, to reduce it to the level of the language of the marketplace. But this levelling is essential to linguistic criticism if the whole range of insights about language provided by linguistics is to be made available. We want to show that a novel or a poem is a complexly structured text; that its structural form, by social semiotic processes, constitutes a representation of a world, characterised by activities and states and values; that this text is a communicative interaction between its producer and its consumers within relevant social and institutional contexts. Now these characteristics of the novel or poem are no more than what functional linguistics is looking for in studying, say, conversations or letters or official documents. Perhaps this is a richer and thus more acceptable characterisation of the aims of linguistic analysis than literary critics usually expect. But for me at any rate, this is what theorisation *as* language involves. No abstract literary properties 'beyond' the medium need to be postulated, for the rhetorical and semiotic properties in question should appear within an ordinary linguistic characterisation, unless linguistics is conceived in too restricted a way.

3. Implicit in what I have just said is my reluctance to accept one further assumption about language which is wide spread in stylistics and criticism. This is the belief that there is a distinct difference between poetic or literary language on the one hand and ordinary language on the other. Critics generally take for granted some version of this distinction; and some linguists have attempted to demonstrate it: we find strong arguments to this effect in the writings of, for example, Jakobson and Mukarovský. But these arguments are not empirically legitimate, and they are a serious obstacle to a linguistic criticism which attempts to allow to literature the communicative fullness that is a common property of language.

I have given some reasons why the apparently simple question 'Can linguistics be applied to literature?' is unlikely to be satisfactorily answered. Because I believe that linguistics *can* very appropriately and revealingly be applied to literature, I want to reorient the issue, in different terms. The solution is, it seems to me, to simply theorise literature *as* language, and to do this using the richest and most suitable linguistic model.

To be adequate to this task, a linguistic model should possess the following broad characteristics. It should be *comprehensive* in accounting for the whole range of dimensions of linguistic structure, particularly pragmatic dimensions. It should be capable of providing an account of the *functions* of given linguistic constructions (in real texts), particularly the thought-shaping (Halliday's 'ideational') function. It should acknowledge the *social* basis of the formation of meanings (Halliday's 'social semiotic').[5]

The requisite linguistics for our purpose, unlike most other, artificially restricted, forms of linguistics, should aim to be comprehensive in offering a complete account of language structure and usage at all levels: semantics, the organisation of meanings within a language; syntax, the processes and orderings which arrange signs into the sentences of a language; phonology and phonetics, respectively the classification and ordering, and the actual articulation, of the sounds of speech; text-grammar, the sequencing of sentences in coherent extended discourse; and pragmatics, the conventional relationships between linguistic constructions and the users and uses of language.

Pragmatics is a part of linguistics which is still very much subject to debate and development,[6] but it is clear that it includes roughly the following topics: the interpersonal and social acts that speakers perform by speaking and writing; thus, the structure of not only conversation but also of all other sorts of linguistic communication as *interaction*; the diverse relationships between language use and its different types of context; particularly the relationships with social contexts and their historical development; and fundamentally, the systems of shared knowledge within communities, and between speakers, which make communication possible – this is where pragmatics and semantics overlap. In various writings I have stressed the need in linguistic criticism to mend the neglect of the interactional facets of 'literary' texts: the rhetorical relationships between addressor and addressee, the dynamics of construction of fictional characters, and the sociolinguistic relationships between the producers and consumers of literature.[7] The second strand of pragmatics, concerning linguistic structure and systems of knowledge, will enrich linguistic criticism even more, and bring it into positive collaboration with literary criticism.

A 'functional' model of language works on the premise that linguistic structures are not arbitrary, nor, as Chomsky claims, broadly constrained by universal properties of Mind. Rather, particular language structures assume the forms they do in response to the communicative uses to which they are put, within a speech community. Halliday proposes three categories of 'function': ideational, interpersonal and textual. The ideational function is a key concept in linguistic criticism. The experience of individuals, and, around them, their communities, is encoded in the language they use as sets of ideas; and the ideational will differ as the dominant ideas of speakers differ. A simple example would be the operational concepts of a science, coded for the relevant speakers in a technical terminology; for these speakers, the terminology is one part of the linguistic organisation of their experience: though this is a specialised part of the ideational, a technical terminology is only an obvious instance of a general principle, namely that language structure, in its ideational function, is constitutive of a speaker's experience of reality.

And of a community's experience; this is what 'social semiotic' means. Although, undoubtedly, some of the meanings encoded in language are natural in origin, reflecting the kind of organism we are (e.g. basic colour, shape and direction terms),[8] most meanings are social: the dominant preoccupations, theories or ideologies of a community are coded in its language, so that the semantic structure is a map of the community's knowledge and its organisation. An important development of this principle follows from the fact that communities are ideologically diverse: the existence of complex and competing sets of ideas gives rise to diverse styles, registers or varieties carrying semiotically distinct versions of reality according to the distinct views of individuals and of subcommunities. For the critics, this is linguistic support for the traditional assumption (formulated by Leo Spitzer but implicit much more widely) that a style embodies a view of the world. The advance in Halliday's and my formulation is that the availability of a formal method of linguistic analysis facilitates the unpicking of relationships between style and the representation of experience.

I want now to look at a textual example; for economy of exposition, a very familiar passage. This will not 'prove the theory', but it will suggest the directions in which this theory of language might take us. The extract is the opening of William Faulkner's *The Sound and the Fury*, a familiar but striking example of the way in which language structure gives form to a view of the world.

Through the fence, between the curling flower spaces, I could see them hitting. They were coming towards where the flag was and I went along the fence. Luster was hunting in the grass by the flower tree. They took the flag out, and they were hitting. Then they put the flag back and they went to the table, and he hit and the other hit. Then they went on, and I went along the fence. Luster came away from the flower tree and we went along the fence and they stopped and we stopped and I looked through the fence while Luster was hunting in the grass.
  'Here, caddie.' He hit. They went across the pasture. I held to the fence and watched them going away.
  'Listen at you, now', Luster said. 'Ain't you something, thirty-three years old, going on that way. After I done went all the way to town to buy you that cake. Hush up that moaning. Ain't you going to help me find that quarter so I can go to the show tonight?'
  They were hitting little, across the pasture. I went back along the fence to where the flag was. It flapped on the bright grass and trees.

The character from whose point of view this part of the narrative is told is Benjy, a 33-year-old man with the mind of a young child. It is obvious that Faulkner has designed this language to suggest the limitations of Benjy's grasp of the world around him. But how does the reader arrive at this almost instinctive realisation? There are some linguistic clues, and these are very suggestive, but by themselves they do not answer the question of how we give the passage the interpretation I have assigned to it.

  Starting with the language: although it is deviant, it is not disintegrated in a haphazard fashion, but systematically patterned in certain areas of structure. Two observations are relevant here. First, random deviance or self-consistent deviance were options for Faulkner; they could be considered different models of mental deficiency. Second, certain types of structure, through repetition, are 'foregrounded' (a process well known to stylisticians): foregrounding implies perceptual salience for readers, a pointer to areas of significance.

Most striking is a consistent oddity in what linguists call *transitivity*: the linguistic structuring of actions and events. In this passage there are almost no transitive verbs; instead, a preponderance of intransitives ('coming', 'went', 'hunting', etc.) and one transitive ('hit') used repeatedly without an object, as if it were intransitive. It is implied that Benjy has little sense of actions and their effects on objects: a restricted notion of causation.

Second, Benjy has no names for certain concepts which are crucial to his understanding of what he is witnessing. In certain cases the word is suppressed entirely: notably, the word 'golf'; in others he uses circumlocutions to designate objects for which he lacks a term: 'the curling flower spaces', 'where the flag was', 'the flower tree'. The implication of this is that he has command of only a part of his society's classification of objects.

Third, he uses personal pronouns in an odd way – look at the sequence 'them. . .they. . .They. . .they. . .they. . .he. . .the other. . .'. He uses these pronouns without identifying who he is referring to and with little variation in the pronoun forms themselves. It is suggested by this that Benjy does not appreciate what is needed if one wishes to specify to another person an object which one knows about but the other person does not. This would obviously be a severe communicative handicap.

Fourth, there is a problem with Benjy's *deictic* terms: the words used to point to and orient objects and actions. There are plenty of these deictics in the passage: 'Through. . .between. . .coming toward where. . .went along. . .' etc. But these words do not add up to a consistent and comprehensible picture of the positions and movements of Benjy himself, his companion Luster, and the golfers whom they are watching. Try drawing diagrams of the sequence of positions and movements. Benjy is literally disoriented, with little sense of his location and of others' relationships with him within a context. The deictic inconsistency produces, for the reader, a sense of incoherence in the narrating, a feeling of being in the presence of a storyteller whose perceptions are disjointed.

In each of the above four paragraphs, I have first noted a recurrent linguistic construction, and then added an interpretative comment. The question arises (or ought to) of what is the authority for these comments. Let us be clear that there are no mimetic considerations involved, and no question of objective criteria for fidelity of representation: what reader could say 'I recognise this as an accurate rendering of the story-telling style of a person with such-and-such a cognitive disability'? and wouldn't this response anyway miss the point that language constructs fictions rather than models reality? But it might be argued, on the 'fiction-constructing' premise, that what happens here is precisely that the specific language of this text somehow creates Benjy's consciousness *ab initio*. This kind of argument, common in literary criticism, has never seemed to me very plausible; since linguistic forms come to the writer already loaded with significances, it is unlikely that words and sentences could be used to create new meanings autonomously in a particular text. It is probable, then, that the significances here are conventional, but having said that, it is necessary to define more precisely what is going on in the interaction between text, reader and culture. At this stage of research, I cannot be absolutely exact, but can indicate something of the complexity of the processes.

Functional grammar maintains that linguistic constructions are selected according to the communicative purposes that they serve. It can be assumed that the total linguistic resources available to a speaker have been cumulatively formed by the communicative practices of the society into which s/he is born, and then by the practices in which s/he participates during socialisation. On this theory, an explanation of my phrase 'loaded with significances' above would be that the linguistic units and structures available to an individual signify their associated functions: e.g. the word 'photosynthesis', in addition to its dictionary meaning of a certain botanical life-process, has the association of a scientific register of language; 'once upon a time' signifies narrative for children; and so on. If it were as simple as this, each individual would possess, in addition to his/her semantic and syntactic and phonological competence, a kind of 'pragmatic dictionary' in which the communicative and social significances of forms were reliably stored. This would, of course, differ from individual to individual depending on their communicative roles within society, but with very substantial overlap.

The catch with this model is that linguistic forms may be pragmatically, as well as semantically, ambiguous. There is not an invariant relationship between form and function. So the linguistic critic, like the ordinary reader or hearer, cannot just recognise the linguistic structure and, consulting his pragmatic competence, assign a significance to it. A more realistic view of linguistic interaction is that we process text as *discourse*, that is, as a unified whole of text and context – rather than as a structure with function attached. We approach the text with a hypothesis about a relevant context, based on our previous experiences of relevant discourse, and relevant contexts: this hypothesis helps us to point an interpretation, to assign significances, which are confirmed or disconfirmed or modified as the discourse proceeds. In the case of face-to-face interaction in conversation, feedback occurs to assist the refining of the hypothesis; with written texts, we are reliant on our existing familiarity with relevant modes of discourse and on our skill (developed in literary education and in other conscious studies of discourse, e.g. sociolinguistics) at bringing appropriate discourse models to bear. As critics know, the reader's realisation of a literary text as discourse takes reading and re-reading, on the basis of the maximum possible previous experience of the canon of literature and of other relevant discourse; to assist this process and to firm up our hypotheses, discussion with other experienced readers of literature is invaluable.

I am not an expert on Faulkner, and can only suggest the direction in which the analysis might go. The features noted can be traced in other texts which characterise various limitations of cognitive ability or of experience. For example, similar peculiarities of transitivity have been noted by Halliday in the language which depicts the thought-processes of William Golding's Neanderthal Man Lok in his novel *The Inheritors*, and he has interpreted them, as I have done here, as suggestions of a weak grasp of causation.[9] Circumlocutions like Benjy's 'the flower tree' are examples of a process called *underlexicalization* which is common in the characterisation of naive, inexperienced people; cf. my comments on Kingsley Amis's treatment of his provincial heroine Jenny Bunn in *Take a Girl like You*.[10] The use of personal pronouns without specifying their referents, according to the sociologist Basil Bernstein, is a sign of an excessive dependence on context characteristic of working-class speakers of 'restricted code'; interestingly, this suggestion is based not on empirical evidence but on an example fabricated by a co-researcher: thus Bernstein is operating with an essentially fictional model.[11]

The fact that the three texts I have referred to all come many years *after* the publication of *The Sound and the Fury* is not especially damaging: I am not, in this paper, discussing sources and influences, direct historical influence of one specific text upon another. I could readily find earlier instances of all four constructions with comparable cognitive significances (in older Gothic, naïve poetry, diaries and letters of poorly educated people, etc.), but the point is to show that there exist for the modern reader established modes of discourse for the characterisation of naïve consciousness and which guide her/him towards the interpretations which I have suggested. This is the only basis on which the contemporary critic can begin to read a text. Later stages of critical practice can, and perhaps ought to be, more strictly historical. Faulkner is building a specific model of idiocy, as in the other sections of the novel, he is constituting other types of consciousness. The moral relationships between these points of view are of course the central concern of the fiction: Faulkner is juxtaposing modes of discourse to involve readers in a practice of evaluation. What literary, psychological and sociological discourses went to mould and articulate his models of deviant personalities is a question in historical sociolinguistics and pragmatics which I am not competent to answer without a great deal of research. But the research would be a kind of historical criticism of discourse and values. Critics may find it comforting that such research is compatible with the present theory of language – though of course not with previous formalist conceptions of linguistic stylistics.

Let me add a brief pedagogical and methodological conclusion. The theory of literature as language as I have articulated it is congruent with the elementary observation that students' critical performance, ability to 'read' in the sense of realising text as significant discourse, is very much dependent on how much and what they have read. Because reading and criticism depend on knowledge of discourse, not ability to dissect text structurally, it should not be expected that teaching formal linguistic analysis to beginning literature students will in itself produce any great advance in critical aptitude. However, linguistics of the kind indicated in this paper, with sociolinguistics, discourse analysis and pragmatics, in the context of a literature course of decent length – in our case three years – is very effective. In this type of course students mature gradually in their command of modes of literary discourse, simultaneously gaining a theoretical knowledge of language and its use, and an analytic method and terminology with which to describe the relationships between linguistic structures and their functions in 'literary' discourses. Finally, since knowledge is formed for the individual in *social* structure, this approach is best taught and discussed in seminar groups rather than lectures and tutorials: thus experience of discourse can be shared.

Underlying these comments on linguistic criticism in literary education are my answers to some basic methodological – or metamethodological – questions which were implicit in my opening discussion. These have to do with whether linguistic criticism is *objective*. The linguistic description of structures in text is certainly objective, particularly at the levels of syntax and phonology (semantic description produces less agreement among linguists). But it is clear that the assignment of functions or significances is not an objective process, because of the noted lack of co-variation of form and function. This does not mean that interpretation is a purely subjective, individual practice (a desperate and anarchic position into which those critics who stress the primacy of individual experience argue themselves). Criticism is an *inter-subjective* practice. The significances which an individual critic assigns are the product of social constitution; cultural meanings coded in the discourses in which the critic is competent. It is understandable, then, that critical interpretation is a matter of public discussion and debate; linguistic description, allowing clear descriptions of structures and a theory of social semiotic, is of fundamental importance in ensuring a clear grasp of the objective and intersubjective elements of texts under discussion.

SOURCE: 'Studying Literature as Language', *Dutch Quarterly Review of Anglo-American Literature* (1984), pp. 171–84.

NOTES

1. Roman Jakobson, 'Concluding Statement: Linguistics and Poetics', in T. A. Sebeok (ed.), *Style in Language* (Cambridge, Mass., 1960), p. 350.
2. David Lodge, *Language of Fiction* (London, 1966), p. 57.
3. See Roger Fowler, 'Linguistics and, and vèrsus, Poetics', *Journal of Literary Semantics*, 8 (1979), pp. 3–21; 'Preliminaries to a Sociolinguistic Theory of Literary Discourse', *Poetics*, 8 (1979), pp. 531–56.
4. Lodge, op. cit., p. ix.
5. For relevant selections from Halliday's writings see G. R. Kress (ed.), *Halliday: System and Function in Language* (London, 1976); M. A. K. Halliday, *Language as Social Semiotic* (London, 1978).
6. For a recent introduction, see G. N. Leech, *Principles of Pragmatics* (London, 1983).
7. See Roger Fowler, *Literature as Social Discourse* (London, 1981).
8. See H. H. Clark & E. V. Clark, *Psychology and Language* (New York, 1977), ch. 14.
9. M. A. K. Halliday, 'Linguistic Fiction and Literary Style: An Inquiry into the Language of William Golding's *The Inheritors*', in S. Chatman (ed.), *Literary Style: A Symposium* (London and New York, 1971), pp. 330–65.
10. Roger Fowler, *Linguistics and the Novel* (London, 2nd edn 1983), pp. 101–3.
11. B. Bernstein, *Class, Codes and Control*, vol. I (London, 1971), pp. 178–9.

4. WHAT IS DECONSTRUCTION?

Jonathan Culler   Jacques Derrida   (1979)

Although the work of Jacques Derrida is a major force in contemporary literary and philosophical debate, it is too early to predict what will prove to have been his most powerful contribution. When we look back in twenty, in fifty, in a hundred years, will he prove to have inaugurated a new era in the history of philosophy? Will he have been responsible for a new mode of reading and interpretation and an accompanying theory of the nature of texts? Will he be seen as a key figure in the development and reorientation of an intellectual movement which will doubtless by then have a new name but which will encompass what we now think of as structuralism and post-structuralism? Rather than venture predictions about the significance future developments will give to his work, the best strategy is to approach his writings from several perspectives, creating, from the texts that bear his name, three Derridas, three projects which are important for us today.

First, as a philosopher, as a reader of philosophical texts, Derrida has demonstrated the persistence in the Western philosophical tradition of what he calls 'logocentrism' or the 'metaphysics of presence'. He argues that the different theories and theses of philosophy are versions of a single system, and though we cannot hope to escape this system we can at least identify the conditions of thought it imposes by attending to that which it seeks to repress. Though we cannot imagine or bring about the *end* of metaphysics, we can undertake a critique of it from within by identifying and reversing the hierarchies it has established. In his dealings with philosophical texts, Derrida has produced a powerful and critical account of Western thought.

Secondly, Derrida is a reader, an interpreter. His readings of a variety of texts – Rousseau, Saussure, Freud, Plato, Genet, Hegel, Mallarmé, Husserl, J. L. Austin, Kant – have become, for those alert to the adventures of intelligence, exemplary analyses, models of a new practice of interpretation. Attentive to the ways in which texts implicitly criticise and undermine the philosophies in which they are implicated, he carries on a double mode of reading, showing the text to be woven from different strands which can never result in a synthesis but continually displace one another. This new practice of reading and writing is making itself felt particularly in the realm of literary criticism.

Finally, Derrida is one of a group of innovative French thinkers, who can be loosely labelled 'structuralist and post-structuralist' and whose efforts in a variety of disciplines have created if not a movement (for they would certainly wish to stress their disagreements with one another), at least a force. The work of each has focused on problems of language and structure and the cumulative effect, even of their disagreements, has been a powerful impetus to a certain style of thought and set of concerns. But precisely because structuralism and its aftermath constitute not a unified theory but a complex network of writings interacting in various ways, it is extremely difficult to map and to interpret them. Derrida's special importance lies in the fact that he alone . . . has written about the works of the others, relating them to central problems of structuralist and post-structuralist theory, and thus providing a perspective which helps us to understand what is at stake in the intellectual enterprises to which the present book refers.

Each of these contributions by Derrida is, of course, a major enterprise, and to attribute all three of them to a single writer must seem to be casting him in the role of supreme master of theory and textuality: author of a comprehensive theory which can place and account for other theories and explicate the works in which they are expressed. . . . But both Derrida and his admirers repeatedly stress that he does not propose a comprehensive or unified theory that would master and explain literature, language, philosophy. Derrida always writes about particular texts, and the kind of writing which he practises and would like to inspire in others explores precisely the impossibility of comprehensive mastery, the impossibility of constructing a coherent and adequate theoretical system. Unlike most theorists, who build a system around several key concepts, Derrida is continually giving strategic roles to new terms, usually taken from the texts he is discussing; and these terms acquire a special salience from the structural complexity of the role they play in the interaction of Derrida's text with that other text. Derrida continually introduces new terms, displacing the old, in order to prevent any of them from becoming the central concepts of a new theory or system. . . .

Derrida was trained in philosophy, the subject which he now teaches at the École Normale Supérieure in Paris. His first work, *L'Origine de la géometrie*, was published in 1962 and consists of a

170-page introduction to a paper by the German philosopher Edmund Husserl on the origin of geometry. . . . *L'Origine de la géométrie* won a philosophical prize but did not attract much attention outside the circle of philosophers concerned with Husserl and phenomenology. Shortly thereafter, however, Derrida began publishing essays in French intellectual periodicals, and in 1967 he suddenly imposed himself on the intellectual scene with three books, *Of Grammatology*, *Writing and Difference*, and *Speech and Phenomena*.

Of Grammatology is perhaps Derrida's best-known work. It concerns the way in which those who write about language have always privileged speech over writing and about what is at stake in that hierarchisation. Arguing that all those qualities which are said to characterise writing, as distinct from speech, turn out to hold for speech also, Derrida considers the possibility, alluded to in his title (grammatology = the science of writing), of inverting the hierarchy and orienting a theory of language not on speech but on a generalised writing. The principal authors discussed in this book are Ferdinand de Saussure, the founder of modern linguistics, and Jean-Jacques Rousseau, one of whose many works is an 'Essay on the Origin of Language'. . . .

Writing and Difference is a collection of essays on the works of major contemporary figures and the general theoretical tendencies they represent: Jean Rousset and structuralist literary criticism, Michel Foucault, Edmond Jabès, Emmanuel Levinas, Husserl, Antonin Artaud, Freud, Georges Bataille, Claude Lévi-Strauss and structuralism in the human sciences. . . .

Speech and Phenomena, unlike the other two books of 1967, is a unified work of philosophical analysis concerned with Husserl's theory of signs and in particular with the role and status in phenomenology of the notions of voice and presence. . . .

These three books made Derrida into a major figure in the theoretical debates which dominated French intellectual life in the late 1960s. Though associated with structuralism by his opponents, Derrida repeatedly produced readings which demonstrated the paradoxes of structuralist positions. In 1972 he once again brought out three books composed of such readings and other material: *Marges de la philosophie*, *La Dissémination*, and *Positions*. . . .

What is the nature of the project to which all these writings contribute? Derrida's readings of various texts and the constructions of his own texts are explorations of Western 'logocentrism'. The 'metaphysics of presence', which these texts can be shown simultaneously to affirm and to undermine, is the only metaphysics we know and underlies all our thinking; but it can be shown to give rise to paradoxes that challenge its coherence and consistency and therefore challenge the possibility of determining or defining being as presence. The framework of the history of metaphysics, Derrida writes,

is the determination of being as *presence* in all the senses of this word. It would be possible to show that all the terms related to fundamentals, to principles, or to the centre have always designated the constant of a presence – *eidos, archè, telos, energeia, ouisa* (essence, existence, substance, subject), *aletheia,* transcendentality, consciousness or conscience, God, man, and so forth.

(Writing and Difference)

Three examples will help to illustrate what is involved in the metaphysics of presence. In the Cartesian *cogito*, 'I think, therefore I am', the *I* is deemed to lie beyond doubt because it is present to itself in the act of thinking. The proposition 'I am, I exist' is necessarily true, Descartes says, 'each time I pronounce it or conceive it in my mind'. Or consider, as a second example, our familiar notion that the present instant is what exists. The future will exist and the past did exist but the reality of each depends on its relation to the presence of a present: the future is an anticipated presence and the past a former presence. A third instance would be the notion of meaning (when we speak to each other) as something present to the consciousness of the speaker, which is then expressed through signs or signals: meaning is what the speaker 'has in mind' at the crucial moment.

As these three examples indicate, the metaphysics of presence is pervasive and familiar. What is perhaps less obvious is the way in which the nature and reality of things in the universe, including numerous things which transcend any given instant, is thought to be grounded on this kind of presence. Thus, Descartes argues for the existence of the self (which we usually think of as the relatively permanent core of an individual) by claiming that at each instant of consciousness there is necessarily something (an *I*) which is conscious. Or again, the reality of a tree is made to depend on the fact that there is a tree there at time x, at time y, and again at time z; its existence is a series of presences. Finally, when we say that a given word means such and such, we can argue that this is a form of shorthand for the fact that at time x someone used the word to signify such and such, which was the concept present in his mind; at time y someone else used the word in the same sense, and so on. Reality is thus made up of a series of present states. These states are what is basic, the elementary constituents which are given and on which our account of the universe depends. This view is powerful and persuasive, but there is a problem which it characteristically encounters. When we invoke these states or moments of presence which are supposedly so basic, we discover that they are themselves already dependent in various ways and therefore cannot serve as the simple givens on which explanation must rest.

Consider, for example, the flight of an arrow. If we focus on a series of present states we encounter a paradox: at any given time the arrow is at a particular spot; it is always in a particular spot and never in motion. Yet we want to insist, quite justifiably, that the arrow *is* in motion at every instant between the beginning and the end of its flight. When we focus on present states, the motion of the arrow is never present, never given. It turns out that motion, which is after all a fundamental reality of our world, is only conceivable in so far as every instant, every present state, is already marked with the traces of the past and the future. An account of what is happening at a given instant requires reference to other instants which are not present. There is thus a crucial sense in which the non-present inhabits and is part of the present. The motion of the arrow is never given as something simple and present which could be grasped in itself; it is always already complex and differential, involving traces of the *not-now* in the *now*.

This is one of the Greek philosopher Zeno's famous paradoxes. Others, less dramatic but no less intractable, arise in whatever domain one investigates. Generally, one can say, with Derrida, that nothing is ever simply present. Anything that is supposedly present and given as such is dependent for its identity on differences and relations which can never be present. But the fact that differences are not present doesn't mean that they are absent. Our language is so suffused with the metaphysics of presence that it seems to offer us only this alternative: either something is present or else it is absent. The Derridean critique of this metaphysics involves, among other things, identifying elements, terms, and functions which, like 'difference', are difficult to conceive within this framework and which, when brought to the fore, work not so much to discredit that framework as to indicate its limits. Difference resists discussion in terms of the opposition presence/absence.

This will perhaps become clearer if we consider a second example of the paradoxes that arise within this system of thinking. This one bears on signification and might be called the paradox (or *aporia*) of structure and event. We tend to think that what we call the meaning of a word depends on the fact that it has been used by speakers on various occasions with the intention of communicating or expressing this meaning, and we thus might want to argue that what can in general be called the structure of a language – the general system of its rules and regularities – is derived from and determined by events: by acts of communication. But if we took this argument seriously and began to look at the events which are said to determine structures, we would find that every event is itself already determined and made possible by prior structures. The possibility of meaning something by an utterance is already inscribed in the structure of the language. The structures, of course, are themselves always products, but however far back we try to push, even when we think about the birth of language itself and try to describe an originating event which might have produced the first structure, we discover that we must assume prior organisation, prior differentiation. For a caveman successfully to originate language by making a special grunt signify something like 'food' is possible only if we assume that the grunt is already distinguished or distinguishable from other grunts and that the world has already been divided into the categories of food and non-food. Signification always depends on difference: contrasts, for example, between food and not-food which allow 'food' to be signified.

And when we think not about concepts but about the signifiers of a language, we find that the same applies. The sound sequence *pet*, for example, can function as a sign only because it contrasts with *bet, met, pat, pen*, etc. The noise one makes when one utters the sign *pet* is thus marked by the traces of these signs which one is not uttering. As we saw in the case of motion, what is present is itself complex and differential, marked by a series of differences. Derrida expands on this theme in *Positions*:

> The play of differences involves syntheses and referalls [*renvois*] which prevent there from being at any moment or in any way a simple element which is *present* in and of itself and refers only to itself. Whether in written or spoken discourse, no element can function as a sign without relating to another element which itself is not simply present. This linkage means that each 'element' – phoneme or grapheme – is constituted with reference to the trace in it of the other elements of the sequence or system. . . . Nothing, in either the elements or the system, is anywhere ever simply present or absent.

Signifying events depend on differences, but these differences are themselves the products of events. When one focuses on events one is led to affirm the priority of differences, but when one focuses on differences one sees their dependence on prior events. One can shift back and forth between these two perspectives which never give rise to a synthesis. Each perspective shows the error of the other in an irresolvable dialectic. This alteration Derrida terms *différance*. The

French verb *différer* means both to differ and to defer. *Différance*, which did not previously exist in French, sounds exactly the same as *différence* (meaning 'difference'), but the ending in *a*, which is used elsewhere to produce noun forms from verbs, makes it a new form meaning 'a differing or a deferring'. *Différance* thus designates both a passive difference already in existence as the condition of signification and an act of differing or deferring which produces differences. A term that behaves similarly in English is *spacing*, which designates both a completed arrangement and an act of distribution or arranging. Derrida does on occasion use the corresponding French term *espacement*, but *différance* is more powerful and apposite precisely because *différence* is a key term in the writings of Nietzsche, Freud, and especially Saussure. Investigating systems of signification, those thinkers were led to stress differences and differentiation; and Derrida's silent deformation of *différence* by substituting an *a* for the *e* is a manoeuvre which makes apparent the problematical complexity of signification by producing what, in our language, is not so much a concept as a contradiction.

Différance, he says,

is a structure and a movement which cannot be conceived on the basis of the opposition presence/absence. *Différance* is the systematic play of differences, of traces of differences, of the *spacing* [*espacement*] by which elements refer to one another. This spacing is the production, both active and passive (the *a* of *différance* indicates this indecision in relation to activity and passivity, indicates that which cannot be governed and organised by that opposition), of intervals without which the 'full' terms could not signify, could not function.   (*Positions*)

This preliminary account of the paradoxes of signification and the role of *différance* prepares us for further explorations of the theory of language in Derrida's reading of Saussure's *Course in General Linguistics* (trans. 1960). Saussure is generally regarded as the father of modern linguistics and his methodological distinctions have formed the basis for much structuralist theory, so a reading of his work can have important implications. Derrida finds in Saussure a powerful critique of the metaphysics of presence and what he calls its 'logocentrism', but also, and simultaneously, an unavoidable affirmation of this logocentrism and an inextricable involvement with it. I shall outline these two movements or moments in turn and then consider their significance.

Saussure begins by defining language as a system of signs – noises count as language only when they serve to express or communicate ideas – and thus the central question for him becomes the nature of the linguistic sign: what gives a sign its identity. He argues that signs are arbitrary and conventional and that each sign is defined not by some essential property but by the differences which distinguish it from other signs. The more rigorously he pursues his investigation, the more uncompromisingly he is led to argue that the sign is a purely relational unit and that 'in language there are only differences, *without positive terms*' (*Course in General Linguistics*). This is a principle wholly at odds with logocentrism and the metaphysics of presence. It maintains, on the one hand, that no terms of the system are ever simply and wholly present, for differences can never be present. And on the other hand it defines identity in terms of common absences rather than in terms of presence. Identity, which is the very cornerstone of any metaphysics, is made purely relational.

At the same time, however, there is in Saussure's argument a powerful affirmation of logocentrism. This emerges, most interestingly for Derrida, in Saussure's treatment of writing, which he relegates to a secondary, derivative status as compared with speaking. The object of linguistic analysis, Saussure writes, 'is not both the written and the spoken forms of words: the spoken forms alone constitute the object' (ibid.). Writing is simply a means of representing speech, a technical device, an external accessory, and need not therefore be taken into consideration when one is studying language. . . .

Voice is privileged so that language can be treated in terms of presence – a necessity if description or analysis is to get under way, since to identify signs one must be able to grasp meanings. But these posited presences, when one focuses on them, always turn out to be already inhabited by *différance*, or marked by absence. Saussure sets aside writing so as to deal with phonic units in their purity and simplicity, but writing returns at a crucial point: when he has to explain the nature of linguistic units. How can one explain that the units of a language have a purely differential nature? 'Since an identical state of affairs is observable in writing, another system of signs, we shall use writing to draw some comparisons that will clarify the whole issue' (*Course in General Linguistics*). For example, the letter *t* can be written in various ways so long as it remains distinct from *l*, *f*, *i*, *d*, etc. There are no essential features which must be preserved; its identity is purely relational.

Thus writing which Saussure claimed ought not to be the object of linguistic enquiry, turns out to be constructed on the very same principles as speech and to be the best illustration of the nature of linguistic units. There is at work here in Saussure's text an operation of 'self-deconstruction', in which the text unmasks its own construction, reveals it as a rhetorical operation rather than a solid foundation. Having established a hierarchy that made writing a form derivative from speech, Saussure's own argument shows that this relationship can be reversed and presents speech as a species of writing, a manifestation of the principles that are at work in writing. Here the 'logic of the supplement' is displayed in the working of Saussure's own text. The marginal in its very marginality turns out to characterise the central object of discussion.

Pursuing this interplay of speech and writing in Saussure and other thinkers – Rousseau, Husserl, Lévi-Strauss, Condillac – Derrida produces a general demonstration that if writing is characterised by the qualities traditionally associated with it, then speech itself is already a form of writing. Not only, as Saussure says, do the units of speech have the relational character especially evident in writing, but precisely the kind of absence which was thought to distinguish writing from speech proves to be the condition of any sign at all. For any form to be a sign it must be repeatable – produceable or reproduceable – even in the absence of a communicative intention. It is part of the nature of every sign to be iterable, to be able to function cut off from any intended meaning, as if it were an anonymous mark. A cry, for example, is a sign only if it can be 'counterfeited', cited, or produced simply as an example. Since this possibility, which is one of the possibilities of writing as traditionally described, always attends the sign, the sign cannot be satisfactorily treated on the model of voice as self-presence. Reversing the hierarchy, we can treat speech as a species of writing, or rather, since the notion of writing must now be broadened to include speech, we might speak, as Derrida does, of an *archi-écriture*, an archi-writing or proto-writing, which is the condition of both speech and writing in the narrow sense.

It is precisely because language is a proto-writing, because presence is always both differed and deferred, that theorists have tried to relegate writing to a status of dependence. Derrida's deconstructive reversal suggests that instead of basing a theory on an idealised speech – in particular the circuit of hearing oneself speak, where meanings seem to be made immediately present by the spoken word – and treating actual utterances or texts as variously attenuated examples of this process, one might think of language as a play of differences, a proliferation of traces and repetitions which, under conditions that can be described but never exhaustively specified, give rise to effects of meaning.

SOURCE: extracts from essay, 'Jacques Derrida', in John Sturrock (ed.), *Structuralism and Since* (Oxford, 1979), pp. 154–9, 161–6, 170–2.

Nicolas Tredell   Euphoria (Ltd) – The
Limitations of Post-structuralism and
Deconstruction   (1987)

When Paris students took to the streets in 1968, Claude Lévi-Strauss, the grand master of structural anthropology, was reported to have said with horror: 'What happens if they touch the libraries?' In 'The Death of the Author', published in the same year, Roland Barthes, no street-fighting man, offered a way of shattering the libraries, the sacred texts of Eternal Truth, without upsetting a single shelf:

literature (it would be better from now on to say *writing*), by refusing to assign a 'secret', an ultimate meaning, to the text (and to the world as text), liberates what may be called an anti-theological activity, an activity that is truly revolutionary since to refuse to fix meaning is, in the end, to refuse God and his hypostases – reason, science, law.[1]

The starting-point of Barthes's essay is by now well-known: an attack on the concept of the 'author' as the source of the text and the guarantee of its meaning. To write is to function as the node of a range of discourses that one does not control or unify; the 'author' is not the cause, but an effect of the text – or rather, of a particular way of reading, of structuring the text; he does not determine or limit its significance. And this is not to say, with the New Critics, that the text is a comfortable liberal plenitude where contraries and ambiguities co-exist in a tense, but ultimately harmonious, equilibrium; it is a site of struggle: 'a multi-dimensional space . . . a variety of writings, none of them original, blend and clash'.[2] It is dispersed, decentred, fragmented, fissured, incorrigibly plural.

The implications of Barthes's essay go far beyond literature, however. They are total; and in that, characteristic of post-structuralism at its most euphoric. All is supposedly shaken: literature, religion, reason, science, law, the individual subject. Barthes, it seems, has rewritten Dostoevsky: if the author does not exist, then everything is permitted; and this is cause, not for terror, but joy. It is the total claims of post-structuralism that account for the passionate intensity of its enthusiasts and enemies, but also for its inability to sustain its liberating promise. By calling all into question, it calls itself into question, giving itself no ground upon which to base its own challenges and to develop constructive possibilities. It is hardly surprising that, even by 1971, only three years after 'The Death of the Author', Barthes's rhetoric can take on an autumnal tone:

In fact, today, there is no language site outside bourgeois ideology: our language comes from it, returns to it, remains closed up in it. The only possible rejoinder is neither confrontation nor destruction, but only theft: fragment the old text of culture, science, literature, and change its features according to formulae of disguise, as one diguises stolen goods.[3]

The optimistic total claim of a 'truly revolutionary activity' has been replaced by a pessmistic total claim: that bourgeois ideology is, for the moment at least, inescapable. The project of shattering the library of Western culture has diminished to a campaign of petty pilfering. We are back inside the whale.

Deconstruction was always more cautious. Consider what might stand as a classic deconstruction statement (if such a thing is possible) – Jacques Derrida's contrast, in 'Structure, Sign and Play in the Human Sciences' (1966) between two kinds, or 'interpretations', of 'interpretation':

The one seeks to decipher, dreams of deciphering a truth or an origin which escapes play and the order of the sign, and which lives the necessity of interpretation as an exile. The other, which is no longer turned towards the origin, affirms play and tries to pass beyond man and humanism, the name of man being the name of that being who, throughout the history of metaphysics or of ontotheology – in other words, throughout his entire history – has dreamed of full presence, the reassuring foundation, of the origin and the end of play.[4]

Derrida's vocabulary – which has been enormously influential – obviously loads the argument. On the one side are the dreamers, who dwell in illusion and seek reassurance; on the other, the deconstructionists, who affirm, who play, who seek to transcend ('pass beyond'). And, like Barthes in 'The Death of the Author', Derrida generates excitement by total claims, encapsulated in the phrase 'throughout his entire history' – a characteristic Derridean locution which gives the exciting sense that we are awakening from a dream as old as man, and that we must choose the side of clarity. But, again characteristically, he moves on almost at once to apparent retraction and qualification: though he has indicated which kind of interpretation we should prefer, he says that he does 'not believe that today there is any question of *choosing*' between the two.[5] By a convenient paradox, however, this serves to add weight to his earlier loading of the case in favour of the view that there can be no truth or origin or foundation that offers ground on which to choose: his denial of the question of choosing in effect makes a choice. But it also provides an exemption clause: we can, if we wish, use the first, less favoured kind of interpretation when appropriate.

This combination of total claims with retractions and qualifications that both confirm those claims but provide an exemption clause is developed in Derrida's most extended iteration of his position, *Of Grammatology* (1967). This seeks to broach 'the de-construction of *the greatest totality* – the concept of the *epistémè* and logocentric metaphysics – within which are produced, without ever posing the radical question of writing, all the Western methods of analysis, explication, reading, or interpretation'.[6] But it is careful to stress that 'the movements of deconstruction do not destroy structures from the outside. They are not possible and effective, nor can they take accurate aim, except by inhabiting those structures. Inhabiting them *in a certain way*, because one always inhabits, and all the more when one does not suspect it.'[7] So although we can begin to deconstruct 'the greatest totality', we can and must only work against it from within; this necessity confirms the existence and scale of the totality, justifies our tactical deployment of logocentric techniques, and partly excuses our unwitting logocentric lapses, indeed turning these into further proofs of the totality's pervasiveness.

Of Grammatology takes matters further, however; for even if we could ever escape logocentric metaphysics – even if we do escape them, momentarily, at the extreme of deconstructive rigour – it is only to become dizzyingly aware of a greater, indeed the truly greatest, totality: the arche-writing, which encompasses both· speech and writing in the more usual sense; the play of differing/deferring that Derrida terms *différance*; the constant movement of the trace, the endless flicker of absence/presence. We can identify three typical moves in Derrida's argument (though these are not necessarily made in linear order): he constructs, by simplification and abstraction, a totality – 'logocentric metaphysics'; contends that we cannot simply break with, and must work within, that totality (contentions which serve to provide circular confirmations of that totality, and an exemption clause for deliberate or inadvertent logocentric behaviour by the deconstructionist); and finally gestures towards the truly total totality – the arche-writing – that lies beyond and within logocentrism. In *Of Grammatology*, even before the euphoria of 1968, Derrida has already enmeshed himself in his own trap: in that, he anticipates the whole history of deconstruction.

The cases of Derrida and Barthes are representative. It is

significant that, as the 1970s proceed, both move, in their respective ways, into a more fragmented mode of writing that more obviously betrays literary longings – for example, Barthes in *Roland Barthes* (1975), *A Lover's Discourse* (1977), *Camera Lucida* (1980); Derrida in *Glas* (1974), *Signsponge* (1975). It is also significant, in a rather different sense, that they increasingly achieve academic respectability. Their itineraries have been and are being repeated by others, with varying degrees of intelligence, insight, style and sophistication, and with many local variations; but always, finally, with a breakdown of the original projects. Post-structuralism and deconstruction are, in a way, inevitably short-lived. Initially they create a sense of euphoria and then, unable to sustain themselves or to develop constructively, they fall back into the old modes they purportedly challenge, and into the practice of a sceptical method that, while it provides a powerful weapon against opponents, and while it may yield specific moments of interest, ineluctably entails self-contradiction, and can too easily become predictable and repetitive. What follows seeks to suggest, in a necessarily broad and provisional manner, the limitations of post-structuralism and deconstruction, and their adverse effects upon literary criticism.

Post-structuralism and deconstruction claim to be anti-theological; but their appeal is in some ways like that of religion. The rhetoric seems to dissolve what it characterises as false, consoling appearances, and to show the world, and one's 'self', as they really are, or are not. The post-structuralist vision – especially in those politicised versions influenced by the earlier Barthes, by Lacan, by Althusser, by Foucault – is lurid: the world, the illusory 'I', is revealed as oppressed, controlled, libidinous, contradictory, fallen. This vision may mix uneasily with Marxism to hold out some hope of salvation. Deconstruction shelves salvation, but it does offer a strenuous ascesis, a constant mortification of what Derrida calls 'the exigent, powerful, systematic, and irrepressible desire' for a transcendent signified.[8] It discloses, not the presence of God, but absence; to be sure, a sophisticated notion of absence, as the constant play of differing/ deferring; but the inversion remains within a theological opposition. This might seem deconstructively inevitable. To try, like the Enlightenment or Marx, to achieve at a stroke a total break with theological modes, may merely be to reinstate God in a new guise: as reason, say, or the relations of production. The first, necessary stage in any deconstructive operation is to reverse the hierarchy: in this case, presence/absence. But is this the relevant hierarchy? Derrida's God, like Barthes's, is the God of totality; he has said: 'The motif of homogeneity [is] the theological motif *par excellence.*'[9] If one did want to deconstruct this God, the relevant hierarchy might be: totality/ non-totality. But Derrida stays within the first term of this hierarchy; he remains a monotheist. He sees absence, the flickering play of the trace, everywhere: his idea of '*différance*' dissolves differences; he finds all appearances both illusory and inescapable. He is, in his way, as totalisingly theological as those he would oppose.[10]

The results of importing totalisingly theological notions into literary criticism are likely to be similar, however secular those notions purport to be. Literary texts that do not conform to them are rejected or deprecated, or – and this is the more sophisticated approach – reinterpreted in such a way as to show that they covertly confirm or anticipate the faith: an allegorical or typological approach. Thus the 1970s saw post-structuralist attacks of the 'classic realist' texts of a Balzac or George Eliot, which were seen as offering a rigid hierarchy of discourses, attempting an imaginary resolution of contradictions, and providing a falsely secure subject-position for the reader. In the 1980s, this gives way to an approach which seeks to show how those 'classic realist' texts are exactly what post-structuralism and deconstruction would lead us to expect them to be: split, dispersed, plural, subverting their preferred hierarchies. Of course, rejection and/or reinterpretation of texts in the light of explicit or implied world-views will, to some extent, characterise any kind of critical approach, not only those permeated by religious or quasi-religious notions (or perhaps one could argue that all critical approaches will inevitably be permeated by quasi-religious notions). But there are different degrees of flexibility, and the totalising tendencies of post-structuralism and deconstruction lead, once their initial innovative impact has worn off, towards rigidity. In a sense, we know what a post-structuralist or deconstructionist reading will say, though it may be interesting to see the details worked out, and to observe the points at which the criticism escapes the ostensible theoretical schema.

Post-structuralism and deconstruction exemplify a failed rebellion which is also a revolt against reason (in this respect, their French provenance is clearly relevant). For all their attempts to exorcise it, the ghost of Cartesian reason – of a mind split from a body, from emotions and instincts – still haunts them. Again, one might say: this is inevitable: all breaks are 'reinscribed in an old cloth'.[11] But the persistence of the Cartesian split has dubious consequences for literary criticism. These are indicated in a comment of Derrida's: 'I believe that the risk of sterility and of sterilisation has always been the price of lucidity.'[12] Post-structuralism and deconstruction depend upon the intellect withdrawing from and analysing experience, as this comment by Christopher Norris inadvertently suggests: 'The truth is that deconstructionist theory can only be as useful and enlightening as the mind that puts it to work.'[13] It is indeed a 'mind', split from a body from emotions and instincts, that goes to work in post-structuralism and deconstruction. They conceive of literary texts, in effect, as deviations from a model of rational, non-contradictory thought, even when such deviation is seen as analogous to similar but concealed deviation in rational thought itself. Supposed *aporiae* or 'blind spots', gaps, silences, contradictions, are eagerly sought out, industriously 'produced', but those very notions – of *aporiae*, gaps, silences, contradictions – are rationalist ones. Though post-structuralism and deconstruction have challenged, in theory, the Cartesian ego, the 'I that thinks', they have set up a new 'I' – or at least, offered a superior subject-position – which watches, dazzled and euphoric, the whirls and turns of the text and of that other 'I' which naively believes itself to be unified and substantial. As Jonathan Culler points out, 'the effect of deconstructive analyses, as numerous readers can attest, is knowledge and feelings of mastery'.[14]

The point here is not to denigrate rational thought, but to recognise its limits; and it is at those limits, perhaps, that art begins. Post-structuralism and deconstruction in fact succeed in denigrating both rationality and art; they employ notions from rational thought, but deny those notions any grounds, and evade the responsibilities of rationality at key moments; they apply those notions to art, to literature, without considering that they might be inappropriate, that other modes of understanding might be required. Literature, or any other art-form, is not a magic mirror in which divisions are dissolved – though the potential healing and unifying power of art should not be scorned in obeisance to some ideological puritanism. Literature can and does, however, arouse emotional and instinctive responses ('felt in the blood, and felt along the heart'[15]) that post-structuralism and deconstruction tend to repress, especially when those responses are stirred by such suspect phenomena as mimesis. Recently, some attempts have been made to rehabilitate proscribed emotions; in particular, Barthes's later work tries to find ways of talking about such taboo topics as pleasure (and not only *jouissance*), love, tenderness. Certain feminist approaches that have drawn upon post-structuralism and deconstruction have nonetheless tried to allow for emotional responses and have pointed out, with some justice, that traditional modes of criticism that have stressed 'spontaneity' have in fact ruled out particular reactions – for instance, women's uneasiness or anger at sexist gender representations – as, say, immature and self-indulgent. One thinks of F. R. Leavis's concern for 'emotional hygiene'.[16] But discriminating among feelings in terms, for example, of 'emotional quality' is different from repressing feeling as philosophically and ideologically illegitimate: the perpetuation of the Cartesian mind/body split in post-structuralism and deconstruction contributes to such repression.

Post-structuralism and deconstruction also abuse the authority of science. The 'scientific' project may seem to belong to an earlier phase of theory; for example, Barthes speaks of the 'petite délire scientifique'[17] of his structuralist period. But the appeal to the prestige of science persists. It is epitomised in the image, much favoured by Althusser and Lacan, and avidly adopted by some later enthusiasts, of the 'Copernican revolution'. 'The decentring of the ego', of the conscious, Cartesian 'I that thinks' begun by Marx and Freud and supposedly developed in structuralism and its successors, is compared with Copernicus's 'decentring' of the earth from the solar system.[18] The image implies an unequivocal breakthrough, which only ignorance and reactionary prejudice can deny. It depends for its effect on the echoes of an almost Victorian faith in science as an authoritative mode of knowledge by which we move steadily, if sometimes uncomfortably, towards greater enlightenment.

The scientific pretensions of post-structuralism and deconstruction are in fact very dubious. Of course, it has now become notoriously difficult to define science; but in a definition derived from, say, Karl Popper,[19] it is not easy to see how the claims of post-structuralism and deconstruction could be tested in ways that would expose them to possible falsification; while by the now influential model of science suggested by Thomas Kuhn,[20] it is questionable whether enough anomalies could ever accumulate, or whether a sufficiently satisfactory solution to a set of problems could ever emerge, to bring about a genuine 'paradigm shift'. (The use of this term as a loose metaphor for current realignments in literary criticism itself demonstrates the persistent desire for quasi-scientific authority.) As 'sciences', post-structuralism and deconstruction suffer a similar problem of validation to psychoanalysis, with which they clearly have close links: it is debatable whether they could ever be proved wrong, since apparently contradictory evidence can always be reinterpreted, with sufficient ingenuity, as concealed confirmation. It is possible to take a wholly relativist view of science, to see the concept of what constitutes a scientific theory, and the procedures by which that theory is supposedly tested, as specific to a particular social and cultural situation, and without universal validity; this view would, in fact, accord with post-structuralist and deconstructionist scepticism; but it would also, by subverting the authority of science, undermine their appeal to that authority.

If post-structuralism and deconstruction can hardly count as scientific, their rhetorical invocation of science nonetheless contributes to their influence, and to their cramping effect upon literary criticism. It implies that they represent the latest and the best in knowledge; it confers upon the critic who employs them an easy sense of superiority over literary texts. Those texts can never surprise him, never teach him anything he does not already know. Assured progress has been made in the human as in the natural sciences, and our knowledge of humanity, as of the physical world, has unequivocally increased; Barthes, or the discourses that constitute him, must know more than Balzac, Derrida than Dickens. Thus Catherine Belsey, who makes much use of the 'Copernican revolution' image, asserts: 'A form of criticism which refuses to reproduce the pseudo-knowledge offered by the text provides a real knowledge of the work of literature.'[21] The uncomfortable possibility that the literature of the past embodies any kind of human wisdom (and not the wisdom of its 'authors' only) is denied. This is the recurrent arrogance of the present – a vulgar scientism indeed, a willed or inadvertent failure of historical memory.

It is true that it is now increasingly allowed that past literary texts (though not their 'authors') may have dimly anticipated the findings of today's luminaries; but 'knowledge' is in the possession of the enlightened critic (or of the discourses that circulate through him), and the appeal to the prestige of science lends this 'knowledge' a spurious authority. To some extent, of course, we will always read past texts in the context of our own time, of currently dominant ideas, and will reject or reinterpret them according to our present preoccupations. Moreover, to discriminate among and within texts is inevitably to assume that, in certain respects, one 'knows better' than those texts. But to acknowledge that we may, in some cases, indeed 'know better' than the past is not to make the assumption, which the 'Copernican revolution' sort of image reinforces, that we unequivocally and indubitably do so.

Though post-structuralism and deconstruction claim to subvert the law, they have, at least as far as literary criticism is concerned, established a new body of binding rules and promoted the careful policing of critical discourse. D. H. Lawrence once protested in a poem: 'They say I wrote a naughty book / With perfectly awful things in it, / putting in all the impossible words / like b— and f— and sh—.'[22] Today, in the field of criticism, we have another set of 'impossible words'; these are conveniently gathered in this passage from Raman Selden's *Reader's Guide to Contemporary Literary Theory*:

> readers may believe that theories and concepts will only deaden the spontaneity of their response to literary works. They may forget that 'spontaneous' discourse about literature is unconsciously dependent on the theorising of older generations. Their talk of 'feeling', 'imagination', 'genius', 'sincerity', and 'reality' is full of dead theory which is sanctified by time and has become part of the language of common sense.[23]

'Realism'; 'sincerity'; 'spontaneity'; 'feeling'; 'imagination'; 'genius'; 'reality': these are the taboo terms now. Selden talks of 'dead theory'; but he leads us into the dead land, where lips that would kiss form prayers to the broken tablets of post-structuralist and de-constructionist law – law which is more powerful, more pervasive, by its fragmentation and dispersal. In the courts of the shifting signifier, there are no judges, no advocates, no rights of appeal: reason and science may be used against you, but cannot be called in support of your own case; and subjective testimony, of the wrong sort, can instantly be discredited.

Post-structuralism and deconstruction have focused particularly on attacking the concept of the individual human subject: the notion of the 'decentring of the ego' as a 'Copernican revolution' exemplifies this, while Barthes's assault on the notion of the 'author' can be situated within a much broader challenge to the idea of the 'individual'. This clearly has major implications for literary criticism, which has often worked in terms of literary texts as expressions of individual authors, as evocations and explorations of individual states of mind, as presenting individual characters, as relating to individual readers. In a complex analysis that draws on Marxist, psychoanalytic, linguistic and semiotic perspectives, the idea of the unified, centred, substantial self (hardly dominant, in fact, in twentieth-century literature and culture) is seen as an illusion: the result of the child's misrecognition of himself as an imaginary unity in the 'mirror stage' and of his insertion into language and the symbolic order; of the suppression of the difference between the 'I' of which one speaks and the 'I' that speaks, the subject of the enounced and the subject of the enunciation; of the reproductive mechanisms of bourgeois society that construct obedient subjects who naively believe that they 'freely' consent to their unperceived subjection.

The concept of the constructed subject has, paradoxically, a strong subjective appeal. Like Calvinism, it ensures that you have at least recognised that most people are damned, even if you cannot be sure of your own salvation. It interpellates you, hails you into a subject-position of privileged knowledge, even if it is the knowledge that the 'I' that thinks it knows is itself no more than a temporary subject-position. Consider this passage, from Althusser's highly influential 'Ideology and Ideological State Apparatuses'; he identifies an 'ideology of the school' that is

universally reigning because it is one of the essential forms of the ruling bourgeois ideology: an ideology which represents the School as a neutral environment purged of ideology ... where teachers respectful of the 'conscience' and 'freedom' of the children who are entrusted to them (in complete confidence) by their 'parents' (who are free, too, i.e. the owners of their children) open up for them the path to the freedom, morality and responsibility of adults by their own example, by knowledge, literature and their 'liberating' virtues.

I ask the pardon of those teachers who, in dreadful conditions, attempt to turn the few weapons they can find in the history and learning they 'teach' against the ideology, the system and the practices in which they are trapped. They are a kind of hero. But they are rare and how many (the majority) do not even begin to suspect the 'work' the system (which is bigger than they are and crushes them) forces them to do, or, worse, put all their heart and ingenuity into performing it with the most advanced awareness (the famous new methods!) So little do they suspect it that their own devotion contributes to the maintenance and nourishment of this ideological representation of the School. . . .[24]

How many, reading this, must have felt themselves called, must have seen themselves among those rare birds who can perceive those realities to which others, the dull majority, are blind. If the subject is put in question in Althusser's essay, analysed as a means of ideological reproduction, the ego – in the ethical sense of the term – is dangerously inflated, granted a licence to scorn any attempt at disinterestedness and to impart its own prejudices and idiosyncracies. It is also provided with a powerful rhetorical weapon. The concept of the constructed subject permits the well-known operation whereby dissent is reinterpreted as unwitting confirmation. If 'I' take the view – or am hailed into the subject-position – that holds individual subjects to be linguistic and ideological constructions, and you deny this, 'your' denial, however it is argued, can be taken as further evidence of the ideological construction to which you are blind and which in fact causes you to want to deny it and to believe that you can freely do so. It is as if one were to say, to a person putting an argument against Christianity: It is the Devil speaking in you. It is an appeal to an agency or process beyond your conscious cognizance and control. You can only 'know' it by accepting the belief-system within which it is held to be true.

The notion of the constructed subject is offered as demystifying. To a degree, this is justified, in so far as it helps to challenge the idea of the 'autonomous individual' abstracted from specific historical, political, social and cultural circumstances. But it can too easily become a new form of mystification, or, more precisely, the revival, in a fresh guise, of an old one: the denial of another's experience (experience itself being seen as an ideological production). In this respect, it contributes to a kind of solipsism; it is a means of trying to eliminate, or diminish the impact of, other persons; in denying the experiencing 'I', in collapsing the 'I' of the other into ideology, one tries to exorcise that other who may dissent, oppose, resist; one engages in a sort of 'magical thinking', an illusory dissolution of obstacles.[25]

The concept of the constructed subject also offers a new, strange refreshing sense of oneself. It is often presented as unnerving, perhaps repellent (thus implying that it needs a certain courage and honesty to accept it); but there is another aspect to the matter, indicated in one of Wittgenstein's comments on Freud: 'He always stresses what great forces in the mind, what strong prejudices work against the idea of psycho-analysis. But he never says what an enormous charm that idea has for people.'[26] The idea of the constructed subject (which owes obvious and acknowledged debts to Freud) also has an enormous charm. If it discloses your subjection, it also enables you to see yourself in a different way, and thus, in a sense, enhances your freedom. If it evacuates you, it also makes you much more interesting. And perhaps it lifts a burden too. Sartre says in *Words*: 'you can get rid of a neurosis but you are never cured of yourself.'[27] But the notion of the constructed subject gives you a cure for yourself, or at least lets you put your 'self' into process in an exciting way. It remains a form of romanticism, and returns into a kind of narcissism; the eye gazes, not into a still pond, but into a vortex in which its image endlessly, thrillingly, breaks and reforms. 'The mind, a single nowhere, swoons to feel / Its multilocal multiplicity.'[28]

It is claimed that the concept of the constructed subject is a radical one, subverting the notion of the 'individual' that is, supposedly, the keystone of bourgeois ideology. But it could be seen, perhaps more convincingly, as a mode of conformity to the dominant demands of our time. It is true that some conservative political rhetoric still appeals to the 'individual'; but the very explicitness of such appeals might make us question whether the idea of the individual is any longer hegemonic, any longer part of what is taken for granted. It is

arguable that one of the major needs of modern societies – whatever their ostensible political creed – is in fact for subjects that can constantly be constructed or manipulated to consume new goods, take up new working practices, subserve new technology. The post-structuralist ideal of the free-flowing subject is close to the ideal modern worker or manager, always able to assume new subject-positions in accordance with productive requirements. The notion of the mobile subject is the post-structuralist and deconstructionist equivalent of 'On yer bike'.

This is not, of course, to deny that it is of immense interest and value to explore the ways in which subjectivity is considered in and across a range of discourses – theological, philosophical, psychological, medical, juridical and, indeed, literary; in fact, it could be argued that literature has always been engaged in such explorations, and with considerably more subtlety, sensitivity and complexity than post-structuralism and deconstruction. Post-structuralism and deconstruction do not offer an adequate theory of the subject; they simply eliminate it, and then become incoherent and self-subverting when they wish to distinguish, descriptively and/or evaluatively, among forms of subjectivity, and when they wish to allow for experience and volition. Rightly rejecting the notion of the absolutely sovereign individual, they shift to a belief in language and ideology as sovereign; *pace* Foucault, they have still not cut off the king's head.[29]

Only apoplectic reaction would deny that post-structuralism and deconstruction have had some stimulating effects upon literary criticism. Their ontological and epistemological challenges have raised important issues for critical theory and practice – for instance: What is an 'author', a 'reader', a 'text'? How do we 'know' the text? Does the text 'know' us? How does 'text' relate to 'world'? They have helped to contest the tyranny of interpretations fixed by an appeal to authority rather than by argument (as well as valuably questioning such distinctions as 'authority/argument'). They have widened our sense of the possibilities of meaning in texts. They have drawn attention to aspects of texts previously ignored, neglected, or deprecated in the drive to discover a univocal message, an organic unity. They have enabled us to see classic texts in different ways – that ponderous monument known as 'the nineteenth-century novel' can now never, thankfully, be quite the same again – and to approach 'difficult' twentieth-century work, from the great texts of Modernism to current 'experimental' writing, with potentially more rewarding reading strategies.

But they have also had restrictive effects, and, with their assimilation and the loss of their innovative force, these are increasing. And these effects are not accidental, not the results of misinterpretation and misapplication; they are inherent in theories that make total claims which destroy their own grounds and any basis for constructive development. In post-structuralism and deconstruction, religion, reason, science, law, the individual subject, all those demons supposedly driven out by Barthes, made deconstructible by Derrida, return, in negative forms, to oppress literature.

SOURCE: This essay is previously unpublished in its present form, but sections of the argument have appeared in the author's contributions to the journal *PN Review*.

NOTES

1. Roland Barthes, 'The Death of the Author', *Image–Music–Text*, essays selected and translated by Stephen Heath (London, 1977), p. 147.

2. Ibid., p. 146.

3. Roland Barthes, *Sade/Fourier/Loyola*, translated by Richard Miller (New York, 1976), p. 10.

4. Jacques Derrida, 'Structure, Sign and Play in the Discourse of the Human Sciences', in Richard Macksey & Eugenio Donato (eds), *The Structuralist Controversy: The Languages of Criticism and the Sciences of Man* (Baltimore, 1970), pp. 264–5; also in Derrida, *Writing and Difference*, translated by Alan Bass (London: 1978), p. 292 (latter translation quoted).

5. *The Structuralist Controversy*, p. 265; *Writing and Difference*, p. 293.

6. Jacques Derrida, *Of Grammatology*, translated by Gayatri Chakravorty Spivak (Baltimore, 1976), p. 46.

7. Ibid., p. 24.   8. Ibid., p. 49.

9. Jacques Derrida, *Positions*, translated by Alan Bass (Athlone, 1981), pp. 63–4.

10. Derrida is particularly sensitive to the 'theological' charge, and works assiduously to counter it. For example, he says in *Positions*: 'the trace is neither a ground, nor a foundation, nor an origin, and . . . in no case can it provide for a manifest or disguised ontotheology' (p. 52). But theology has, arguably, always been as much concerned with absence as with presence, with non-being as with being. Sometimes more so. Consider the Buddhist Nagarjuna, as described by Ninian Smart: 'He used subtle arguments to undermine commonsense views of reality . . . [he] and his followers tried to show that all views about reality are contradictory. He concluded that reality is empty, or void' – *The Religious Experience of Mankind* (New York, 1968; London, 1971), pp. 138–9. Of course, it would be crudely reductive (in both directions) to simply assimilate Derrida's notions to any particular set of religious ideas. But the whole question of his relationship to religion, Western and Eastern, merits detailed examination.

11. Cf. Derrida, *Positions*: 'I do not believe in decisive ruptures, in an unequivocal "epistemological break" . . . Breaks are always, and fatally reinscribed in an old cloth that must continually, interminably be undone' (p. 24).

12. 'Discussion' after 'Structure, Sign and Play . . .' in *The Structuralist Controversy* (note 4, above), p. 271.

13. Christopher Norris, *Deconstruction: Theory and Practice* (London, 1982), p. 133.

14. Jonathan Culler, *On Deconstruction: Theory and Criticism after Structuralism* (London, 1983), p. 225.

15. William Wordsworth, 'Lines written a few miles above Tintern Abbey' (1798), *Lyrical Ballads*, edited by R. L. Brett & A. R. Jones (London, 1965), p. 114, line 29.

16. F. R. Leavis, *The Living Principle: 'English' as a Discipline of Thought* (London, 1975), p. 75.

17. *Roland Barthes par Roland Barthes* (Paris, 1975), p. 148.

18. For a convenient summary of 'Copernican revolution' imagery, see Catherine Belsey, *Critical Practice* (London, 1980), pp. 130–6.

19. See Karl Popper, *The Logic of Scientific Discovery* 3rd edn (London, 1972).

20. See Thomas Kuhn, *The Structure of Scientific Revolutions*, 2nd edn (Chicago, 1980).

21. Belsey, op. cit., p. 129.

22. D. H. Lawrence, 'My Naughty Book', *Complete Poems*, edited by Vivian de Sola Pinto & Warren Roberts (London, 1972), vol. 1, p. 491.

23. Raman Selden, *A Reader's Guide to Contemporary Literary Theory* (Brighton, 1985), p. 3.

24. Louis Althusser, 'Ideology and Ideological State Apparatuses', *Lenin and Philosophy and Other Essays*, translated by Ben Brewster, 2nd edn (London, 1971), p. 148.

25. See Jean-Paul Sartre, *Sketch for a Theory of the Emotions*, translated by Philip Mairet (London, 1962).

26. Norman Malcolm, *Ludwig Wittgenstein: A Memoir*, 2nd edn (Oxford, 1984), pp. 100–1. Frank Cioffi, who quotes this in his essay 'Wittgenstein's Freud', points out that in fact Freud once wrote to Fliess: 'The sexual business attracts people' – Peter Winch (ed.), *Studies in the Philosophy of Wittgenstein* (London, 1969), p. 186n.

27. Jean-Paul Sartre, *Words*, translated by Irene Clephane (Harmondsworth, 1967), p. 157.

28. G. S. Fraser, 'Paul Valéry', *Poems of G. S. Fraser*, edited by Ian Fletcher & John Lucas (Leicester University Press, 1981), p. 98.

29. Cf. Michel Foucault, *Power/Knowledge: Selected Interviews and Other Writings, 1972–1977*, edited by Colin Gordon, translated by Colin Gordon, Leo Marshall, John Mepham, Kate Sopar (Brighton, 1980): 'What we need . . . is a political philosophy that isn't erected around the problem of sovereignty. . . . We need to cut off the King's head' (p. 121). But Foucault's theory of power makers the King all-pervasive.

5. WHAT IS THE READER'S PLACE?

Wolfgang Iser   The Reading Process   (1972)

I

The phenomenological theory of art lays full stress on the idea that, in considering a literary work, one must take into account not only the actual text but also, and in equal measure, the actions involved in responding to that text. Thus Roman Ingarden confronts the structure of the literary text with the ways in which it can be *konkretisiert* (realised).[1] The text as such offers different 'schematised views' through which the subject matter of the work can come to light, but the actual bringing to light is an action of *Konkretisation*. If this is so, then the literary work has two poles, which we might call the artistic and the esthetic: the artistic refers to the text created by the author, and the esthetic to the realisation accomplished by the reader. From this polarity it follows that the literary work cannot be completely identical with the text, or with the realisation of the text, but in fact must lie halfway between the two. The work is more than the text, for the text only takes on life when it is realised, and furthermore the realisation is by no means independent of the individual disposition of the reader – though this in turn is acted upon by the different patterns of the text. The convergence of text and reader brings the literary work into existence, and this convergence can never be precisely pinpointed, but must always remain virtual, as it is not to be identified either with the reality of the text or with the individual disposition of the reader.

It is the virtuality of the work that gives rise to its dynamic nature, and this in turn is the precondition for the effects that the work calls forth. As the reader uses the various perspectives offered him by the text in order to relate the patterns and the 'schematised views' to one another, he sets the work in motion, and this very process results ultimately in the awakening of responses within himself. Thus, reading causes the literary work to unfold its inherently dynamic character.

. . . A literary text must therefore be conceived in such a way that it will engage the reader's imagination in the task of working things out for himself, for reading is only a pleasure when it is active and creative. In this process of creativity, the text may either not go far enough, or may go too far, so we may say that boredom and overstrain form the boundaries beyond which the reader will leave the field of play.

The extent to which the 'unwritten' part of a text stimulates the reader's creative participation is brought out by an observation of Virginia Woolf's in her study of *Jane Austen*:

Jane Austen is thus a mistress of much deeper emotion than appears upon the surface. She stimulates us to supply what is not there. What she offers is, apparently, a trifle, yet is composed of something that expands in the reader's mind and endows with the most enduring form of life scenes which are outwardly trivial. Always the stress is laid upon character. . . . The turns and twists of the dialogue keep us on the tenterhooks of suspense. Our attention is half upon the present moment, half upon the future. . . . Here, indeed, in this unfinished and in the main inferior story, are all the elements of Jane Austen's greatness.[2]

The unwritten aspects of apparently trivial scenes and the unspoken dialogue within the 'turns and twists' not only draw the reader into the action but also lead him to shade in the many outlines suggested by the given situations, so that these take on a reality of their own. But as the reader's imagination animates these 'outlines', they in turn will influence the effect of the written part of the text. Thus begins a whole dynamic process: the written text imposes certain limits on its unwritten implications in order to prevent these from becoming too blurred and hazy, but at the same time these implications, worked out by the reader's imagination, set the given situation against a background which endows it with far greater significance than it might have seemed to possess on its own. In this way, trivial scenes suddenly take on the shape of an 'enduring form of life'. What constitutes this form is never named, let alone explained in the text, although in fact it is the end product of the interaction between text and reader. . . .

II

. . . Whatever we have read sinks into our memory and is foreshortened. It may later be evoked again and set against a different background with the result that the reader is enabled to develop hitherto unforeseeable connections. The memory evoked, however, can never reassume its original shape, for this would mean that memory and perception were identical, which is manifestly not so.

The new background brings to light new aspects of what we had committed to memory; conversely these, in turn, shed their light on the new background, thus arousing more complex anticipations. Thus, the reader, in establishing these inter-relations between past, present and future, actually causes the text to reveal its potential multiplicity of connections. These connections are the product of the reader's mind working on the raw material of the text, though they are not the text itself – for this consists just of sentences, statements information, etc.

This is why the reader often feels involved in events which, at the time of reading, seem real to him, even though in fact they are very far from his own reality. The fact that completely different readers can be differently affected by the 'reality' of a particular text is ample evidence of the degree to which literary texts transform reading into a creative process that is far above mere perception of what is written. The literary text activates our own faculties, enabling us to recreate the world it presents. The product of this creative activity is what we might call the virtual dimension of the text, which endows it with its reality. This virtual dimension is not the text itself, nor is it the imagination of the reader: it is the coming together of text and imagination.

As we have seen, the activity of reading can be characterised as a sort of kaleidoscope of perspectives, preintentions, recollections. Every sentence contains a preview of the next and forms a kind of viewfinder for what is to come; and this in turn changes the 'preview' and so becomes a 'viewfinder' for what has been read. This whole process represents the fulfilment of the potential, unexpressed reality of the text, but it is to be seen only as a framework for a great variety of means by which the virtual dimension may be brought into being. The process of anticipation and retrospection itself does not by any means develop in a smooth flow.

. . . If one regards the sentence sequence as a continual flow, this implies that the anticipation aroused by one sentence will generally be realised by the next, and the frustration of one's expectations will arouse feelings of exasperation. And yet literary texts are full of unexpected twists and turns, and frustration of expectations. Even in the simplest story there is bound to be some kind of blockage, if only because no tale can ever be told in its entirety. Indeed, it is only through inevitable omissions that a story gains its dynamism. Thus whenever the flow is interrupted and we are led off in unexpected directions, the opportunity is given to us to bring into play our own faculty for establishing connections – for filling the gaps left by the text itself.[3]

These gaps have a different effect on the process of anticipation and retrospection, and thus on the 'gestalt' of the virtual dimension, for they may be filled in different ways. For this reason, one text is potentially capable of several different realisations, and no reading can ever exhaust the full potential, for each individual reader will fill in the gaps in his own way, thereby excluding the various other possibilities; as he reads, he will make his own decision as to how the gap is to be filled. In this very act the dynamics of reading are revealed. By making his decision he implicitly acknowledges the inexhaustibility of the text; at the same time it is this very inexhaustibility that forces him to make his decision. With 'traditional' texts this process was more or less unconscious, but modern texts frequently exploit it quite deliberately. They are often so fragmentary that one's attention is almost exclusively occupied with the search for connections between the fragments; the object of this is not to complicate the 'spectrum' of connections, so much as to make us aware of the nature of our own capacity for providing links. In such cases, the text refers back directly to our own preconceptions – which are revealed by the act of interpretation that is a basic element of the reading process. With all literary texts, then, we may say that the reading process is selective, and the potential text is infinitely richer than any of its individual realisations. This is borne out by the fact that a second reading of a piece of literature often produces a different impression from the first. The reasons for this may lie in the reader's own change of circumstances; still, the text must be such as to allow this variation. On a second reading familiar occurrences now tend to appear in a new light and seem to be at times corrected, at times enriched. . . .

In whatever way, and under whatever circumstances the reader may link the different phases of the text together, it will always be the process of anticipation and retrospection that leads to the formation of the virtual dimension, which in turn transforms the text into an experience for the reader. The way in which this experience comes about through a process of continual modification is closely akin to the way in which we gather experience in life. And thus the 'reality' of the reading experience can illuminate basic patterns of real experience:

We have the experience of a world, not understood as a system of relations which wholly determine each event, but as an open totality the synthesis of which is inexhaustible. . . . From the moment that experience – that is, the opening on to our *de facto* world – is recognised as the beginning of knowledge, there is no longer any way of distinguishing a level of *a priori* truths and one of factual ones, what the world must necessarily be and what it actually is.[4]

The manner in which the reader experiences the text will reflect his own disposition, and in this respect the literary text acts as a kind of mirror; but at the same time, the reality which this process helps to create is one that will be *different* from his own (since, normally, we tend to be bored by texts that present us with things we already know perfectly well ourselves). Thus we have the apparently paradoxical situation in which the reader is forced to reveal aspects of himself in order to experience a reality which is different from his own. The impact this reality makes on him will depend largely on the extent to which he himself actively provides the unwritten part of the text, and yet in supplying all the missing links, he must think in terms of experiences different from his own; indeed, it is only by leaving behind the familiar world of his own experience that the reader can truly participate in the adventure the literary text offers him.

III

We have seen that, during the process of reading, there is an active interweaving of anticipation and retrospection, which on a second reading may turn into a kind of advance retrospection. The impressions that arise as a result of this process will vary from individual to individual, but only within the limits imposed by the written as opposed to the unwritten text. In the same way, two people gazing at the night sky may both be looking at the same collection of stars, but one will see the image of a plough, and the other will make out a dipper. The 'stars' in a literary text are fixed; the lines that join them are variable. The author of the text may, of course, exert plenty of influence on the reader's imagination – he has the whole panoply of narrative techniques at his disposal – but no author worth his salt will ever attempt to set the *whole* picture before his reader's eyes. If he does, he will very quickly lose his reader, for it is only by activating the reader's imagination that the author can hope to involve him and so realise the intentions of his text. . . .

IV

The 'picturing' that is done by our imagination is only one of the activities through which we form the 'gestalt' of a literary text. We have already discussed the process of anticipation and retrospection, and to this we must add the process of grouping together all the different aspects of a text to form the consistency that the reader will always be in search of. While expectations may be continually modified, and images continually expanded, the reader will still strive, even if unconsciously, to fit everything together in a consistent pattern. 'In the reading of images, as in the hearing of speech, it is always hard to distinguish what is given to us from what we supplement in the process of projection which is triggered off by recognition . . . it is the guess of the beholder that tests the medley of forms and colours for coherent meaning, crystalising it into shape when a consistent interpretation has been found.'[5] By grouping together the written parts of the text, we enable them to interact, we observe the direction in which they are leading us, and we project onto them the consistency which we, as readers, require. This 'gestalt' must inevitably be coloured by our own characteristic selection process. For it is not given by the text itself; it arises from the meeting between the written text and the individual mind of the reader with its own particular history of experience, its own consciousness, its own outlook. The 'gestalt' is not the true meaning of the text; at best it is a configurative meaning; 'comprehension is an individual act of seeing-things-together, and only that.' With a literary text such comprehension is inseparable from the reader's expectations, and where we have expectations, there too we have one of the most potent weapons in the writer's armory – illusion.

Whenever 'consistent reading suggests itself . . . illusion takes over'.[7] Illusion, says Northrop Frye, is 'fixed or definable, and reality is best understood as its negation'.[8] The 'gestalt' of a text normally takes on (or, rather, is given) this fixed or definable outline, as this is essential to our own understanding, but on the other hand, if reading were to consist of nothing but an uninterrupted building up of illusions, it would be a suspect, if not downright dangerous, process: instead of bringing us into contact with reality, it would wean us away from realities. Of course, there is an element of 'escapism' in all literature, resulting from this very creation of illusion, but there are some texts which offer nothing but a harmonious world, purified of all contradiction and deliberately excluding anything that might disturb the illusion once established, and these are the texts that we generally do not like to classify as literary. Women's magazines and the brasher forms of the detective story might be cited as examples.

However, even if an overdose of illusion may lead to triviality, this does not mean that the process of illusion-building should ideally be dispensed with altogether. On the contrary, even in texts that appear to resist the formation of illusion, thus drawing our attention to the cause of this resistance, we still need the abiding illusion that the resistance itself is the consistent pattern underlying the text. This is especially true of modern texts, in which it is the very precision of the written details which increases the proportion of indeterminacy; one detail appears to contradict another, and so simultaneously stimulates and frustrates our desire to 'picture', thus continually causing our imposed 'gestalt' of the text to disintegrate. Without the formation of illusions, the unfamiliar world of the text would remain unfamiliar; through the illusions, the experience offered by the text becomes accessible to us, for it is only the illusion, on its different levels of consistency, that makes the experience 'readable'. If we cannot find (or impose) this consistency, sooner or later we will put the text down. The process is virtually hermeneutic. The text provokes certain expectations which in turn we project onto the text in such a way that we reduce the polysemantic possibilities to a single interpretation in keeping with the expectations aroused, thus extracting an individual, configurative meaning. The polysemantic nature of the text and the illusion-making of the reader are opposed factors. If the illusion were complete, the polysemantic nature would vanish; if the polysemantic nature were all-powerful, the illusion would be totally destroyed. Both extremes are conceivable, but in the individual literary text we always find some form of balance between the two conflicting tendencies. The formation of illusions, therefore, can never be total, but it is this very incompleteness that in fact gives it its productive value.

With regard to the experience of reading, Walter Pater once observed: 'For to the grave reader words too are grave; and the ornamental word, the figure, the accessory form or colour or reference, is rarely content to die to thought precisely at the right moment, but will inevitably linger awhile, stirring a long "brainwave" behind it of perhaps quite alien associations.'[9] Even while the reader is seeking a consistent pattern in the text, he is also uncovering other impulses which cannot be immediately integrated or will even resist final integration. Thus the semantic possibilities of the text will always remain far richer than any configurative meaning formed while reading. But this impression is, of course, only to be gained through reading the text. Thus the configurative meaning can be nothing but a *pars pro toto* fulfilment of the text, and yet this fulfilment gives rise to the very richness which it seeks to restrict, and indeed in some modern texts, our awareness of this richness takes precedence over any configurative meaning.

   This fact has several consequences which, for the purpose of analysis, may be dealt with separately, though in the reading process they will all be working together. As we have seen, a consistent, configurative meaning is essential for the apprehension of an unfamiliar experience, which through the process of illusion-building we can incorporate in our own imaginative world. At the same time, this consistency conflicts with the many other possibilities o' fulfilment it seeks to exclude, with the result that the configurative meaning is always accompanied by 'alien associations' that do not fit in with the illusions formed. The first consequence, then, is the fact that in forming our illusions, we also produce at the same time a latent disturbance of these illusions. Strangely enough, this also applies to texts in which our expectations are actually fulfilled – though one would have thought that the fulfilment of expectations would help to complete the illusion. 'Illusion wears off once the expectation is stepped up; we take it for granted and want more.'[10]

The experiments in gestalt psychology referred to by Gombrich in *Art and Illusion* make one thing clear: 'though we may be intellectually aware of the fact that any given experience *must* be an illusion, we cannot, strictly speaking, watch ourselves having an illusion'.[11] Now, if illusion were not a transitory state, this would mean that we could be, as it were, permanently caught up in it. And if reading were exclusively a matter of producing illusion – necessary though this is for the understanding of an unfamiliar experience – we should run the risk of falling victim to a gross deception. But it is precisely during our reading that the transitory nature of the illusion is revealed to the full.

As the formation of illusions is constantly accompanied by 'alien associations' which cannot be made consistent with the illusions, the reader constantly has to lift the restrictions he places on the 'meaning' of the text. Since it is he who builds the illusions, he oscillates between involvement in and observation of those illusions; he opens himself to the unfamiliar world without being imprisoned in it. Through this process the reader moves into the presence of the fictional world and so experiences the realities of the text as they happen. . . .

As we read, we oscillate to a greater or lesser degree between the building and the breaking of illusions. In a process of trial and error, we organise and reorganise the various data offered us by the text. These are the given factors, the fixed points on which we base our 'interpretation', trying to fit them together in the way we think the author meant them to be fitted. 'For to perceive, a beholder must *create* his own experience. And his creation must include relations comparable to those which the original producer underwent. They are not the same in any literal sense. But with the perceiver, as with the artist, there must be an ordering of the elements of the whole that is in form, although not in details, the same as the process of organisation the creator of the work consciously experienced. Without an act of recreation the object is not perceived as a work of art.'[12]

The act of recreation is not a smooth or continuous process, but one which, in its essence, relies on *interruptions* of the flow to render it efficacious. We look forward, we look back, we decide, we change our decisions, we form expectations, we are shocked by their nonfulfilment, we question, we muse, we accept, we reject; this is the dynamic process of recreation. This process is steered by two main structural components within the text: first, a repertoire of familiar literary patterns and recurrent literary themes, together with allusions to familiar social and historical contexts; second, techniques or strategies used to set the familiar against the unfamiliar. Elements of the repertoire are continually backgrounded or foregrounded with a resultant strategic overmagnification, trivialisation, or even annihilation of the allusion. This defamiliarisation of what the reader thought he recognised is bound to create a tension that will intensify his expectations as well as his distrust of those expectations. Similarly, we may be confronted by narrative techniques that establish links between things we find difficult to connect, so that we are forced to reconsider data we at first held to be perfectly straightforward. One need only mention the very simple trick, so often employed by novelists, whereby the author himself takes part in the narrative, thus establishing perspectives which would not have arisen out of the mere narration of the events described. Wayne Booth once called this the technique of the 'unrealiable narrator',[13] to show the extent to which a literary device can counter expectations arising out of the literary text. The figure of the narrator may act in permanent opposition to the impressions we might otherwise form. The question then arises as to whether this strategy, opposing the formation of illusions, may be integrated into a consistent pattern, lying, as it were, a level deeper than our original impressions. We may find that our narrator, by opposing us, in fact turns us against him and thereby strengthens the illusion he appears to be out to destroy; alternatively, we may be so much in doubt that we begin to question all the processes that lead us to make interpretative decisions. Whatever the cause may be, we will find ourselves subjected to this same interplay of illusion-forming and illusion-breaking that makes reading essentially a recreative process.

We might take, as a simple illustration of this complex process, the incident in Joyce's *Ulysses* in which Bloom's cigar alludes to Ulysses's spear. The context (Bloom's cigar) summons up a particular element of the repertoire (Ulysses's spear); the narrative technique relates them to one another as if they were identical. How are we to 'organise' these divergent elements, which, through the very fact that they are put together, separate one element so clearly from the other? What are the prospects here for a consistent pattern? We might say that it is ironic – at least that is how many renowned Joyce readers have understood it.[14] In this case, irony would be the form of organisation that integrates the material. But if this is so, what is the object of the irony? Ulysses's spear, or Bloom's cigar? The uncertainty surrounding this simple question already puts a strain on the consistency we have established and, indeed, begins to puncture it, especially when other problems make themselves felt as regards the remarkable conjunction of spear and cigar. Various alternatives come to mind, but the variety alone is sufficient to leave one with the impression that the consistent pattern has been shattered. And even if, after all, one can still believe that irony holds the key to the mystery, this irony must be of a very strange nature; for the formulated text does not merely mean the opposite of what has been formulated. It may even mean something that cannot be formulated at all. The moment we try to impose a consistent pattern on the text, discrepancies are bound to arise. These are, as it were, the reverse side of the interpretative coin, an involuntary product of the process that creates discrepancies by trying to avoid them. And it is their very presence that draws us into the text, compelling us to conduct a creative examination not only of the text but also of ourselves.

This entanglement of the reader is, of course, vital to any kind of text, but in the literary text we have the strange situation that the reader cannot know what his participation actually entails. We know that we share in certain experiences, but we do not know what happens to us in the course of this process. This is why, when we have been particularly impressed by a book, we feel the need to talk about it; we do not want to get away from it by talking about it – we simply want to understand more clearly what it is in which we have been entangled. We have undergone an experience, and now we want to know consciously *what* we have experienced. Perhaps this is the prime usefulness of literary criticism – it helps to make conscious those aspects of the text which would otherwise remain concealed in the subconscious; it satisfies (or helps to satisfy) our desire to talk about what we have read.

The efficacy of a literary text is brought about by the apparent evocation and subsequent negation of the familiar. What at first seemed to be an affirmation of our assumptions leads to our own rejection of them, thus tending to prepare us for a re-orientation. And it is only when we have outstripped our preconceptions and left the shelter of the familiar that we are in a position to gather new experiences. As the literary text involves the reader in the formation of illusion and the simultaneous formation of the means whereby the illusion is punctured, reading reflects the process by which we gain experience. Once the reader is entangled, his own preconceptions are continually overtaken, so that the text becomes his 'present' while his own ideas fade into the 'past'; as soon as this happens he is open to the immediate experience of the text, which was impossible so long as his preconceptions were his 'present'.

V

Any 'living event' must, to a greater or lesser degree, remain open. In reading, this obliges the reader to seek continually for consistency, because only then can he close up situations and comprehend the unfamiliar. But consistency-building is itself a living process in which one is constantly forced to make selective decisions – and these decisions in their turn give a reality to the possibilities which they exclude, in so far as they may take effect as a latent disturbance of the consistency established. This is what causes the reader to be entangled in the text-'gestalt' that he himself has produced.

Through this entanglement the reader is bound to open himself up to the workings of the text and so leave behind his own preconceptions. This gives him the chance to have an experience in the way George Bernard Shaw once described it: 'You have learnt something. That always feel at first as if you had lost something.' Reading reflects the structure of experience to the extent that we must suspend the ideas and attitudes that shape our own personality before we can experience the unfamiliar world of the literary text. But during this process, something happens to us.

This 'something' needs to be looked at in detail, especially as the incorporation of the unfamiliar into our own range of experience has been to a certain extent obscured by an idea very common in literary discussion: namely, that the process of absorbing the unfamiliar is labeled as the *identification* of the reader with what he reads. Often the term 'identification' is used as if it were an explanation, whereas in actual fact it is nothing more than a description. What is normally meant by 'identification' is the establishment of affinities between oneself and someone outside oneself – a familiar ground on which we are able to experience the unfamiliar. The author's aim, though, is to convey the experience and, above all, an attitude toward that experience. Consequently, 'identification' is not an end in itself, but a strategem by means of which the author stimulates attitudes in the reader.

This of course is not to deny that there does arise a form of participation as one reads; one is certainly drawn into the text in such a way that one has the feeling that there is no distance between oneself and the events described. This involvement is well summed up by the reaction of a critic to reading Charlotte Brontë's *Jane Eyre*: 'We took up *Jane Eyre* one winter's evening, somewhat piqued at the extravagant commendations we had heard, and sternly resolved to be as critical as Croker. But as we read on we forgot both commendations and criticism, identified ourselves with Jane in all her troubles, and finally married Mr Rochester about four in the morning.'[15] The question is how and why did the critic identify himself with Jane?

In order to understand this 'experience', it is well worth considering Georges Poulet's observations on the reading process. He says that books only take on their full existence in the reader.[16] It is true that they consist of ideas thought out by someone else, but in reading the reader becomes the subject that does the thinking. Thus there disappears the subject-object division that otherwise is a prerequisite for all knowledge and all observation, and the removal of this division puts reading in an apparently unique position as regards the possible absorption of new experiences. This may well be the reason why relations with the world of the literary text have so often been misinterpreted as identification. From the idea that in reading we must think the thoughts of someone else, Poulet draws the following conclusion: 'Whatever I think is a part of *my* mental world. And yet here I am thinking a thought which manifestly belongs to another mental world, which is being thought in me just as though I did not exist. Already the notion is inconceivable and seems even more so if I reflect that, since every thought must have a subject to think it, this *thought* which is alien to me and yet in me, must also have in me a *subject* which is alien to me. . . . Whenever I read, I mentally pronounce an *I*, and yet the *I* which I pronounce is not myself.'[17]

But for Poulet this idea is only part of the story. The strange subject that thinks the strange thought in the reader indicates the potential presence of the author, whose ideas can be 'internalised' by the reader: 'Such is the characteristic condition of every work which I summon back into existence by placing my consciousness at its disposal. I give it not only existence, but awareness of existence.'[18] This would mean that consciousness forms the point at which author and reader converge, and at the same time it would result in the cessation of the temporary self-alienation that occurs to the reader when his consciousness brings to life the ideas formulated by the author. This process gives rise to a form of communication which, however, according to Poulet, is dependent on two conditions: the life-story of the author must be shut out of the work and the individual disposition of the reader must be shut out of the act of reading. Only then can the thoughts of the author take place subjectively in the reader, who thinks what he is not. It follows that the work itself must be thought of as a consciousness, because only in this way is there an adequate basis for the author-reader relationship – a relationship that can only come about through the negation of the author's own life-story and the reader's own disposition. This conclusion is actually drawn by Poulet when he describes the work as the self-presentation or materialisation of consciousness: 'And so I ought not to hesitate to recognise that so long as it is animated by this vital inbreathing inspired by the act of reading, a work of literature becomes (at the expense of the reader whose own life it suspends) a sort of human being, that it is a mind concious of itself and constituting itself in me as the subject of its own objects.'[19] Even though it is difficult to follow such a substantialist conception of the consciousness that constitutes itself in the literary work, there are, nevertheless, certain points in Poulet's argument that are worth holding onto. But they should be developed along somewhat different lines.

If reading removes the subject-object division that constitutes all perception, it follows that the reader will be 'occupied' by the thoughts of the author, and these in turn will cause the drawing of new 'boundaries'. Text and reader no longer confront each other as object and subject, but instead the 'division' takes place within the reader himself. In thinking the thoughts of another, his own individuality temporarily recedes into the background, since it is supplanted by these alien thoughts, which now become the theme on which his attention is focussed. As we read, there occurs an artificial division of our personality, because we take as a theme for ourselves something that we are not. Consequently when reading we operate on different levels. For although we may be thinking the thoughts of someone else, what we are will not disappear completely – it will merely remain a more or less powerful virtual force. Thus, in reading there are these two levels – the alien 'me' and the real, virtual 'me' – which are never completely cut off from each other. Indeed, we can only make someone else's thoughts into an absorbing theme for ourselves, provided the virtual background of our own personality can adapt to it. Every text we read draws a different boundary within our personality, so that the virtual background (the real 'me') will take on a different form, according to the theme of the text concerned. This is inevitable, if only for the fact that the relationship between alien theme and virtual background is what makes it possible for the unfamiliar to be understood.

In this context there is a revealing remark made by D. W. Harding, arguing against the idea of identification with what is read: 'What is sometimes called wish-fulfilment in novels and plays can . . . more plausibly be described as wish-formulation or the definition of desires. The cultural levels at which it works may vary widely; the process is the same. . . . It seems nearer the truth . . . to say that fictions contribute to defining the reader's or spectator's values, and perhaps stimulating his desires, rather than to suppose that they gratify desire by some mechanism of vicarious experience.'[20] In the act of reading, having to think something that we have not yet experienced does not mean only being in a position to conceive or even understand it; it also means that such acts of conception are possible and successful to the degree that they lead to something being formulated in us. For someone else's thoughts can only take a form in our consciousness if, in the process, our unformulated faculty for deciphering those thoughts is brought into play – a faculty which, in the act of deciphering, also formulates itself. Now since this formulation is carried out on terms set by someone else, whose thoughts are the theme of our reading, it follows that the formulation of our faculty for deciphering cannot be along our own lines of orientation.

Herein lies the dialectical structure of reading. The need to decipher gives us the chance to formulate our own deciphering capacity – i.e., we bring to the fore an element of our being of which we are not directly conscious. The production of the meaning of literary texts – which we discussed in connection with forming the 'gestalt' of the text – does not merely entail the discovery of the unformulated, which can then be taken over by the active imagination of the reader; it also entails the possibility that we may formulate ourselves and so discover what had previously seemed to elude our consciousness. These are the ways in which reading literature gives us the chance to formulate the unformulated.

SOURCE: extracts from essay, 'The Reading Process: A Phenomenological Approach' (1972) – translated by Catherine Macksey & Richard Macksey – in Iser's *The Implied Reader: Patterns of Communication in Prose Fiction from Bunyan to Beckett* (Baltimore, 1974), excerpted from pp. 274–94.

NOTES

[Reorganised and renumbered from the original – Ed.]

1. [Ed.] Roman Ingarden's work of the 1930s, which examined the relationship between text and reader in the literary work of art, greatly

influenced the German 'reception theorists' of the 1960s, especially Wolfgang Iser himself.

2. Virginia Woolf, *The Common Reader*, first series (London, 1925; reprinted 1957), p. 174.

3. For a more detailed discussion of the function of 'gaps' in literary texts see Wolfgang Iser, 'Indeterminacy and the Reader's Response in Prose Fiction', in J. Hillis Miller (ed.), *Aspects of Narrative* (New York, 1971), pp. 1–45.

4. Maurice Merleau-Ponty, *Phenomenology of Perception*, trans. Colin Smith (New York, 1962), pp. 219–21.

5. E. H. Gombrich, *Art and Illusion: A Study in the Psychology of Pictorial Representation* (London, 1962), p. 204.

6. Louis O. Mink, 'History and Fiction as Modes of Comprehension', *New Literary History*, 1 (Spring, 1970).

7. Gombrich, op. cit., p. 278.

8. Northrop Frye, *Anatomy of Criticism* (Princeton, N.J., 1957; paperback edn, 1967), pp. 169ff.

9. Walter Pater, *Appreciations, With an Essay on Style* (London, 1889; reprinted 1895), p. 15.

10. Gombrich, op. cit., p. 54.   11. Ibid., p. 5.

12. John Dewey, *Art as Experience* (New York, 1958), p. 54.

13. Cf. Wayne Booth, *The Rhetoric of Fiction* (Chicago, 1961), pp. 211ff., 339ff.

14. Richard Ellmann classified this particular allusion as 'Mock-heroic' – see his essay, 'Ulysses, The Divine Nobody', in Charles Shapiro (ed.), *Twelve Original Essays on Great English Novels* (Detroit, 1960), p. 247.

15. William George Clark, review article in *Fraser's Magazine* (Dec. 1849), p. 692 – quoted by Kathleen Tillotson, *Novels of the Eighteen-Forties* (Oxford, 1961), pp. 19ff.

16. Cf. Georges Poulet, 'Phenomenology of Reading', *New Literary History*, 1 (Autumn 1969), p. 54.

17. Ibid., p. 56.   18. Ibid., p. 59.   19. Ibid.

20. D. W. Harding, 'Psychological Process in the Reading of Fiction', *British J. of Aesthetics*, 2 (April 1962), p. 144.

Terry Eagleton   'Reception Theory'   (1983)

. . . Reception theory examines the reader's role in literature, and as such is a fairly novel development. Indeed one might very roughly periodise the history of modern literary theory in three stages: a preoccupation with the author (Romanticism and the nineteenth century); an exclusive concern with the text (New Criticism); and a marked shift of attention to the reader over recent years. The reader has always been the most underprivileged of this trio – strangely, since without him or her there would be no literary texts at all. Literary texts do not exist on bookshelves: they are processes of signification materialised only in the practice of reading. For literature to happen, the reader is quite as vital as the author.

What is involved in the act of reading? Let me take, almost literally at random, the first two sentences of a novel: ' "What did you make of the new couple?" The Hanemas, Piet and Angela, were undressing.' (John Updike, *Couples*.) What are we to make of this? We are puzzled for a moment, perhaps, by an apparent lack of connection between the two sentences, until we grasp that what is at work here is the literary convention by which we may attribute a piece of direct speech to a character even if the text does not explicitly do this itself. We gather that some character, probably Piet or Angela Hanema, makes the opening statement; but why do we presume this? The sentence in quotation marks may not be spoken at all: it may be a thought, or a question which someone else has asked, or a kind of epigraph placed at the opening of the novel. Perhaps it is addressed to Piet and Angela Hanema by somebody else, or by a sudden voice from the sky. One reason why the latter solution seems unlikely is that the question is a little colloquial for a voice from the sky, and we might know that Updike is in general a realist writer who does not usually go in for such devices; but a writer's texts do not necessarily form a consistent whole and it may be unwise to lean on this assumption too heavily. It is unlikely on realist grounds that the question is asked by a chorus of people speaking in unison, and slightly unlikely that it is asked by somebody other than Piet or Angela Hanema, since we learn the next moment that they are undressing, perhaps speculate that they are a married couple, and know that married couples, in our suburb of Birmingham at least, do not make a practice of undressing together before third parties, whatever they might do individually.

We have probably already made a whole set of inferences as we read these sentences. We may infer, for example, that the 'couple' referred to is a man and woman, though there is nothing so far to tell us that they are not two women or two tiger cubs. We assume that whoever poses the question cannot mind-read, as then there would be no need to ask. We may suspect that the questioner values the judgement of the addressee, though there is not sufficient context as yet for us to judge that the question is not taunting or aggressive. The phrase 'The Hanemas', we imagine, is probably in grammatical apposition to the phrase 'Piet and Angela', to indicate that this is their surname, which provides a significant piece of evidence for their being married. But we cannot rule out the possibility that there is some group of people called the Hanemas in addition to Piet and Angela, perhaps a whole tribe of them, and that they are all undressing together in some immense hall. The fact that Piet and Angela may share the same surname does not confirm that they are husband and wife: they may be a particularly liberated or incestuous brother and sister, father and daughter or mother and son. We have assumed, however, that they are undressing in sight of each other, whereas nothing has yet told us that the question is not shouted from one bedroom or beach-hut to another. Perhaps Piet and Angela are small children, though the relative sophistication of the question makes this unlikely. Most readers will by now probably have assumed that Piet and Angela Hanema are a married couple undressing together in their bedroom after some event, perhaps a party, at which a new married couple was present, but none of this is actually said.

The fact that these are the first two sentences of the novel means, of course, that many of these questions will be answered for us as we read on. But the process of speculating and inferring to which we are driven by our ignorance here is simply a more intense and dramatic example of what we do all the time when reading. As we read on we shall encounter many more problems, which can be solved only by making further assumptions. We will be given the kinds of *facts* which are withheld from us in these sentences, but we will still have to construct questionable interpretations of them. Reading the opening of Updike's novel involves us in a surprising amount of complex, largely unconscious labour: although we rarely notice it, we are all the time engaged in constructing hypotheses about the meaning of the text. The reader makes implicit connections, fills in gaps, draws inferences and tests out hunches; and to do this means drawing on a tacit knowledge of the world in general and of literary conventions in particular. The text itself is really no more than a series of 'cues' to the reader, invitations to construct a piece of language into meaning. In the terminology of reception theory, the reader concretises the literary work, which is in itself no more than a chain of organised black marks on a page. Without this continuous active participation on the reader's part, there would be no literary work at all. However solid it may seem, any work for reception theory is actually made up of 'gaps', just as tables are for modern physics – the gap, for instance, between the first and second sentences of *Couples*, where the reader must supply a missing connection. The work is full of 'indeterminates', elements which depend for their effect upon the reader's interpretation, and which can be interpreted in a number of different, perhaps mutually conflicting ways. The paradox of this is that the more information the work provides, the more indeterminate it becomes. Shakespeare's 'secret black and midnight hags' in one sense narrows down what kind of hags are in question, makes them more determinate, but because all three adjectives are richly suggestive, evoking different responses in different readers, the text has also rendered itself less determinate in the act of trying to become more so.

The process of reading, for reception theory, is always a dynamic one, a complex movement and unfolding through time. The literary work itself exists merely as what the Polish theorist Roman Ingarden calls a set of 'schemata' or general directions, which the reader must actualise. To do this, the reader will bring to the work certain 'pre-understandings', a dim context of beliefs and expectations within which the work's various features will be assessed. As the reading process proceeds, however, these expectations will themselves be modified by what we learn, and the hermeneutical circle – moving from part to whole and back to part – will begin to revolve. Striving to construct a coherent sense from the text, the reader will select and organise its elements into consistent wholes, excluding some and foregrounding others, 'concretising' certain items in certain ways; he or she will try to hold different perspectives within the work together, or shift from perspective to perspective in order to build up an integrated 'illusion'. What we have learnt on page one will fade and become 'foreshortened' in memory, perhaps to be radically qualified by what we learn later. Reading is not a straightforward linear movement, a merely cumulative affair: our initial speculations generate a frame of reference within which to interpret what comes next, but what comes next may retrospectively transform our original understanding, highlighting some features of it and backgrounding others. As we read on we shed assumptions, revise beliefs, make more and more complex inferences and anticipations; each sentence opens up a horizon which is confirmed, challenged or undermined by the next. We read backwards and forwards simultaneously, predicting and recollecting, perhaps aware of other possible realisations of the text which our reading has negated. Moreover, all of this complicated activity is carried out on many levels at once, for the text has 'backgrounds' and 'foregrounds', different narrative viewpoints, alternative layers of meaning between which we are constantly moving.

Wolfgang Iser, of the so-called Constance school of reception aesthetics, whose theories I have been largely discussing, speaks in *The Act of Reading* (1978) of the 'strategies' which texts put to work, and of the 'repertoires' of familiar themes and allusions which they contain. To read at all, we need to be familiar with the literary techniques and conventions which a particular work deploys; we must have some grasp of its 'codes', by which is meant the rules which systematically govern the ways it produces its meanings. Recall . . . the London underground sign . . .: 'Dogs must be carried on the escalator.' To understand this notice I need to do a great deal more than simply read its words one after the other. I need to know, for example, that these words belong to what might be called a 'code of reference' – that the sign is not just a decorative piece of language there to entertain travellers, but is to be taken as referring to the behaviour of actual dogs and passengers on actual escalators. I must mobilise my general social knowledge to recognise that the sign has been placed there by the authorities, that these authorities have the power to penalise offenders, that I as a member of the public am being implicitly addressed, none of which is evident in the words themselves. I have to rely, in other words, upon certain social codes and contexts to understand the notice properly. But I also need to bring these into interaction with certain codes or conventions of reading – conventions which tell me that by 'the escalator' is meant *this* escalator and not one in Paraguay, that 'must be carried' means 'must be carried *now*', and so on. I must recognise that the 'genre' of the sign is such as to make it highly improbable that the ambiguity I mentioned in the Introduction is actually 'intended'.* It is not easy to distinguish between 'social' and 'literary' codes here: concretising 'the escalator' as 'this escalator', adopting a reading convention which eradicates ambiguity, itself depends upon a whole network of social knowledge.

I understand the notice, then, by interpreting it in terms of certain codes which seem appropriate; but for Iser this it not all of what happens in reading literature. If there were a perfect 'fit' between the codes which governed literary works and the codes we applied to interpret them, all literature would be as uninspiring as the London underground sign. The most effective literary work for Iser is one which forces the reader into a new critical awareness of his or her customary codes and expectations. The work interrogates and transforms the implicit beliefs we bring to it, 'disconfirms' our routine habits of perception and so forces us to acknowledge them for the first time for what they are. Rather than merely reinforce our given perceptions, the valuable work of literature violates or transgresses these normative ways of seeing, and so teaches us new codes for understanding. There is a parallel here with Russian Formalism: in the act of reading, our conventional assumptions are 'defamiliarised',

---

*The ambiguity in question is that the sign, read literally, could be understood as ordering all escalator-users to carry dogs.

objectified to the point where we can criticise and so revise them. If we modify the text by our reading strategies, it simultaneously modifies us: like objects in a scientific experiment, it may return an unpredictable 'answer' to our 'questions'. The whole point of reading, for a critic like Iser, is that it brings us into deeper self-consciousness, catalyses a more critical view of our own identities. It is as though what we have been 'reading', in working our way through a book, is ourselves.

Iser's reception theory, in fact, is based on a liberal humanist ideology: a belief that in reading we should be flexible and open-minded, prepared to put our beliefs into question and allow them to be transformed. Behind this case lies the influence of Gadamerian hermeneutics, with its trust in that enriched self-knowledge which springs from an encounter with the unfamiliar.[1] But Iser's liberal humanism, like most such doctrines, is less liberal that it looks at first sight. He writes that a reader with strong ideological commitments is likely to be an inadequate one, since he or she is less likely to be open to the transformative power of literary works. What this implies is that in order to undergo transformation at the hands of the text, we must only hold our beliefs fairly provisionally in the first place. The only good reader would *already* have to be a liberal: the act of reading produces a kind of human subject which it also presupposes. This is also paradoxical in another way: for if we only hold our convictions rather lightly in the first place, having them interrogated and subverted by the text is not really very significant. Nothing much, in other words, will have actually happened. The reader is not so much radically upbraided, as simply returned to himself or herself as a more thoroughly liberal subject. Everything about the reading subject is up for question in the act of reading, except what kind of (liberal) subject it is: these ideological limits can be in no way criticised, for then the whole model would collapse. In this sense, the plurality and open-endedness of the process of reading are permissible because they presuppose a certain kind of closed unity which always remains in place: the unity of the reading subject which is violated and transgressed only to be returned more fully to itself. As with Gadamer, we can foray out into foreign territory because we are always secretly at home. The kind of reader whom literature is going to affect most profoundly is one already equipped with the 'right' kind of capacities and responses, proficient in operating certain critical techniques and recognising certain literary conventions; but this is precisely the kind of reader who needs to be affected least. Such a reader is 'transformed' from the outset, and is ready to risk further transformation just because of this fact. To read literature 'effectively' you must exercise certain critical capacities, capacities which are always problematically defined; but it is precisely these capacities which 'literature' will be unable to call into question, because its very existence depends on them. What you have defined as a 'literary' work will always be closely bound up with what you consider 'appropriate' critical techniques: a 'literary' work will mean, more or less, one which can be usefully illuminated by such methods of enquiry. But in that case the hermeneutical circle really is a vicious rather than virtuous one: what you get out of the work will depend in large measure on what you put into it in the first place, and there is little room here for any deep-seated 'challenge' to the reader. Iser would seem to avoid this vicious circle by stressing the power of literature to disrupt and transfigure the reader's codes; but this itself, as I have argued, silently assumes exactly the kind of 'given' reader that it hopes to generate through reading. The closedness of the circuit between reader and work reflects the closedness of the academic institutions of Literature, to which only certain kinds of texts and readers need apply.

The doctrines of the unified self and the closed text surreptitiously underlie the apparent open-endedness of much reception theory. Roman Ingarden in *The Literary Work of Art* (1931) dogmatically presumes that literary works form organic wholes, and the point of the reader's filling in their 'indeterminancies' is to complete this harmony. The reader must link up the different segments and strata of the work in a 'proper' fashion, rather in the manner of those children's picture books which you colour in according to the manufacturer's instructions. The text for Ingarden comes ready-equipped with its indeterminacies, and the reader must concretise it 'correctly'. This rather limits the reader's activity, reducing him at times to little more than a kind of literary handyman, pottering around and filling in the odd indeterminacy. Iser is a much more liberal kind of employer, granting the reader a greater degree of co-partnership with the text: different readers are free to actualise the work in different ways, and there is no single correct interpretation which will exhaust its semantic potential. But this generosity is qualified by one rigorous instruction: the reader must construct the text so as to render it internally *consistent*. Iser's model of reading is fundamentally functionalist: the parts must be made to adapt coherently to the whole. Behind this arbitrary prejudice, in fact, lies the influence of *Gestalt* psychology, with its concern to integrate discrete perceptions into an intelligible whole. It is true that this prejudice runs so deep in modern critics that it is difficult to see it as just that – a doctrinal predilection, which is no less arguable and contentious than any other. There is absolutely no need to suppose that works of literature either do or should constitute harmonious wholes, and many suggestive frictions and collisions of meaning must be blandly 'processed' by literary criticism to induce them to do so. Iser sees that Ingarden is a good deal too 'organicist' in his views of the text, and appreciates modernist, multiple works partly because they make us more self-conscious about the labour of interpreting them. But at the same time the 'openness' of the work is something which is to be gradually eliminated, as the reader comes to construct a working hypothesis which can account for and render mutually coherent the greatest number of the work's elements.

Textual indeterminacies just spur us on to the act of abolishing them, replacing them with a stable meaning. They must, in Iser's revealingly authoritarian term, be 'normalised' – tamed and subdued to some firm structure of sense. The reader, it would seem, is engaged in fighting the text as much as interpreting it, struggling to pin down its anarchic 'polysemantic' potential within some manageable framework. Iser speaks quite openly of 'reducing' this polysemantic potential to some kind of order – a curious way, one might have thought, for a 'pluralist' critic to speak. Unless this is done, the unified reading subject will be jeopardised, rendered incapable of returning to itself as a well-balanced entity in the 'self-correcting' therapy of reading.

It is always worth testing out any literary theory by asking: How would it work with Joyce's *Finnegans Wake*? The answer in Iser's case is bound to be: Not too well. He deals, admittedly, with Joyce's *Ulysses*; but his major critical interests are in realist fiction since the eighteenth century, and there are ways in which *Ulysses* can be made to conform to this model. Would Iser's opinion that the most valid literature disturbs and transgresses received codes do for the contemporary readers of Homer, Dante or Spenser? Is it not a viewpoint more typical of a modern-day European liberal, for whom 'systems of thought' is bound to have something of a negative rather than positive ring, and who will therefore look to the kind of art which appears to undermine them? Has not a great deal of 'valid' literature precisely confirmed rather than troubled the received codes of its time? To locate the power of art primarily in the negative – in the transgressive and defamiliarising – is with both Iser and the Formalists to imply a definite attitude to the social and cultural systems of one's epoch: an attitude which, in modern liberalism, amounts to suspecting thought-systems as such. That it can do so is eloquent testimony to liberalism's obliviousness of one particular thought-system: that which sustains its own position.

SOURCE: extract from *Literary Theory: An Introduction* (Oxford, 1983), pp. 74–82.

NOTE

1. [Ed.] Hans Georg Gadamer, in his book *Truth and Method* (1960), argued the importance in hermeneutics (the science of understanding and interpretation) of the preconceptions, or 'prejudices' which form our mental horizons. In the act of understanding this existing horizon is fused with that of newly encountered material. Gadamer's thinking has been widely influential, particularly on the reception theorists, but is criticised for ignoring socially-specific factors.

PART THREE

New Theories in Practice

1. FICTION

Rachel M. Brownstein 'On Jane Austen's Heroines' (1982)

A heroine moves toward her inevitable end, death or marriage, along lines her body generates: the domestic novel binds her over and over to the sexual plot. For her, for sure, anatomy is destiny. One of two courses of action is possible: she will either get virtue's earthly reward, a rich husband, or be seduced and die of it. The conscious heroine must work out a view of this absurdly simple pair of alternatives by which to transcend them. Clarissa Harlowe imagines the perfect marriage, death, transcendence that realises her self. Trapped in the constraints of the heroine's story, she triumphs – paradoxically, ambiguously – by writing her own variation on it.

A number of factors account for the novel's long marriage to the marriage plot. Eighteenth- and nineteenth-century women had little chance of living comfortable or fulfilling lives outside of marriage, social historians explain. And, they add, middle-class women liked to dream in their increased leisure time over undemanding fiction, which was provided for them in increasingly large part by women like themselves, who made novels out of the usual stuff of women's gossip. Feminists argue that in patriarchal society woman is defined as simply a sexual creature, and that novels that show women's lives as gender-determined help to define her thus. Meanwhile, literary critics observe that the novel is peculiarly suited to weigh the relationships between character and plot, to show how they make one another problematic, and that therefore the case of a conscious being who feels too narrowly defined by what Moll Flanders called her 'carcase' is a natural for a novelist. I think all these points are worth making.

There are exceptions to the rule that the heroine of an eighteenth- or nineteenth-century English novel can only marry or not. Defoe's pioneering Moll and Roxana start off seduced and abandoned, and go on to have busy long lives. Jeanie Deans, of Sir Walter Scott's *The Heart of Midlothian* (1817), is another kind of exception. Scott's friend Lady Louisa Stuart commended him for unconventionally casting

Jeanie as the heroine rather than her sister Effie, who is the victim of a standard sexual plot. Jeanie's story, like Clarissa's, is intricately involved with language; she is quite as literal minded, as bound to the letter, as any conscious heroine. She refuses to tell a lie to save the life of her sister, who has been condemned to death for infanticide, because she takes her own word too seriously to lie; she gives her sister her word to help her; so she walks to London to seek the King's word of pardon for the criminal. Scott recalled the Old Testament doctrine Richardson cites in *Clarissa*, that the promise of an unmarried girl, given when she is in her father's house, doesn't really signify: Jeannie, in defiance of the maiden's privilege, insists her word has meaning. She does not see herself as a creature defined by her gender. Jeanie is no beauty, and she is Scottish, not English, and lower-class. The marriage that occurs at the end of it is beside the point of her story, which is about a journey and not a courtship, a long and arduous walk in the course of which she is explicitly compared – by a wandering madwoman – to Bunyan's Christiana. The small world of courtship novels is hermetically sealed off from a wider world like Jeanie's, where there are mountains and revolutions and cheeses and cows, pregnancies and prisons and wandering wild women. Jeanie is not a lady. She is heroic, but she is not a heroine as I have been using the term here. Partly this is because her story is too rare. The main thing about the heroine is that hers is always the same old story.

The paradigmatic hero is an overreacher; the heroine of the domestic novel, the descendant of the Rose, is overdetermined. The hero moves toward a goal; the heroine tries to be it. He makes a name for himself; she is concerned with keeping her good name. (But at the end of her story, when it's happy, she takes her husband's name.) A hero is extraordinary, exempt from the rules of society; a heroine must stick to the social code and then some. She is governed by constraints as rigid as the ones that make a sonnet. The instructive contrast is between Richardson's good girls and Fielding's bad boy, Tom Jones, who proves the neighbors were wrong when they said he was born to be hanged. What the neighbors say can ruin a girl's life, and run like water off a duck's back off a boy's. A heroine must be perfectly well-behaved, well-spoken and well-spoken-of. She must be just like other girls and also she must be better, to be singled out once for all by the best of men.

At the end of Richardson's third novel, *Sir Charles Grandison* (1753–54), a discussion of marrying leads to a discussion of the bad effects of romance. The venerable Mrs Shirley, the heroine Harriet Byron's grandmother, says that the popular literature of her youth, the heroic romances of the seventeenth century, misled girls by celebrating the overwhelming importance of first and passionate love. A second love, Mrs Shirley maintains, can be as true and powerful as a first; and a first love may turn out to have been not true love at all; and an arranged marriage, based on reason not passion, may prove a most successful one. Richardson's last novel argues that while love is best, self-restraint and courtesy are very, very important, and fatal passions are not the only ones there are. *Sir Charles Grandison* has two heroines instead of one, as if to amend the emphasis on the singular that is central to romance and also central in Richardson's first two novels. Jane Austen admired *Grandison*, remembered it often as she went about her daily domestic life and, no doubt, when she wrote her books. By Austen's time, to reflect as Mrs Shirley had done on the effects of reading fiction was to consider a large body of literature. Jane Austen rewrote romance and Richardson when she described a young woman's struggle to define herself by reflecting on and revising, doubting and reaffirming, the truth of the heroine's old story. . . .

Implicit in Austen's novels are these truths no longer universally acknowledged: that women are interesting only in the brief time they are marriageable, that marrying is the most significant action a woman can undertake, and that after she marries her story is over. Her goal achieved, a lady may lounge out her life on a sofa, dote on her children or neglect them, even run off with a lover, and be equally unworthy of attention. A retired Jane Austen heroine will of course do none of these foolish things, being a valuable person who has learned in the strenuous course of courtship precisely what she is worth. Married, she will concern herself with her cows' pasturage, or entertain and educate deserving relatives, and love and manage her husband and her house, and fall on rainy days upon her 'resources', her pencils and her instruments and her powers of reflection. But no matter what admirable things she does, she will never again be the focus of serious interest, a heroine. Married, she is finished. Austen wrote ominously to her niece Fanny as if the ceremony put an end to the character as well as to plot: 'Oh! what a loss it will be when you are married. You are too agreable in your single state, too agreable as a Niece. I shall hate you when your delicious play of Mind is all settled down into conjugal & maternal affections' (*Letters*, pp. 478–9). . . .

Except for *Emma*, all Austen's novels are about girls who are in some sense homeless and in the end find homes.[1] The heroine's story is always, like Clarissa's, about defining and being defined by a space, about finding a space of one's own. Austen's novels are about attaining the external correlative (husband, social position, house) that makes inner potential real. The heroines are not orphans, as so many fictitious maidens were in the eighteenth century; one of the difficult tasks before Catherine, Elinor and Marianne, Elizabeth, Fanny, Emma and Anne, is to separate themselves from their parents or surrogate parents, and come to judge their families correctly. (It is a large part of Clarissa Harlowe's problem, too.) Austen's good girls will be rewarded by having families of their own. Elinor and Marianne Dashwood in *Sense and Sensibility*, Elizabeth Bennet in *Pride and Prejudice* and Anne Elliot in *Persuasion* are victims of the patriarchal law of entail, which prevents them from inheriting their father's houses, favoring selfish and obnoxious men like John Dashwood and Mr Collins, and even scheming hypocrites like Mr Elliot, over deserving young women. No wonder the heroines must find husbands. Young women of sensibility, they of course do not go pragmatically husband-hunting, but it is as clear to them as it is to us that for their comfort they must marry. The Dashwood estate is already settled on the sisters' half-brother John when their story begins, and Marianne is mourning the prospect of leaving the house where she grew up. One of the things Willoughby does to make her fall in love with him is to show her through the 'charming' house he will inherit; from the point of view of even so romantic a girl as Marianne, a man's attractions include his real property. The heroine of *Pride and Prejudice* deflects the charge by making it herself, but to some degree she does, as she claims, fall in love with Darcy 'upon first seeing his beautiful grounds at Pemberly'. 'To be mistress of Pemberley might be something!' she reflects when she first sees the great estate. To be Mr Bennet's daughter, whose entailed home will go to Mr Collins, is to be not very much. Elizabeth is some*one*: personal merit makes her that. But she must also become some*thing*. When she does she becomes the image of all a woman may hope to be.

Mansfield Park (1814), with its witty anti-heroine, Mary Crawford, and its enervated protagonist, Fanny Price, is a revision of *Pride and Prejudice* (1813), which Austen on second thought decided was too 'light, and bright, and sparkling'. It is determinedly sober. Fanny, most remarkable for her tenacity, is an adopted poor relation at grand Mansfield Park; fastidious and high-minded, she prefers to be away from her parents' small, disorderly house. (Fanny is a model of filial piety to *surrogate* parents, as Anne Elliot is to Lady Russell in *Persuasion*; like Anne but with less justification, she is disdainful of her own. The 'family romance' fantasy Freud described, of choosing parents worthy of one's superior tastes, is proposed and quietly exploded as Fanny's aunt and uncle, the Bertrams, prove, like Lady Russell, to be also inadequate.) Fanny's image of Mansfield Park is purer than the actual place. When she triumphs in the end by marrying her cousin Edmund, she becomes mistress of its parsonage and of the spirit of Mansfield Park. The poor girl excels her rich uncle's daughters, in the end, not only in moral but also in material good. The bad elements are purged from Fanny's Mansfield; her ideal becomes the real estate.

Of Austen's protagonists only the heroine of *Emma* (1816) is a middle-class princess. 'Handsome, clever, and rich', she is the flower of Hartfield, her father's house, and the first lady of the neighboring village of Highbury. Like Clarissa Harlowe, Emma Woodhouse suffers from 'real evils' of a 'situation' which imposes on her the idea that she is uniquely set on a pedestal. In the course of her story she must discover 'the beauty of truth and sincerity in all our dealings with each other', as Mr Knightley puts it, and move closer to the rest of the world. When she gives up her fantasies and embraces reality, Emma joins together her father's and Knightley's estates, *Hart*field and *Don*well, to unite desire with doing.

In *Persuasion* (1818) Austen raises the revisionary possibility that personal fulfilment cannot be translated into terms of real property. Twenty-seven-year-old Anne Elliot is the daughter of Sir Walter Elliot of Kellynch Hall, a vain and empty baronet whose extravagance has driven him to rent out to tenants the property which will eventually go to a male relation. In the course of the novel Anne thinks of marrying her cousin, very briefly, when she imagines herself taking her mother's place at Kellynch. But Mr Elliot is repellently reserved and careful; and Anne loves another. Since she broke her engagement to Frederick Wentworth eight years before the novel's beginning, she has lived as a displaced person, either making long visits or being overlooked by her father and older sister at home. Supposing she will never marry and continuing to think of Wentworth, Anne is alone among relatives very unlike her, and reflects with melancholy on where her eventual place might be. She is miraculously saved by a second chance to revise her life's plot. Wentworth's worth is not embodied in a permanent, stable home, but earned via new goings, piratical, nautical adventures; in the world of Austen's last novel, a new economy is replacing the old land-based one. Anne will be happy ever after with a man national emergencies will call from time to time to his country's service on the seas: 'She gloried in being a sailor's wife, but she must pay the tax of quick alarm for belonging to that profession which is, if possible, more distinguished in its domestic virtues than in its national importance' [*P.* II, 12]. Glory, importance, virtue, happiness – all these abstractions, as Anne has learned, are taxed. The economics of *Persuasion* are different from those of the earlier novels, where man and woman are seen as consumers and commodities: here both sexes struggle for rare and elusive immaterial goods in a changing world where people are very concerned with aging and altering.

The symptoms of Anne's intense love for Wentworth are rushes of dizzying feeling that come and go, which perhaps foreshadow the 'quick alarm' of the sailor's wife. For Austen's younger, earlier heroines, sexual feeling takes the cooler, chaster, eighteenth-century forms of esteem, respect and determination to marry. But their passion is also strong, being equal to the forms that côntain it. When 'it darted through her, with the speed of an arrow, that Mr Knightley must marry no one but herself', Emma Woodhouse was pierced by sexual desire so thoroughly implicated in the desire to exclusive legal possession of a male property that it is impossible to say whether she wishes really to be pierced or really to do the piercing herself. Both Emma, through whom 'it darted', and Mr Knightley, who 'must marry', are rendered passive by the syntax: what is revealed to Emma is that the grand design of marriage must join the two of them to one another. Desire is as forceful as what organises it.

The paradoxical conclusion of the marriage plot, the comic resolution that symbolises social coherence, requires that the heroine distinguish and separate herself from the social world she lives in. She learns in the course of her story that apparently charming young men are not necessarily the best ones; by marrying she puts herself out of their reach. She learns that well-intentioned women are often wrong about whom to marry; becoming a matron herself, she escapes matronly power. But before she can escape both men and matrons she must separate herself from her sisters: she must learn from the fate of another girl, who has fallen or allied herself stupidly or indecorously, and so choose correctly herself. There is a witty turn on this in *Persuasion*, where Louisa Musgrove falls literally from the Cob at Lyme Regis, and events devolving from the accident move Anne and Wentworth toward marrying. (Louisa's fall renders her unconscious: Anne's consciousness, in contrast, is exquisite.) The heroine's wise marriage is a rejoinder to another young woman's foolish engagement with a man. To the extent that they affirm feminine capacity and value and are radiant in their context of less special and successful girls, Jane Austen's heroines are in a way exemplars. . . .

'Happiness in marriage is entirely a matter of chance', Charlotte Lucas says in ch. 6 of *Pride and Prejudice*. 'If the dispositions of the parties are ever so well known to each other, or ever so similar before-hand, it does not advance their felicity in the least. They always continue to grow sufficiently unlike afterwards to have their share of vexation; and it is better to know as little as possible of the defects of the person with whom you are to pass your life.' It is on the strength of this philosophy that Charlotte marries the insufferable Mr Collins and manages to suffer him rather well, busying herself first with her poultry and later, probably, with her babies, keeping for herself a little back parlor away from the side of the house where her husband sits hoping for Lady Catherine to pass by. Elizabeth says Charlotte makes her laugh, and she protests that her doctrine 'is not sound. You know it is not sound, and that you would never act in this way yourself', she says, and on rereading the novel we note her characteristic errors in judging character and predicting the future. But it is harder to know if we are meant to perceive her notion that Charlotte's view 'is not sound' as an error. Jane Austen clearly puts stock in knowing people's defects, and Charlotte's cynical counsel that ignorance may lead to bliss is the opposite of what *Pride and Prejudice* would seem to be preaching. Elizabeth attains perfect happiness by coming to know Mr Darcy and thus learning to know herself. And the process by which she attains happiness does not seem a matter of chance, as it unfolds, but rather the logical, inevitable expression of her character in an action. In other words, *Pride and Prejudice* is not a picture of real life but a plausible fiction.

Charlotte does not believe that life is logical, or that we get what we deserve. Her 'realistic' maxim is one of the many anti-romantic elements in this novel, which mocks as it exploits the conventions of romance. Elizabeth Bennet, who attains perfect happiness, is, for all her defiance of the ideal of woman, a novel heroine after all: her love story figures forth the novel's fantasies, that character determines fate, that virtue is rewarded, that to know oneself is to know and control one's destiny. A heroine, unlike other women, controls her life, shapes herself, makes her happiness; for other, real women, happiness is a matter of chance quite as Charlotte says. It is significant that of all the weddings in *Pride and Prejudice*, only Charlotte's will certainly produce what Mr Bennet refers to with gingerly distaste, alluding to Mr Collins's platitude about peace-making, as 'a young olive-branch'; Elizabeth's marriage is the long-promised end to a perfectly made story, art not life. *Pride and Prejudice II* is unimaginable. Elizabeth is framed in the end.

SOURCE: extracts from *Becoming a Heroine: Reading about Women in Novels* (New York, 1982; paperback edn, Harmondsworth, 1984), pp. 81–3, 90, 96–9, 133–4.

NOTE

1. Partial exceptions increase the rule's resonance: Catherine Morland in *Northanger Abbey*, like Charlotte Heywood in Austen's unfinished *Sanditon*, is merely away from home visiting; Anne Elliot, marrying Captain Wentworth, gains true love and improves her social position, but, since she marries a sailor, she remains unsettled for life.

Penny Boumelha   'The Narrator in Hardy's *Tess of the d'Urbervilles*'   (1982)

... *Tess* presses the problem of what I have earlier called Hardy's urge towards narrative androgyny to the point where a break becomes necessary.[1] John Bayley claims that 'Tess is the most striking embodiment in literature of the woman realised both as object and as consciousness, to herself and to others'. But this even-handed statement of the case smooths out the tension inherent in this androgynous mode of narration, which has as its project to present woman, 'pure woman', as known from within and without, explicated and rendered transparent. In short, she is not merely spoken by the narrator, but also spoken *for*. To realise Tess as consciousness, with all that that entails of representation and display, inevitably renders her all the more the object of gaze and of knowledge for reader and narrator. John Goode has drawn attention to the erotic dimension of this interplay between reader and character.

Tess is the subject of the novel: that makes her inevitably an object of the reader's consumption (no novel has ever produced so much of what Sontag required in place of hermeneutics, namely, an erotics of art).

And so it is that all the passionate commitment to exhibiting Tess as the subject of her own experience evokes an unusually overt maleness in the narrative voice. The narrator's erotic fantasies of penetration and engulfment enact a pursuit, violation and persecution of Tess in parallel with those she suffers at the hands of her two lovers. Time and again the narrator seeks to enter Tess, through her eyes – 'his [eyes] plumbed the deepness of the ever-varying pupils, with their radiating fibrils of blue, and black, and gray, and violet' [p. 198] – through her mouth – 'he saw the red interior and her mouth as if it had been a snake's' [p. 198] – and through her flesh – 'as the day wears on its feminine smoothness is scarified by the stubble, and bleeds' [p. 117].

The phallic imagery of pricking, piercing and penetration which has repeatedly been noted, serves not only to create an image-chain linking Tess's experiences from the death of Prince to her final penetrative act of retaliation, but also to satisfy the narrator's fascination with the interiority of her sexuality, and his desire to take possession of her. Similarly, the repeated evocations of a recumbent or somnolent Tess awakening to violence, and the continual interweaving of red and white, blood and flesh, sex and death, provide structuring images for the violence Tess suffers, but also repeat that violence. It has even been suggested that the novel takes the form it does in part because the narrator's jealous inability to relinquish his sole possession of her causes both the editing out of her seduction by Alec, and the denial to her of consummated marriage or lasting relationship.[2]

But this narrative appropriation is resisted by the very thing that the narrator seeks above all to capture in Tess: her sexuality, which remains unknowable and unrepresentable. There is a sense here in which James's comment that 'The pretence of "sexuality" is only equalled by the absence of it' could be justified. It is as if Tess's sexuality resides quite literally *within* her body, and must be wrested from her by violence. The most telling passage in this respect is Angel Clare's early morning sight of Tess:

She had not heard him enter and hardly realised his presence there. She was yawning, and he saw the red interior of her mouth as if it had been a snake's. She had stretched one arm so high above her coiled-up cable of hair that he could see its satin delicacy above the sunburn; her face was flushed with sleep, and her eyelids hung heavy over their pupils. The brim-fulness of her nature breathed from her. It was a moment when a woman's soul is more incarnate than at any other time; when the most spiritual beauty bespeaks itself flesh; and sex takes the outside place in the presentation   [p. 198]

It is most revealing here that, as Mary Jacobus has remarked, the language of incarnation is destabilised by the physicality and interiority of the 'woman's soul', co-extensive with the 'brimfulness of her nature', that it seeks to represent. Jacobus has also significantly noted that 'The incarnate state of Tess's soul appears to be as close to sleep – to unconsciousness – as is compatible with going about her work.'[3] Here, as elsewhere, and particularly at moments of such erotic response, consciousness is all but edited out. Tess is asleep, or in reverie, at almost every crucial turn of the plot: at Prince's death, at the time of her seduction by Alec, when the sleep-walking Angel buries his image of her, at his return to find her at the Herons, and when the police take her at Stonehenge. Important moments of speech are absent, too – her wedding-night account of her past life, for example, or the 'merciless polemical syllogism', learnt from Angel, with which she transforms Alec from evangelical preacher to sexual suitor once more [p. 345]. Tess is most herself – and that is, most woman – at points where she is dumb and semi-conscious. The tragedy of Tess Durbeyfield, like that in *The Return of the Native*, turns upon an ideological basis, projecting a polarity of sex and intellect, body and mind, upon an equally fixed polarity of gender. In this schema, sex and nature are assigned to the female, intellect and culture to the male. That this is so would have been even more clearly the case had Hardy retained the Ur-*Tess* version of the relation between Tess and Angel. The relatively crude feminist point made by Angel's flagrant application of a double standard of sexual morality replaces what might have been a rather subtler counterpointing of the varieties of heterodoxy available to (intellectual) man and (sexual) woman: there is some evidence that his original wedding-night 'confession' was to have been primarily of lost faith. Angel Clare's dilemma is compounded primarily of elements given a historical and social location: the difficulties of class transition, the confrontation of liberal education and Christian faith, the establishment of a standard of morality in the absence of transcendentally ratified principles. Tess's situation, unlike that of Eustacia Vye, calls upon similar elements: her entrapment in mutually reinforcing economic and sexual oppression, for example, and the characteristically Victorian morality of the double standard. But still, the source of what is specifically *tragic* in her story remains at the level of nature. Tess is identified with nature – or, more accurately, constructed as an instance of the natural – in a number of ways. She is, for instance, particularly associated with instinct and intuition, those 'natural' modes of knowledge which Clare too will ascribe to her, and which form part of a collision in the novel between formal and heuristic education. So, the 'invincible instinct towards self-delight' [p. 128] sends her to Talbothays in relatively good heart; her 'instincts' tell her that she must not play hard to get with Angel Clare, 'since it must in its very nature carry with it a suspicion of art' [p. 221]; and the 'appetite for joy' moves her to accept Clare's proposal of marriage [p. 218]. It is noticeable, too, that Tess is often bound doubly to her sex and to intuition or instinct by a generalising commentary: 'the woman's instinct to hide' [p. 224], 'it would have denoted deficiency of womanhood if she had not instinctively known what an argument lies in propinquity' [p. 269], 'the intuitive heart of woman knoweth not only its own bitterness, but its husband's' [p. 269]. Then, too, there is her explicitly remarked continuity with the natural world: she (again in common with other members of her sex) is 'part and parcel of outdoor nature . . . a portion of the field' [p. 116]; images of animals and birds, hunting and traps, cluster around her; and in the latter part of the novel she becomes increasingly 'like . . . a lesser creature than a woman' [p. 418]. Kathleen Rogers has remarked that 'Tess herself is almost less a personality than a beautiful portion of nature violated by human selfishness and over-intellectualising. She is the least flawed of Hardy's protagonists, but also the least human.'[4] But what might otherwise be simply a process of diminution is modified by the new degree of consciousness with which Tess's assimilation to nature is evoked. The ideological elision of woman, sex and nature remains a structuring element of the tragedy, but at the same time presses 'the vulgarism of the "natural woman"'[5] to a point where it becomes disruptively visible. Angel Clare, who is patently implicated in Hardy's continuing dialogue with both Shelley and Arnold, is also the bearer of the vestiges of certain Romantic and Christian views of nature in his responses to Tess. For him, Tess is 'a mate from unconstrained Nature, and not from the abodes of Art' [p. 202]; during their courtship, he creates for himself a pastoral in which the farm life is 'bucolic' and Tess herself 'idyllic' [p. 232]; her wedding-night confession transforms her, for him, from 'a child of nature' [p. 259] to an instance of 'Nature, in her fantastic trickery' [p. 263]. It is through Clare, through the obvious contradictions and inadequacies of his response to Tess, that the novel throws into question the ideological bases of its own tragic polarities. . . .

[Boumelha discusses 'discontinuities' in the novel – viz, the way crucial narrative moments (such as the seduction scene) often occur in the break between one phase and the next, the effect being that 'Tess's sexuality eludes the circumscribing narrative voice' – Ed.] These discontinuities, incidentally, have enabled a critical dismembering of Tess. For some, concentrating on such scenes as the Lady-Day move and the threshing-machine, she is the representative of an order of rural society threatened by urbanism, mechanisation, and the destruction of stable working communities. Thus, for Kettle, she typifies the proletarianisation of the peasantry; for the agrarian traditionalist Douglas Brown, she embodies 'the agricultural community in its moment of ruin'; for the Weberian Lucille Herbert, she marks the moment of transition from *Gemeinschaft* to *Gesellschaft*; and John Holloway finds in her evidence of Hardy's increasing awareness of flaws within the traditional rural order that has hitherto functioned to establish a moral norm.[6] For all of these, the significance of Tess's womanhood is negligible, except insofar as it provides an appropriate image of passivity and victimisation. Others, seizing on the way in which Tess is singled out from her community, both by her own outstanding qualities and by her aristocratic descent with its encumbering heritage of omens and legends, have followed Lawrence to find in 'the deeper-passioned Tess' [p. 164], who can assert that '"I am only a peasant by position, not by nature!"' [p. 258], a natural aristocrat, the suitable subject of a tragedy.[7] Alternatively, by taking up the novel's allusions to, or recapitulations of, Biblical and literary plots (Eden and Fall, *Paradise Lost*, *Pilgrim's Progress*, and so on), or by following through the chains of imagery centring upon altars, druids and sacrifices, it is possible to find in Tess the shadow of innumerable cultural archetypes (Patient Griselda, the scapegoat, the highborn lady in disguise).[8] That each of these views finds its point of departure in the detail of the text indicates how complex and contradictory Tess is, viewed in the light of a critical practice that demands a stable and coherent consolidation of character.

And there is more to the discontinuity than this. The narrator shifts brusquely between dispassionate, long-distance observation (Tess as 'a fly on a billiard-table of indefinite length, and of no more consequence to the surroundings than that fly' [p. 133]) and a lingering closeness of view that particularises the grain of her skin, the texture of her hair. The transparency of her consciousness is punctuated by the distancing reflections of a meditative moralist who can generalise ('women whose chief companions are the forms and forces of outdoor Nature retain in their souls far more of the Pagan fantasy of their remote forefathers than of the systematised religion taught their race at later date' [p. 132]), allude ('But, might some say, where was Tess's guardian angel?. . . Perhaps, like that other god of whom the ironical Tishbite spoke, he was talking, or he was pursuing, or he was in a journey, or he was sleeping and not to be awaked' [p. 101]), and abstract ('But for the world's opinion those experiences would have been simply a liberal education' [p. 127]). Equally, the narrator's analytic omniscience is threatened both by his erotic commitment to Tess, and by the elusiveness of her sexuality. The novel's ideological project, the circumscribing of the consciousness and experience of its heroine by a scientifically dispassionate mode of narration, is undermined by the instability of its 'placing' of Tess through genre and point of view. Structured primarily as tragedy, the novel draws also on a number of other genres and modes of writing: on realism, certainly, but also on a melodrama that itself reaches into balladry, and, of course, on polemic.

SOURCE: extracts from *Thomas Hardy and Women: Sexual Ideology and Narrative Form* (Brighton, 1982), pp. 120–3, 127–8.

NOTES

[Reorganised and renumbered from the original – Ed.]

1. [Ed.] Narrative androgyny is defined earlier by Boumelha as the narrator's ability to 'shuttle between, or for moments yoke together, the responses of the two sexes', allowing both dismissive generalisations about women and an attempt to make the female characters the subjects of their own experience rather than just the instrument of man's. For the quotations which follow, see note 2 for John Bayley and note 3 for the collection which contains John Goode's essay. The New Wessex Edition of the novel is cited throughout.

2. John Bayley, *An Essay on Hardy* (Cambridge, 1978), p. 183.

3. Mary Jacobus, 'The Difference of View', in M. Jacobus (ed.), *Women in Writing and Writing about Women* (London, 1979), p. 13.

4. Kathleen Rogers, 'Women in Thomas Hardy', *Centennial Review*, 19 (1975), pp. 249–50.

5. Bayley, op. cit., p. 176.

6. See, respectively, Arnold Kettle's Introduction to *Tess*, reprinted in Albert J. LaValley (ed.), *Twentieth-Century Interpretations of 'Tess of the d'Urbervilles'* (Englewood, Cliffs, N.J., 1969), pp. 14–29; Douglas Brown, *Thomas Hardy* (London, 1954), p. 91; Lucille Herbert, 'Hardy's Views in *Tess of the d'Urbervilles*', *English Literary History*, 37 (1970), pp. 77–94; and John Holloway, 'Hardy's Major Fiction', in his *The Charted Mirror: Literary and Critical Essays* (London, 1960), pp. 94–107.

7. D. H. Lawrence, 'Study of Thomas Hardy', in *Phoenix: The Posthumous Papers of D. H. Lawrence*, edited by Edward McDonald (London, 1936; reprinted 1961), pp. 482–8.

8. Myth critics include Jean Brooks, *Thomas Hardy: The Poetic Structure* (London, 1971), pp. 233–53; Henry Kozicki, 'Myths of Redemption in Hardy's *Tess of the d'Urbervilles*', *Papers on Language and Literature*, 10 (1974), pp. 150–8; and James Hazen, 'The Tragedy of Tess Durbeyfield', *Texas Studies in Literature and Language*, 11 (1969), pp. 779–94.

Mikhail Bakhtin   'Heteroglossia in Dickens's *Little Dorrit*'   (1934–35)

... The compositional forms for appropriating and organising heteroglossia in the novel, worked out during the long course of the genre's historical development, are extremely heterogeneous in their variety of generic types. Each such compositional form is connected with particular stylistic possibilities, and demands particular forms for the artistic treatment of the heteroglot 'languages' introduced into it. We will pause here only on the most basic forms that are typical for the majority of novel types.

The so-called comic novel makes available a form for appropriating and organising heteroglossia that is both externally very vivid and at the same time historically profound: its classic representatives in England were Fielding, Smollett, Sterne, Dickens, Thackeray and others. . . .

In the English comic novel we find a comic-parodic re-processing of almost all the levels of literary language, both conversational and written, that were current at the time. . . . Depending on the subject being represented, the story-line parodically reproduces first the forms of parliamentary eloquence, then the eloquence of the court, or particular forms of parliamentary protocol, or court protocol, or forms used by reporters in newspaper articles, or the dry business language of the City, or the dealings of speculators, or the pedantic speech of scholars, or the high epic style, or Biblical style, or the style of the hypocritical moral sermon or finally the way one or another concrete and socially determined personality, the subject of the story, happens to speak.

This usually parodic stylisation of generic, professional and other strata of language is sometimes interrupted by the direct authorial word (usually as an expression of pathos, of Sentimental or idyllic sensibility), which directly embodies (without any refracting) semantic and axiological intentions of the author. But the primary source of language usage in the comic novel is a highly specific treatment of 'common language'. The 'common language' – usually the average norm of spoken and written language for a given social group – is taken by the author precisely as the *common view*, as the verbal approach to people and things normal for a given sphere of society, as the *going point of view* and the going *value*. To one degree or another, the author distances himself from this language, he steps back and objectifies it, forcing his own intentions to refract and diffuse themselves through the medium of this common view that has become embodied in language (a view that is always superficial and frequently hypocritical). . . .

We will pause for analysis [of two] examples from Dickens, from his novel *Little Dorrit*.

The conference was held at four or five o'clock in the afternoon, when all the region of Harley Street, Cavendish Square, was resonant of carriage-wheels and double-knocks. It had reached this point when Mr Merdle came home *from his daily occupation of causing the British name to be more and more respected in all parts of the civilised globe capable of the appreciation of worldwide commercial enterprise and gigantic combinations of skill and capital.* For, though nobody knew with the least precision what Mr Merdle's business was, except that it was to coin money, these were the terms in which everybody defined it on all ceremonious occasions, and which it was the last new polite reading of the parable of the camel and the needle's eye to accept without inquiry. [book 1, ch. 33]

The italicised portion represents a parodic stylisation of the language of ceremonial speeches (in parliaments and at banquets). The shift into this style is prepared for by the sentence's construction, which from the very beginning is kept within bounds by a somewhat ceremonious epic tone. Further on – and already in the language of the author (and consequently in a different style) – the parodic meaning of the ceremoniousness of Merdle's labours becomes apparent: such a characterisation turns out to be 'another's speech', to be taken only in quotation marks ('these were the terms in which everybody defined it on all ceremonious occasions').

Thus the speech of another is introduced into the author's discourse (the story) in *concealed form*, that is, without any of the *formal* markers usually accompanying such speech, whether direct or indirect. But this is not just another's speech in the same 'language' – it is another's utterance in a language that is itself 'other' to the author as well, in the archaicised language of oratorical genres associated with hypocritical official celebrations.

It was a dinner to provoke an appetite, though he had not had one. The rarest dishes, sumptuously cooked and sumptuously served; the choicest fruits, the most exquisite wines; marvels of workmanship in gold and silver, china and glass; innumerable things delicious to the senses of taste, smell, and sight, were insinuated into its composition. *O, what a wonderful man this Merdle, what a great man, what a master man, how blessedly and enviably endowed* – in one word, what a rich man! [book 2, ch. 12]

The beginning is a parodic stylisation of a high epic style. What follows is an enthusiastic glorification of Merdle, a chorus of his admirers in the form of the concealed speech of another (the italicised portion). The whole point here is to expose the real basis for such glorification, which is to unmask the chorus's hypocrisy: 'wonderful', 'great', 'master', 'endowed' can all be replaced by the single word 'rich'. This act of authorial unmasking, which is openly accomplished within the boundaries of a single simple sentence, merges with the unmasking of another's speech. The ceremonial emphasis on glorification is complicated by a second emphasis that is indignant, ironic, and this is the one that ultimately predominates in the final unmasking words of the sentence.

We have before us a typical double-accented, double-styled *hybrid construction.*

What we are calling a hybrid construction is an utterance that belongs, by its grammatical (syntactic) and compositional markers, to a single speaker, but that actually contains mixed within it two utterances, two speech manners, two styles, two 'languages', two semantic and axiological belief systems. We repeat, there is no formal – compositional and syntactic – boundary between these utterances, styles, languages, belief systems; the division of voices and languages takes place within the limits of a single syntactic whole, often within the limits of a simple sentence. It frequently happens that even one and the same word will belong simultaneously to two languages, two belief systems that intersect in a hybrid construction – and, consequently, the word has two contradictory meanings, two accents. . . . [Such] hybrid constructions are of enormous significance in novel style. . . .

SOURCE: extracts from 'Discourse in the Novel' (1934–35), included in *The Dialogic Imagination: Four Essays by M. M. Bakhtin*, edited by Michael Holquist, translated by Caryl Emerson & Michael Holquist (Austin, Texas, 1981), pp. 301–2, 304–5.

Robert Scholes Semiotic Approaches to Joyce's 'Eveline' (1982)

. . . In *S/Z*, his book-length analysis of Balzac's story 'Sarrasine', Barthes works his way through the text, a few phrases or sentences at a time, interpreting these 'lexias', as he calls them, according to the ways they generate meanings in five signifying systems or codes. His five codes are as follows:

1. The proairetic code or code of actions, which he calls 'the main armature of the readerly text' – by which he means, among other things, all texts that are in fact narrative. Where most traditional critics . . . would look only for major actions or plots, Barthes (in theory) sees all actions as codable, from the most trivial opening of a door to a romantic adventure. In practice, he applies some principles of selectivity. We recognise actions because we are able to name them.

In most fiction (Barthes's readerly texts) we expect actions begun to be completed; thus the principal action becomes the main armature of such a text. . . .

2. The hermeneutic code or code of puzzles plays on the reader's desire for 'truth', for the answers to questions raised by the text. In examining 'Sarrasine' Barthes names ten phases of hermeneutic coding, from the initial posing of a question or thematisation of a subject that will become enigmatic, to the ultimate disclosure and decipherment of what has been withheld. Like the code of actions, the code of enigmas is a principal structuring agent of traditional narrative. Between the posing of a riddle and its solution in narrative, Barthes locates eight different ways of keeping the riddle alive without revealing its solution, including equivocations, snares, partial answers, and so forth. In certain kinds of fiction, such as detective stories, the hermeneutic code dominates the entire discourse. Together with the code of actions it is responsible for narrative suspense, for the reader's desire to complete, to finish the text.

3. The cultural codes. There are many of these. They constitute the text's references to things already 'known' and codified by a culture. Barthes sees traditional realism as defined by its reference to what is already known. Flaubert's 'Dictionary of Accepted Ideas' is a realist Bible. The axioms and proverbs of a culture or a subculture constitute already coded bits upon which novelists may rely. Balzac's work is heavily coded in this way.

4. The connotative codes. Under this rubric we find not one code but many. In reading, the reader 'thematises' the text. He notes that certain connotations of words and phrases in the text may be grouped with similar connotations of other words and phrases. As we recognise a 'common nucleus' of connotations we locate a theme in the text. As clusters of connotation cling to a particular proper name we recognise a character with certain attributes. (It is worth noting that Barthes considers denotation as simply the 'last' and strongest of connotations.)

5. The symbolic field. This is the aspect of fictional coding that is most specifically 'structuralist' – or, more accurately, post-structuralist – in Barthes's presentation. It is based on the notion that meaning comes from some initial binary opposition or differentiation – whether at the level of sounds becoming phonemes in the production of speech; or at the level of psychosexual opposition, through which a child learns that mother and father are different from each other and that this difference also makes the child the same as one of them and different from the other; or at the level of primitive cultural separation of the world into opposing forces or values that

may be coded mythologically. In a verbal text this kind of symbolic opposition may be encoded in rhetorical figures such as antithesis, which is a privileged figure in Barthes's symbolic system.

Since the space and time for a Barthesian amble through the lexias of 'Eveline' are not available, I shall invert his procedure and simply locate some elements of each code as found in Joyce's text.

1. Code of Actions (Proairetic)

In 'Eveline' these range from the relatively trivial 'She sat', completed four pages later by 'She stood up', to the more consequential action of her leaving Dublin for good, which of course never occurs. This is a story of paralysis, which is a major connotative code in all the *Dubliners* stories. Significantly, we never see Eveline move a single step. Even in the last climactic scene her actions are described as 'She stood. . . .She gripped. . . .She set her face'. This increasing rigidity thematises the connotative code of paralysis.

2. Code of Enigmas (Hermeneutic)

Joyce does not rely heavily on this code. Above all, he does not feel a need to complete it. We begin with some questions about who Eveline is, why she is tired, and the like, but there is no mystery about this. Frank is an enigma, of course. The discourse tells us something about him, but only gives us Eveline's thoughts about Frank's version of his life. There is also some mystery attached to Eveline's mother, the cause of her death, and the mysterious phrase she uttered which no one can decipher. But the discourse does not complete 'or solve' these mysteries. Like the priest who went to Melbourne, they suggest a world not completely fathomable, beyond the comfortable realism of Balzacian discourse. The final enigma, the reason for Eveline's refusal, forces us back into the text, and out to the other *Dubliners* stories to find solutions that will never have the assurance of discursive 'truth'.

3. Cultural Codes

Cultural coding in this tale is not so much the property of any narrative voice, or of the discourse itself, as it is something in the minds of the characters. Eveline's father sees Frank under a code of cynical parental wisdom: 'I know these sailor chaps.' Eveline sees him as codified by romantic fiction: 'Frank was very kind, manly, open-hearted'. The discourse ratifies neither view. It avoids the cultural codes of Dublin, which so dominate the characters' lives. Of these, the most powerful is the code of Irish Catholicism, which would classify Eveline's action as a sin.

4. Connotative Codes

The dominant connotative code is the code of paralysis, which is a major element in Eveline's character as well as in the world around her. It is connoted by Eveline's motionlessness throughout the story. It is even conveyed by the dreary, monotonous sentence structure – subject, verb, predicate, over and over again. And it is signified by such details as the promises made to Blessed Margaret Mary Alacoque, who was paralysed until she vowed to dedicate herself to a religious life. The way in which this saintly lady's life comments on Eveline's own introduces another level of connotation, the ironic. Through its ironic combination of signs, the discourse paraleptically leads us to a view of Eveline's situation beyond her own perception of it. She sees herself as weighing evidence and deciding. But the discourse ironically indicates that she has no choice. She is already inscribed as a Dubliner in Joyce's code, and a Dubliner never decides, never escapes. As Diderot's *Jacques le fataliste* would have it, *il est écrit en haut*, it is written above – in Joyce's text.

5. The Symbolic Code

For Joyce in *Dubliners* the primal opposition is not male versus female but sexed versus unsexed, usually presented as celibate versus profligate: an opposition that is almost unmediated by any linking term. Only the dead are fruitful or potent in Joyce's wasteland. In 'Eveline', the sailor Frank is set in opposition to the father as a rival for Eveline, who is filling her mother's role in the household. In this symbolic opposition Frank is associated with water, freedom, the unknown, the future and sexual potency. The father's house is dusty, Eveline is a slavey in it, but it is known, rooted in the past, and fruitless. As her father's slave/wife, Eveline will be sterile, impotent, celibate, a kind of nun, a Dubliner. This symbolic opposition emerges most powerfully from the clash of connotations in a single sentence in the final scene, when Eveline sees 'the black mass of the boat, lying beside the quay'. This 'black mass' is an innocent descriptive phrase which also connotes the sacrilegious power of the act Eveline is contemplating here. To board that boat, leave the land and enter upon the sea, would be to leave what is known, safe, already coded. It would be above all to flout the teachings of the church, to sin. The

virgin, the nun, a celibate safely within the cultural codification of
ritual, is opposed to the defiled woman upon whose belly the black
mass is blasphemously consummated. But look more closely. In that
other harmless descriptive phrase, 'lying in', another terror is
connoted. To 'lie in' is to be delivered of child, to be fruitful, to be
uncelibate, not to play the mother's role for the father, but to displace
her and the father both, sending them into the past. It is to accept life
– and the danger of death. These connotations activate the symbolic
level of the text by their juxtaposition of its antitheses. And in that
extraordinary figure, 'All the seas of the world tumbled about her
heart', the discourse connotes both the heart surrounded by amniotic
fluid ready to burst with life, and also the fear of drowning in life itself,
lured beyond her depth by a person she can no longer allow herself to
recognise.

   Our final vision of Eveline is of a creature in a state of symbolic
deprivation. If the symbolic code is rooted in the fundamental
processes of cognition and articulation, what is signified in that code
at the end of 'Eveline' is a creature who has lost those fundamental
processes, not only at the level of speech and language but even the
more fundamental semiotic functions of gesture and facial signals:
'She set her white face to him, passive, like a helpless animal. Her eyes
gave him no sign of love or farewell or recognition.' However we
interpret the story, we are surely intended to regard with pity and fear
the situation of this young woman absolutely incommunicado,
capable of giving 'no sign'. . . .

SOURCE: extract from chapter, 'Semiotic Approaches to Joyce's
"Eveline"', in *Semiotics and Interpretation* (New Haven, Conn., 1982),
pp. 99–104.

Lucette Finas   The Charge: On the Short
Story *The Brigands* by Villiers de l'Isle
Adam   (1978)

The Brigands,[1] a 7-page short story from Villiers's *Contes Cruels* (1883),
has something in common with a *hoax*. But this 'charge' – in the
French sense of 'caricature' – which ends up with a charge, in the
sense of an assault – is apocalyptic. The 'same' gets caught by the
'same' and annihilates it. The play of catastrophe depends entirely on

cliché, the banality of which Villiers works up to the point of excess.

The tale can be summarised. Under cover of darkness, the old fiddler of Nayrac demands money from the sexton of Pibrac, a *sous-préfecture* twinned with Nayrac. The frightened sexton plays up without recognising the fiddler, and transforms the account of his misadventure into a story of highway robbery. The bourgeois (of both towns) are not fooled but exploit popular fears and encourage the reverberation of the echo. When rent collection day comes round, the fourteen landlords of Nayrac go as a body to their farmers to collect their dues. On the way back, their spirits lowered by the rumour they have helped to spread, they become terrified of the brigands. The latter appear suddenly at nightfall. A shot is fired, it prompts a massacre. In fact, the brigands were none other than the fourteen landlords of Pibrac who, having had the same idea as those of Nayrac, were on the way home after collecting their rents. The two parties wipe each other out without recognising each other. Along comes the fiddler, trembling with fright, who quickly assesses the situation: 'THEY WILL PROVE ... THAT IT WAS US.'[2] And he advises his confederates to pick up the money of 'these worthy bourgeois'.

Tradition, at once transmission (*traditio*) and betrayal (*traditor*), is busy in *The Brigands*. First of all a rumour circulates, a *fama est* . . . which soon turns the petty extortion of money ('quelque monnaie') into a legend. *Illusion* takes hold of the event.

A sophisticated play mingles the abstract and the concrete: 'le bruit' (in the French sense of news, echo, rumour) and 'le bruit' (noise, din); blindness (delusion) and blindness (the darkness of the night). At the moment of the massacre, the bourgeois are nothing more than their 'bruit': as if the rumour they had rendered plausible – the growing volume of their falsification – were assuming a material form all of a sudden; as if the abstract rumour, become audible, were physically assassinating them.

The epigraph, a quotation from Sieyès: 'What is the Third Estate? – Nothing. What should it be? – Everything.'[3] makes the narrative' hang on a historical and political thread. The proximity of the brigands (in the title) and the Third Estate (in the epigraph) prepares us for the avenging allusion which will punctuate the dénouement.

The short story is constructed according to a movement of *amplification* and *repercussion*, beginning with a tiny act of aggression, the reality of which is shrouded in illusion from the outset. Amplification and repercussion lead the bourgeois to an apotheosis which consists in dying for a rumour.

STAGE 1: THE SEXTON'S PANIC

'Taking advantage of the shadows',[4] the fiddler demands money from the sexton in 'a peremptory tone of voice' (he is therefore imposing on him, creating an illusion) and the sexton does not recognise the fiddler (a second illusion, or rather the obverse of the first).

The man without a profession, the busker, attacks the sexton entrusted with the upkeep of the church. This opposition is expressed musically: the violin man (less than a violinist) is opposed to the man of the Bells (in French 'L'homme des Cloches', with a capital letter). The function of the bell ringer parodies the diffusion of the story: indeed, thanks to the sexton, the fiddler's little fraud (his fiddle) rings out like a peal of bells.

The fiddler's action is motivated by shortage of money, and he appears out of nowhere, like the god Pan (the man of the Bells 'in his panic. . .'). A surprise, a commotion, of an almost mythological type, presides over the releasing of the illusion.

STATE 2: THE SEXTON'S NARRATIVE

The sexton's account obeys two considerations: the narrator-victim's need to exaggerate, and the listener-public's frenzy. Exaggeration and frenzy repeat the fiddler's initial act of daring and orchestrate it. The fiddler thus becomes 'a whole band of famished brigands infesting the Midi, and laying waste the . . . highroad with their murders, arson and robberies'. The amplifications of this sentence suggest the amplifications of the sexton and the proliferation of the rumour in his listeners' minds.

STATE 3: THE BOURGEOIS KNOWINGLY KEEP THE MYTH ALIVE

The sexton has given himself away; the bourgeois know; the masses will be taken in: a game of knowledge and illusion; of the secret uncovered then exploited and preserved. The bourgeois keep the secret for political ends, to maintain their government.

STAGE 4: THE BOURGEOIS STAGE THE PANIC AND ACT IN THEIR OWN PLAY

The fourteen landlords of Nayrac, wanting to put on a show of adventure and heroism for their wives, proceed to make preparations for war and organise a knightly vigil. Just as the meeting between the fiddler and the sexton was amplified, so the two protagonists give way to fourteen (twice seven) landlords. At the end of the story, twice fourteen landlords will meet their death.

STAGE 5: THE BOURGEOIS TORMENTED BY THE ECHO

'Still, a shadow had cast himself over their spirits!' The moral singular ('a shadow') reiterates the concrete plural ('shadows').

The insistence on 'shadow', in the literal and figurative sense, in the singular and plural, draws the shadows of the Beyond to the text and casts a veil over the action. Fear descends with the night. Shadow divides the narrative into two halves, the first of which, the happy half ('The day was fine'), ends at 'dusk'.

The shadow which casts itself over the spirits of the landlords translates their concern over the first echo which generated the intrigue. The growing concern, for the initial echo has been amplified: 'The old rogue, it appears, had [recruited]⁵ a gang of real thieves.' A little further up: 'the fiddler had founded a school'. And so, just like the sexton, the fiddler propagates. But, unlike his adversary who transforms fact into fiction, he specialises in action. He propagates deeds, and not rumours or false appearances. He transforms fiction into fact, legend into history. The point where the illusion ends (the event behind the image) is, however, not *certain*: we only know about the fiddler's doings indirectly, via 'certain tales of the peasants'.

On the other hand, the bourgeois are victims of a rebound effect. The illusion they have kept alive in the population returns to torment them.

STAGE 6: THE GHOST-CART

The burghers' carriage, drawn by 'three Mecklenburg mares', is gradually transformed into a ghost-cart, carrying along the clichés of nightmare and of the supernatural: the black outlines of the poplars, the sinister howling of a stray dog, the bats, the pale moonbeams strike terror into the hearts of the hallucinated bourgeois.

STAGE 7: THE ILLUSIONS COMES TO LIFE . . . IN THE WRONG FORM

Don Quixotes of rent collectors, the bourgeois of Nayrac take the bourgeois of Pibrac for bandits. It is as if their expectations were finally bringing this chimera of 'the brigands' to life. Their battle is like a battle of shadows possessed by madness. They are led to the carnage by the wrongness of their interpretation. The last survivor kills himself by mistake.

STAGE 8: ROLE REVERSAL

There are false brigands (the bourgeois) who take each other for brigands and are, in a sense, brigands.

There are true brigands (the fiddler and his companions) who are not all brigands to the same extent (the fiddler is more a rogue than a brigand) and who are all afraid of the brigands. 'Brigands' is not the right word for them.

Finally, they too, the brigands who are not exactly brigands, hear, not the rumours (*des* bruits), but a real din (*du* bruit). The tumult is incomprehensible, even to them, until it begins to dawn on their leader what has happened.

The relation between shrewdness and gullibility is reversed. Whereas up until then the crafty bourgeois were opposed to the poor gullible wretches, henceforth the bourgeois die from gullibility and the fiddler begins to understand and then to analyse the situation.

STAGE 9: THE EMPTY PLACE OF JUDICIAL ERROR

Faced with the 'formidable spectacle' of the slaughter, the fiddler discovers that his guilt and that of his gang appears not only as likely but even as probable, i.e., provable. As it is presented to us, the 'scene of the crime' is the theatre of the improbable. Because it cannot imagine the improbable, bourgeois judgement is doomed to judicial error. The fiddler has understood this, while also understanding that 'they' (the others) are not going to understand. Hence the penetrating conclusion: 'THEY WILL PROVE . . . THAT IT WAS US.' *Prove* and not simply *think*, the ultimate fact of the carnage constituting in every respect the triumph of opinion, its coincidence with reality.

The final theft of the fiddler, the unpremeditated repetition on a larger scale of his original crime, can be explained in at least two ways: by the need for money, and by the giddy desire to perform the deed which the situation, on the face of it, required. The opinion which will prevail, according to which the fiddler and his gang are the authors of the massacre, imposes a model of behaviour to which the suspect conforms before taking flight and which justifies the virtuous cynicism of the injunction: 'quick, my good friends, gather up the money of these worthy bourgeois'.

Expenditure unto death in *The Brigands* is motivated by rent collection and the hoarding of money. This is to say that accumulation does not pay, or rather, that beyond a certain point it pays the price of death. The story's frenzied dénouement brings together:

1. the general din of history,
2. the libidinal discharge of the worried and over-excited bourgeois,
3. the dispersal of the rents,
4. the annihilation of a social class which looks at itself without recognising itself, which frightens itself and destroys itself,
5. the confounding of the law,
6. myth derided or the return of the scapegoat,
7. numerical escalation.

1. Sensory Expenditure

The Brigands brings in a great variety of voices:
- (a) Human voices, individual or collective: monologues, dialogues, stories, songs, shouts . . .
- (b) Animal voices: the sinister howling of a stray dog, the regular trot of the three Mecklenburg mares.
- (c) Voices 'of nature': 'myriad sounds'.
- (d) Voices of instruments: violin, bells.
- (e) Voices of weapons: guns.

The first line of the French text contains the word *duo*, suggesting vocal or instrumental music. The two *sous-préfectures* appear from the outset as a grotesque duo singing in *unison* ('unisson'), that is to say cancelling out the duo. Moreover, the bloody ending of the tale reveals the threat which unison conceals! The musical progression of the narrative begins with a *duo*, continues with a *chorus*, and ends with a *solo* (in the French text, the fiddler's 'voix affreusement basse', terribly low voice, evokes 'une voix de basse affreuse', a terrible bass voice). The fiddler is also a 'chanteur', a little 'maître-chanteur' (singer/master singer/blackmailer).

From the beginning of the narrative to the end, the noises get physically louder, while still continuing to play their metaphorical part. And it is in the silence which follows the paroxysm, when 'the terrible and growing noise' of the gunfire and 'the fearful cries of the bourgeois' die out, that the voice of the fiddler is heard. The latter will therefore have had both the first word and the last in the narrative: the first by demanding money from the sexton in a peremptory tone of voice, the last by ordering, in a low, contrite voice, the gathering up of the rents he had never coveted. The amplification and deflection of the *echo* have as their corollary the amplification and deflection of the *profit*.

2. Libidinal Expenditure

If the fiddler's action answers a need: the need to subsist, the bourgeois, for their part, alienate themselves in the desire to collect money. Like Harpagon, what they love is their strong-box.

On the other hand, desire is absent from conjugal relationships, lived solely in the register of cliché. Each of them claims 'One last kiss!' from his wife. This banal formula is rendered impossible by the fact that the bourgeois, each of them having gone home, are supposed to say it in unison, as if the dictates (the dictation) of unison crossed the dividing walls. The transposing of an individual expression of desire into a collective cliché constitutes a caricature ('une charge') accentuated by the funereal word-play on 'last' kiss.

The bourgeois have no qualms at all about simulating the confrontation with death, but their blustery night-time dreams, which repeat the day-time show, reveal a premonition: 'The bourgeois dreamed of assaults and carnage. . .'.

What is unexpected is the real fear which rouses and kills them right in the middle of the sham. They finish up as heroes in spite of themselves, killing their doubles, killing each other because they do not recognise each other: the anecdote of the last survivor who blows his brains out reloading his weapon has a symbolic value. The attitude of the bourgeois is unconsciously suicidal. Only the mad will to conserve can bring them to the point of release. . .

3. Economic Expenditure

The repercussion of the fiddler's original theft, the concert of noises which results from it, are motivated by financial considerations. In the fiddler, poverty and anarchy are rampant; the sexton is comfortably off, respectable, law-abiding. Of the two, it is the one who possesses a certain amount – the sexton – who practises *inflation*. As for the fiddler, he knows only brutal demand, primitive forms of interchange.

Thus the sexton triggers off the inflation of the event, and the bourgeois maintain it. Villiers establishes a link between 'keeping a secret' and 'keeping' pure and simple: 'Our worthy burghers kept the secret to themselves, as they love to keep everything they own', a link between monetary accumulation and the private accumulation of phantasies. This capitalisation, as we would say today, is what Villiers cruelly calls wisdom – the wisdom of the Third Estate which opposes the foolish, spendthrift, aristocratic class to which he belongs. Bourgeois morality, the morality of the cliché, goes hand in hand with accumulation.

And of course – through a justice 'immanent' in the narration – the rents will disappear on the same day that they materialise, confiscated by the fiddler who reappears at the end of the tale specifically for this purpose. And so the tale dissipates, laughs away, financial savings as well as vital savings (your money *and* your life). Financial savings like vital savings are lost over a phantasy. The fiddler reaps the fruits along with the suspicion.

4. Political Expenditure

Two classes confront each other: that of the fiddler and that of the bourgeois. That of the fiddler is also that of the sexton, give or take a degree. This degree is important: it divides the two men, while the crafty bourgeois treat the people like children so as to stay in power with the help of a fable.

Before leaving to collect the rents, the bourgeois sing the 'Parisienne'.[6] The 'virile accents' of the political hymn remind them of their past revolutionary action, and also their historical betrayal. Their song is a parody twice over, because it is a warrior's song and because it is revolutionary. The action of the fathers is lived as a memory-cliché; the sons become the usurpers. The political shame extends to the Orléans, upholders of the Third Estate and responsible for the parish road which brings Pibrac and Nayrac together at the beginning of the tale.

The fiddler and his gang do not attack the bourgeois order directly. The fiddler's initial action is an isolated, spontaneous one; and the robbers' den is not the scene of a plot but of an innocent game of cards. The revolutionary explosion, like a gun going off on its own, passes them all by. And yet, the ringleader, like someone exploited who eventually perceives the nature of his oppression, suddenly *understands* what is happening and draws the necessary conclusions. But the tone remains deferent, not to say obsequious, unless it is cynical: 'these worthy bourgeois'. All is not transparent in the fiddler.

5. Confounding the Law

'. . . just as ten o'clock struck from the belfry of the justiciary building of Nayrac . . .' The reference to the law is not fortuitous. The massacre which ends the story renders inevitable the intervention of the law, of the Third Estate. For the Third Estate, like a sad phoenix, dies always to be reborn. 'THEY WILL PROVE . . . THAT IT WAS US . . .' is written in capital letters in the French text, like the punishment of the same name which awaits the fiddler and his confederates if they cannot cross the frontier.

The guilt of the fiddler may be deduced from the final scene in a way which is as rigorous as it is false. From this moment on it is installed in the empty place left by the 'real' culprit. But then, there is no more a real culprit than a subject of the massacre. The massacre is a *massacre without a subject*, or again a massacre where the subjects are the victims: a self-massacre.

The fiddler, if he stays around, will be *substituted* for the absent culprit, as in *La Reine Ysabeau*, where we read that after the escape of the sire de Maule, the queen puts her lawyer on the wheel instead. By picking up the money left lying on the battleground, the fiddler is not only giving in to the temptation to do a little later what, in any case, people will think he did a little earlier: he promotes the working out of the *legal fiction* by what Villiers scornfully calls 'the *Honour* of the Third Estate'.

6. The Return of the Scapegoat

The fiddler was on the margins of the society of the twin *sous-préfectures*. His attack on the sexton has made it necessary for him to stay away and so fulfil the secret wish of the bourgeois. The dénouement assures the return of the repressed fiddler. But his victory is only a half-victory. Forced, after the massacre, to leave the country with his gang, he flees further than he did the first time, and he is no longer alone. A double amplification which partakes of and contributes to the *overflowing* (la *crue*) of the narrative.

The Brigands includes the barest suggestion of a mythological layer. The god Pan emerges effortlessly from the *panic* of the sexton. Morpheus, expressly invoked, ties the foulard of sleep round the heads of the bourgeois. One of them, on the scene of the action, uses a pot of *foie gras* as a shield (*'égide'*: aegis). The mythological metaphor is more than a rhetorical flourish: it has a function. Mythology acts as a foil to prosaicism. Conversely, prosaicism when taken to the limit meets up with mythology again by degrading it. The attack of the bourgeois has something in common with Picrochole's war or the *Virgile Travesti*. Their ridiculous charge across the ground (of the narrative) is the negative projection of the frenzied 'charge' (caricature) of Villiers who, as he discharges his hatred on them, 'charges' them to death, precisely.

7. Numerical Escalation: One, Two, Three

The Brigands constitutes a crazy exercise on unison, the duo and the
third. Here are some examples:

One:

 a parish road
 a perfect harmony ('unisson') in morals

Two:

 a pair ('duo') of twin *sous-préfectures*
 the fiddler/the sexton
 the fiddler/his gang
 the fiddler/the last bourgeois
 the bourgeois/the brigands
 the chorus of bourgeois/the chorus of wives
 the married men/the bachelors
 twice seven landlords
 twice fourteen landlords
 the two ends of the silk handkerchief
 the fork ('bifurcation') of the road
 the middle of November
 the half dozen poor devils
 two black clouds

Three:

 three Mecklenburg mares

The burlesque concern for symmetry can be found in the rich rhyme
bourgeois/mecklembourgeois (Mecklenburg mares) which fits the
bourgeois into the horse and transforms the latter into a centaur. The
three in 'trois mecklembourgeois' (three Mecklenburg mares[7]) is the
sum of one and two. It also happens that the name Mecklenburg
designated two Grand Duchies of northern Germany: those of
Mecklenburg-Schwerin and Mecklenburg-Strelitz. A distant and
august reminder of Pibrac and Nayrac: a deliberate reminder (did
Villiers know these twin duchies?) or a chance encounter seized
on by the text. The poor rhyme *trois/mecklembourgeois* ironically sup-
ports the magic and religious symbolism of three attached to the
horses of misfortune. Fourteen is a multiple of *two* and *seven*, a sacred
number . . .
 Progressively, in the tale, the struggle between the same and the
other has given way to the stuggle of the same against the same. The

bourgeois wipe themselves out, while in the face of the banditry of the bourgeois who perform the work of brigands on each other, the brigands corrupt their pseudo-essence and speak the language of the bourgeoisie: 'these worthy bourgeois'. The funeral oration in praise of the bourgeois delivered by the brigand is an appropriation which goes with a theft (of money). But appropriation and theft happen after the sacrifice. The bourgeois are victims only of themselves: it is themselves they have struck while aiming at the *others*. Their blow has boomeranged.

The return of the echo which strikes its point of origin and the *real* effect of this repercussion makes for a similarity between *The Brigands* by Villiers de l'Isle Adam and *Florville et Courval* by Sade. Both narratives stage an author's struggle to exploit the echo-effect so as to bring about the downfall of the 'same'.

SOURCE: essay 'La Charge . . .', in Finas's *Le Bruit d'Iris* (Paris, 1978), pp. 77–91; translation by Annwyl Williams, in *Oxford Literary Review*, 5 (double issue), nos 1 & 2 (1982), pp. 154–69.

Translator's comment: my notes, supplementing those by Finas, are given below within square brackets. I wish to thank Lucette Finas, Karel Williams, Celia Britton and Ann Wordsworth for their comments on various drafts of the translation, revised subsequent to its first publication in 1982. In quotations from the text of Villiers de l'Isle Adams's short story, I have used the version ('The Brigands') in Hamish Miles's translation of *Contes Cruels* – i.e., *Sardonic Tales* (New York, and London, 1925), but I have also made some use, as indicated in the Notes, of the version in Robert Baldick's translation – *Cruel Tales* (Oxford, 1963). Where the differences between Miles's translation and Villiers's original are significant for the purposes of Finas's discussion, I have added Villiers's French terms or have referred, for example, to the 'French text'.

NOTES

[Reorganised and renumbered from the original – Ed.]

1. *Brigand*: first an armed man, then a highwayman. The name 'brigands' was given by public opinion to those who burned down the gates [*barrières*] of Paris on 12 July 1789. It was in order to repress these 'brigands' that the bourgeois militia was created on the following day. The theme of the brigand was very popular at the end of the eighteenth century – cf. Schiller, *The Brigands* (1782), Hoffman & Kreutzer, *The Brigand* (1785) – and in the nineteenth century – cf. Maillan & Dutertre, *The Brigands of the Loire* (1842) – the period which saw the spread of brigand ballads, and even the emergence of the brigand as a clock motif.

2. [Capital letters in the French text.]

3. The title of Sieyès's pamphlet is 'What is the Third Estate?' The text is

slightly deformed by Villiers: 'What is the Third Estate? – Everything – What has it been up to now in the political order? – Nothing – What does it ask to be? – Something?' According to *Larousse de XIXe siècle*, Sieyès got the idea of the title from Chamfort. [*The Third Estate* is the name given, in French society before the Revolution, to those who belonged neither to the aristocracy nor to the clergy: i.e., the bourgeois, the artisans and the peasants; the bourgeois were the most active element.]

    4. [Trans. Baldick.]   5. [Trans. Baldick.]

    6. *La Parisienne*: lyrics by Casimir Delavigne, music by Aubert (1830). Delavigne wrote the words in the middle of the barricades, the cannon and the gunfire, to music that Auber had composed as a marching tune. It is a bourgeois hymn which salutes the advent of the July Monarchy – i.e., the Orléanist régime, Villiers's target. Here is the first stanza:

> Peuple français, peuple de braves,
> La Liberté rouvre ses bras.
> On nous disait: Soyez esclaves;
> Nous avons dit: Soyons soldats!
> Soudain Paris dans sa mémoire
> A retrouvé son cri de gloire:
> En avant, marchons!
> Contre leurs canons,
> A travers le fer, le feu des bataillons,
> Courons à la victoire,
> Courons à la victoire!

Rough translation (last 5 lines = H. Miles's translation):

> People of France, people of courage,
> Freedom welcomes us again.
> They told us: Be slaves;
> We said: We'll be soldiers!
> Suddenly Paris has remembered
> Its erstwhile shout of glory:
> Forward we go
> To face the foe!
> Through flame and through steel
> Haste we to victory,
> Haste we to victory!

    7. I hardly need say that, outside this particular context or some other which might lend itself to the operation, the reader would not *necessarily* find, 'bourgeois' in 'mecklembourgeois', 'vol' [theft] and 'viol' [rape] in 'violoneux' [fiddler], or be tempted to link 'marguillier' [sexton] to 'margouillis' [mess, as in 'to get someone in a mess'] or 'margoulin' [swindler].

Villiers de l'Isle Adam   The Brigands   (1883)

What is the Third Estate? – Nothing.
What should it be? – Everything.
SULLY, later SIEYÈS

Pibrac and Nayrac were a pair of twin sous-préfectures, linked by a parish road opened under the d'Orléans régime. And from them there rose to the delighted heavens the hum of a perfect harmony in morals, occupations and outlooks.

As elsewhere, the municipality in each was distinguished by passions; as everywhere, the bourgeoisie won public esteem for itself and its own esteem as well. So, in these fortunate regions, everyone was living in peace and happiness when, one October evening, it chanced that the old fiddler of Nayrac, finding himself short of coin, stopped the sexton of Pibrac on the highroad and, profiting by the darkness, demanded money from him in very peremptory tones.

The gentleman of the bells, in his panic, did not recognise the fiddler, and graciously paid up. But, returning to Pibrac, he related his adventure in such a way that, in the imaginations inflamed by his story, the poor old fiddler of Nayrac took on the semblance of a whole band of famished brigands infesting the Midi, and laying waste the line of the highroad with their murders, arson and robberies.

Sagaciously, the bourgeois gentry of both towns had encouraged these rumours: so true is it that every good man of property inevitably exaggerates the faults of people who might cherish any designs on his capital. Not that they had been taken in! They had gone direct to the source, and had questioned the beadle in his cups. The beadle had let the cat out of the bag – and now they knew the long and the short of the business a great deal better than he did! But nevertheless, with a wink for the credulity of the masses, our worthy burghers kept the secret to themselves, as they love to keep everything they own – a tenacity which, anyhow, is the outward and visible sign of sensible and enlightened persons.

Towards the middle of the following November, just as ten o'clock sounded from the belfry of the justiciary building of Nayrac, each one of them returned to his home with a rather more swaggering air than usual, and his hat (upon my word!) pushed over one ear; with the result that their wives, fondling their whiskers, addressed them as

'Musketeer!' – which gave a touch of reciprocal warmth to the cockles of their hearts.

'Well, Madame N――, to-morrow I must be off.'

'Oh, dear, dear!'

'It's the day for the rent collections. I must go out myself to the tenants . . .'

'You shan't go!'

'And why not, pray?'

'The brigands, of course!'

'Pooh! I've seen plenty of them in my time!'

'You shan't go!' concluded each of the wives, as is fitting between people who know how to play up to each other.

'Come, come my little one . . . I anticipated this anxiety. But to reassure you, we have agreed to set off all together, with our guns, in a big trap hired for the purpose. Our properties are contiguous, and we shall be back in the evening. So dry your tears. And now Morpheus calls, so give me peace to tie the two ends of my silk handkerchief over my head.'

'Ah, well, provided you're all going together, well and good! You must do as the others do', murmured each of the wives, suddenly calmed.

A delightful night! The citizens dreamed of assaults and carnage, collisions and tourneys and laurels. So, fresh and eager, they awoke to the gay sunlight.

'Now then!' they all murmured, drawing on their stockings with a fine gesture of recklessness – and in such a way that the phrase could be heard by their wives – 'off we go! The hour has struck; a man can only die once!'

Filled with admiration, the ladies gazed on these modern paladins, and in view of the autumn season stuffed their pockets with cough-lozenges.

The paladins, deaf to sobs, quickly tore themselves from the arms which strove, all in vain, to hold them back . . .

'One last kiss!' they said, each man of them, on the landing.

And debouching from their respective streets they arrived on the principal square. Already a few of them (the bachelors) were awaiting their colleagues round the great gig, making the hammers of their guns shine in the morning sunlight, and priming them with knitted eyebrows.

Six o'clock struck; the trap set off to the masculine accents of *La Parisienne*, thundered out by the fourteen men of property packed into it. Meanwhile, at far-off windows, fevered hands waved despairing handkerchiefs, and the heroic song could be heard:

Forward we go
To face the foe
Through flame and through steel –
Forward we go!

And then, with the right arm flung up, and with a great bellowing:

Haste we to vic-tor-y!

time being beaten for the whole by the sturdy lashes of the whip wherewith the proprietor on the box, with turns of his wrist, encircled the three horses.

The day was fine.

Good citizens of this sort are good livers, and straightforward in their business. But under the heading of honesty – stop! – they are strict enough to hang a child for a stolen apple.

Well, each of them took dinner with his farmer, chucked the daughter under the chin at dessert, pocketed the moneybag of the farm, and exchanged with the family a few approved proverbs, such as 'Good accounts make good friends', or 'One good turn deserves another', or 'To work is to pray', or 'No trade's a fool's trade', or 'Pay your debts and grow rich', and other customary dicta. And each of them, escaping from the usual benedictions, came out in turn to take his place in the collecting trap, which came to pick them up in this way from farm to farm. And as dusk was falling they turned back on the road to Nayrac.

Still, a shadow had cast itself over their spirits! – The truth was that certain tales of the peasants had given our good proprietors reason to believe that the fiddler had founded a school. His example had been contagious. The old rogue, it appeared, had reinforced himself with a gang of real thieves, and the road – especially at the time of rent collections – was no longer by any means safe. So that now, notwithstanding the fumes of the claret, which moreover were fast dispersing, our heroes were muting the strains of *La Parisienne*.

Night fell. The poplars lengthened their black outlines along the road. The wind shook the hedges. Amid the myriad sounds of nature, and alternating with the regular trot of the three Mecklenburg mares, could be heard afar off the ill-omened howling of a lost dog. Bats flitted around our pale travellers, and the first beams of the moon shone sadly on their faces . . . Brrr! They gripped the guns now between their knees with convulsive tremors; noiselessly, from time to time, they made sure that the moneybags were safe and sound beside them. Not a word was heard. What an agony for honest men!

Suddenly, at the fork of the road – great heavens! Dreadful

crouching figures were seen; there was a glint of guns; and a clatter of horses' hooves was heard, and a terrible '*Who goes there?*' rang out in the darkness, for at that very moment the moon slipped behind two black clouds.

A large vehicle, packed with armed men, was barring the main road.

What were they, these men? – Obviously malefactors! Bandits! – Obviously!

Alas, no! It was the twin band of honest citizens from Pibrac. The Pibrac men – who had had precisely the same idea as those of Nayrac!

Returning from their business, the peaceable and propertied citizens of both towns had simply crossed each other's path on the homeward way.

For a moment they looked into each other's pale faces. The intense terror they had caused themselves, what with this fixed idea that had possessed their minds, had brought out the true instincts on all these prosperous-looking faces – just as a gust of wind passing over a lake and forming a whirlpool, will force its depths up to the surface – and it was only natural that each should mistake the other for those same brigands of whom they stood in mutual dread.

In one instant their whisperings in the darkness brought them to such a point of panic that the Pibrac gentlemen, trembling, snatched up their guns in headlong speed to keep themselves in countenance. The hammer of one gun caught on the edge of the seat, a shot went off, and the charge struck one of the Nayrac party, shattering on his chest a pot of excellent *foie gras* which he had mechanically held up as a breastplate.

Ah, that shot! It was the fatal spark which exploded the powder. The paroxysm of their emotions turned them into raving madmen. A furious sustained fusillade opened out. The instinct of the preservation of self and of property blinded them. With tremblingly rapid fingers they rammed cartridges into their guns and fired into the mass. The horses fell, and one of the gigs capsized, spilling the wounded and the moneybags all together. The wounded, in the perturbation of their terror, rose like stricken lions and began firing again on each other, though they could not distinguish one from another in the smoke! Had the gendarmes come upon this scene of raging madness in the starlight, no doubt but they would have paid for their devotion with their lives. In short, it was a battle of extermination, despair having inflamed them with the most murderous energy – the energy, in a word, which always distinguishes the class of honourable people when they are pushed to extremes!

Meanwhile, the real brigands (that is to say, the half-dozen poor devils who were guilty, at the most, of having stolen a few crusts, a few pieces of lard, or a few ha'pence, here and there) were trembling with apprehension in a distant cave, as they listened to the terrible and growing noise that came across the wind from the highroad: explosions and the fearful cries of the good citizens.

Imagining, in the moment of the shock, that a huge onslaught had been organised against themselves, the bandits had interrupted their innocent game of cards round their pot of wine, and had risen, livid, and looking to their leader. The old fiddler seemed ready to faint away. His long shanks were trembling. Taken completely by surprise, the poor fellow was haggard. What he heard was beyond his comprehension.

But still, after a few minutes of bewilderment, as the fusillade did not die down, the worthy brigands saw that he was suddenly trembling. He put a meditative finger against the extremity of his nose, and raising his head, he said:

'My lads, it is impossible!' It's not us they're after . . . There is something wrong . . . It's a big mistake of some sort. . . . Run! Bring your blind lanterns! We must bring help for the poor wounded! That noise comes from the highroad.'

And so, with infinite precautions, and pushing their way through the thickets, they reached the scene of the catastrophe. The moon was now lighting up all its horror.

The last surviving bourgeois, in his haste to reload his red-hot gun, had just inadvertently, without the slightest desire to do so, blown out his own brains.

At the sight of this formidable spectacle, and all these corpses scattered on the blood-stained roadway, the brigands stood speechless with consternation, dazed and stupefied, unable to believe their eyes. And then an obscure comprehension of what had happened began to dawn in their minds.

Suddenly the ringleader whistled, and at a signal the lanterns drew together round the fiddler.

'My good friends!' he muttered in a voice of fearful lowness, his teeth chattering with a dread that seemed still more terrified than his first, 'quick, my good friends, gather up the money of these worthy bourgeois! And then make for the frontier! Get away at all speed! Never let us set foot in this country again!

And as his acolytes gazed at him, gaping and muddle-headed, he pointed a finger to the corpses, and added with a shudder this single but electric remark, one which came very surely from a profound experience, an eternal recognition of the vitality, the *Honour* of the Third Estate:

'They will prove . . . that it was us . . .'

SOURCE: Villiers de l'Isle Adam, 'Les Brigands', in *Contes Cruels* (Paris, 1883); translated by Hamish Miles as 'The Brigands', in *Sardonic Tales* (New York and London, 1927).

2. POETRY

H. G. Widdowson   The Conditional Presence of Larkin's Mr Bleaney   (1982)

Imagined medieval monsters like the basilisk were weird and wonderful because they were in part familiar and commonplace. The basilisk, or cockatrice, was part reptile and part domestic fowl, and it had a mysterious effect on men. Metaphors can be thought of as monsters of a linguistic kind created from the elements of ordinary language. They also have a mysterious, if less fatal, effect. We are accustomed to thinking of metaphors as composed of lexical parts. What I propose to do in this paper is to consider hybrids of a syntactic kind which have the same effect of estrangement and oblige us to see a new significance in ordinary language and everyday experience. I shall take as my text a poem by Philip Larkin called 'Mr Bleaney'. My argument will be that an appreciation of this poem depends, in some degree at least, on an understanding of the peculiarities of certain grammatical features. These have to do with person, tense and the conditional clause. Here is the poem:

MR BLEANEY

'This was Mr Bleaney's room. He stayed
The whole time he was at the Bodies, till
They moved him.' Flowered curtains, thin and frayed,
Fall to within five inches of the sill,

Whose window shows a strip of building land,   5
Tussocky, littered. 'Mr Bleaney took
My bit of garden properly in hand.'
Bed, upright chair, sixty-watt bulb, no hook

Behind the door, no room for books or bags –
'I'll take it.' So it happens that I lie   10
Where Mr Bleaney lay, and stub my fags
On the same saucer-souvenir, and try

Stuffing my ears with cotton-wool, to drown
The jabbering set he egged her on to buy.
I know his habits – what time he came down,   15
His preference for sauce to gravy, why

He kept on plugging at the four aways –
Likewise their yearly frame: the Frinton folk
Who put him up for summer holidays,
And Christmas at his sister's house in Stoke.   20

But if he stood and watched the frigid wind
Tousling the clouds, lay on the fusty bed
Telling himself that this was home, and grinned,
And shivered, without shaking off the dread

That how we live measures our own nature,   25
And at his age having no more to show
Than one hired box should make him pretty sure
He warranted no better, I don't know.

The first thing to notice is that two scenes are presented here which
have the same spatial setting, in that they both occur in Mr Bleaney's
room, but distinct temporal settings. The first scene involves two
characters: the landlady and the new lodger. It is presented in
theatrical mode with dialogue and description of décor: the flowered
curtains and the window with a view of building land appear like
stage scenery. The second scene, which begins in the second half of
line 10, involves only the lodger. Or so it seems at first sight. Later in
the discussions we shall find that we need to revise this view.
Meanwhile, let us note that although the two scenes represent
different occasions, they both apparently take place in the present:

> . . . Flowered curtains, thin and frayed
> *Fall* to within five inches of the sill,
>
> Whose window *shows*. . . .   (Scene 1)
>
> So it *happens* that I *lie*
> . . . and stub my fags   (Scene 2)

Thus, the first person, whose point of view informs the poem as a
whole (the new lodger) is simultaneously present, in both a temporal
and spatial sense, in two different periods of time.

But he is also present in two different ways. As I have indicated, the
first scene is theatrically described and, although the lodger appears
in it, it is presented in terms of his detached observations. In this sense
he is apart from the scene. In the second scene, on the other hand, he
is a part of it, and now the present tense is used to describe not his
observations but his actions. His role shifts from onlooker to
participant. So, although the two scenes share the same spatial
setting, the first-person lodger's relationship with the setting is
different in each case.

I have spoken of two characters: the landlady and the new lodger. There is another character of course: the previous lodger, Mr Bleaney himself. Unlike the others, he is a third-person figure, and furthermore never actually appears in the present. Everything about him is reported in the simple past tense, in both scenes. Thus, his existence is associated with the same spatial setting as the two scenes presented in the poem, but his temporal setting is in the past. Or is it? For just as the present lodger appears in the present in two different ways in the two scenes, so the previous lodger appears in the past in two different ways. In the first scene, reference to him occurs exclusively in the landlady's direct speech, and for the prospective lodger, therefore, his actions are to be noted in detachment, like the details of the room. He is, as it were, part of the scenery. In the second scene, on the other hand, reference to Mr Bleaney and his activities is made by the new lodger in relation to his own activities. Mr Bleaney has come into the reality of the new lodger's own present life. He is associated now with the physical props of the setting with which the lodger is now fully engaged as a participant:

> . . . So it happens that I lie
> Where Mr Bleaney lay, and stub my fags
> On the same saucer-souvenir, and try
>
> Stuffing my ears with cotton-wool, to drown
> The jabbering set he egged her on to buy.

In the first scene, then, the physical setting and Mr Bleaney, though described in the present and past tense respectively, are alike in being dissociated from the lodger, the detached observer. In the second scene, the past existence of Mr Bleaney converges with the present existence of the person replacing him; and aspects of the physical setting (the saucer-souvenir, the jabbering radio set) are a focus of this convergence. First and third persons, present and past time, so clearly distinct in the first scene, become fused in the second. The first-person present of the new lodger merges with the third-person past of the previous one. Mr Bleaney, though not present, is nevertheless a presence in the second scene of the poem.

The consequence of this convergence of person and time reference is worked out in the last two stanzas. And here we come to the significance of the conditional clause. Up to line 20, the syntax of the poem is simple enough and easy to process: it realises a serial presentation of observations about Mr Bleaney and his room. Up to this point, the new lodger still retains his detachment to some degree, expressed in ironic undertones, even though Mr Bleaney has begun to encroach on his individual identity. The syntax of the last two stanzas, however, is complicated in the extreme. And as the syntax changes so does the attitude expressed. These two stanzas consist of one complex sentence whose completion is deferred by one syntactic elaboration after another until the very last three words of the poem. This sentence begins with what appears to be a conditional clause:

> But if he stood and watched the frigid wind. . . .

But *is* it a conditional clause? The initial *if* seems to indicate that it is. On the other hand, there are other facts we must note that indicate that it is not.

If clauses in English are not necessarily adverbial. They can also be nominal. Consider the following examples:

(1) If he stood here, he would see the clouds.
(2) I do not know if he stood here and saw the clouds.

In the first of these sentences, the *if* clause is adverbial, but in the second it is nominal, functioning as object. Hence *if* can be replaced by *whether* in the second sentence but not in the first. Compare:

(3) *Whether he stood here, he would see the clouds.
(4) I do not know whether he stood here and saw the clouds.

There are other features which distinguish the two types of *if* clause and which have a direct bearing on the convergence of person and time that I have referred to. First, the normal, or unmarked, order of appearance relative to the other constituents of the sentence is different in each case. Thus, although the adverbial may precede or follow the main clause, the nominal must normally follow subject and verb to complete the main-clause structure of which it is an intrinsic part. Thus, the following, as an alternative version of sentence 2, exhibits a marked and so abnormal ordering:

(5) *If he stood here and saw the clouds I do not know.

Such a sentence presents us with an interpretative problem. On the one hand, the fronting of the *if* clause disposes us to think of it as an adverbial but, on the other hand, the normal transitivity of the verb *know* leads us to interpret the clause as its object and the sentence, therefore, as a version of sentence 2. In other words, sequence inclines us to understand the *if* clause as adverbial but structure inclines us to understand it as nominal.

And so it is with the *if* clause of the last two stanzas of this poem. We begin by assuming that it is an adverbial clause of condition since it occurs initially, and we therefore expect the main clause to appear quite promptly afterwards. This appearance is delayed by a prolonged elaboration of the conditional clause itself, and our expectation is dulled by this intervening elaboration which seems to increase in obscurity and inconsequence as it develops. Then comes the main clause to provide the necessary syntactic completion, and it takes us by surprise because it requires us to recategorise everything that has preceded as a nominal clause, a displaced object of the verb *know*. This has the effect of making us reconsider the structure of the syntax and of directing our attention to what is actually being said in the meandering phrases that precede. By initially interpreting the *if* clause as an adverbial we necessarily assign it subsidiary status. But this is inconsistent with the elaboration, which provides more and more information and so approximates more and more to the function of a main clause. The effect of this is that the reader initially assumes a pitch pattern appropriate to a subsidiary clause, and then, as information builds up, he either attempts to contain it within one tone group, which results in a dull monotone tailing off into inconsequence, or he varies the pattern to give independent value to the units of information as if they had main-clause status. The reader, faced with this difficulty, really does not know where he is.

But neither does the lodger. The syntactic complexity is a direct expression of his own confusion, a confusion which has its origins in the convergence of person and time in the earlier lines. This is further borne out by another distinction between adverbial and nominal *if* clauses that has yet to be mentioned. It has to do with the value of the past tense in such constructions. In the case of the nominal clause, as exemplified by sentence 2, the simple past tense is used to make reference to a possible event in past time. This event may or may not have taken place, but the temporal context is firmly fixed in the past. With the adverbial clause, however, matters are somewhat different. In this case, the past tense may be associated either with a temporal context in the past or with a temporal context in the present. Compare sentence 1 with sentence 6:

   (1) If he stood here, he would see the clouds.

   (6) If he stood here, he would have seen the clouds.

The utterance of sentence 1 expresses the hypothetical possibility of the third person appearing in the present: it refers to a state of affairs alternative to that which actually obtains. Sentence 6, on the other hand, refers to a possible state of affairs in the past. Since in the poem there is no indication in a main clause as to which of these values for the past tense is intended, the ambiguity remains unresolved. We do not know as we read through these last two stanzas whether reference is being made to a possible state of affairs in the past or in the present. We do not know whether the past tense in the expression *lay on the fusty bed* [22] has the same value as the expression *Where Mr Bleaney lay* [11] or whether it does not rather serve to invoke Mr Bleaney's presence, and so to fuse his identity with that of his successor. For, although all the activities referred to in the last two stanzas are, by virtue of the *if* clause, represented as hypothetical activities of Mr Bleaney, as phrase follows phrase the reader recognises that what is being expressed are the present lodger's own actual experiences, for why else would he be led to wonder whether Mr Bleaney underwent them?

The *if* clause, then, is in this poem a syntactic hybrid: part adverbial and part nominal. If we read it, in retrospect, by reference to normal structure, we derive something like the following meaning:

> I do not know whether Mr Bleaney stood and watched the frigid wind tousling the clouds, etc.

And this sets up a parallel with what is expressed in lines 15ff. Thus

> I *know* his habits – what time he came down,
> His preference for sauce to gravy, why   etc.

contrasts with

> But if he stood and watched . . .
>   . . .   I *don't* know.

If we read the last verses by reference to sequence, however, retain our adverbial interpretation and ignore the normal structural implications of the last three words, then these words themselves constitute an independent main clause with *know* as an intransitive verb requiring no object: 'I don't know.'

This is an expression of resignation to a general state of unknowing, a failure to understand. It is as if the complexity of the preceding lines, after the simple detachment of the earlier parts of the poem, creates a confusion which cannot be resolved. There are, then, two possible ways of interpreting this clause, but it is not a matter of choosing one and rejecting the other. They co-exist. The clause is both adverbial and nominal, and so neither, a newly created syntactic metaphor devised to express precisely a confusion of thought and attitude which could not be otherwise expressed. The meaning depends on the ambiguity remaining unresolved.

I have tried to show how this poem moves from confident detachment to confused involvement, and how this development is mediated through certain peculiarities of language use. The normally distinct categories of first and third person conflate so that the identity of Mr Bleaney is superimposed on that of the present lodger. They begin by occupying different worlds, one in the past and the other in the present, but end up in the same world, both occupants of Mr Bleaney's room. This is a world which is both past and present, both actual and hypothetical, both experienced and observed. Such a world is not one which is given sanction by normal language usage, and so the poet has to create it by devising new linguistic categories which must of their nature be intrinsically ambiguous. In this way he can directly represent a reality in a different dimension from that which is recorded by convention. And this is where the basilisk and Mr Bleaney have their being.

SOURCE: essay, 'The Conditional Presence of Mr Bleaney', in Ronald Carter (ed.), *Language and Literature: An Introductory Reader in Stylistics* (London, 1982), pp. 19–25.

Bernard Sharratt   'On George Herbert's "Prayer (1)"'   (1984)

. . . The first essay* – which I will consider in some detail – worries away at a short poem by George Herbert that I have always regarded as pleasing and harmless; it is entitled 'Prayer (1)' in Hutchinson's sadly superseded edition:

> Prayer the Churches banquet, Angels age,
>   Gods breath in man returning to his birth,
>   The soul in paraphrase, heart in pilgrimage,
> The Christian plummet sounding heav'n and earth;
> Engine against th'Almightie, sinners towre,
>   Reversèd thunder, Christ-side-piercing spear,
>   The six-daies world transposing in an houre,
> A kinde of tune, which all things heare and fear;
> Softnesse, and peace, and joy, and love, and blisse,
>   Exalted Manna, gladnesse of the best,
>   Heaven in ordinarie, man well drest,
> The milkie way, the bird of Paradise,
>   Church-bels beyond the starres heard, the souls bloud.
>   The land of spices; something understood.

---

* [Ed.] The essay and the reading discussed here have no material existence outside the pages of this essay which *may* therefore be taken as a reading of the poem in its own right.

For Dr Andrews there lurks in that last phrase, 'something understood', a deep and devious device, the import of which is that the poem itself is something *not* understood. Not at first glance, mind; it is only after devoted critical attention that the poem ceases to be understood. (A sad paradigm perhaps of fashionable critical practices?) As Dr Andrews takes us through the peom in detail (twice), those apparently lucid analogues dissolve into grammatical ambiguities (line 2: 'his' birth as man's or as 'its'?), directional uncertainties (line 4: do plummets go down or up?), and metaphysical conundra (line 1: how old are angels?). Even more drastically, prayer becomes a kind of blasphemy (a siege-engine assaulting God, a new Babel, a Jovian thunderbolt hurled back to heaven, a jab into the dead Saviour's side) – though some of these disrespectful suggestions can be theologically redeemed by appropriate exegetical effort (the spear in John XIX releases sacramental succour in eucharistic blood and baptismal water) or by appeal to seventeenth-century emblem books (where prayers are already arrows shot into the very eye of God). Other lines are revealed as quivering with multiple associations ('Heaven in ordinarie' yields at least five distinct senses), or as too bafflingly simple to delineate any properly illuminating 'definition' of prayer (line 9 suffers from this); while still others defeat our best attempts at clarity [7] or at apropriate interpretation (the phrase 'and fear' [8] proves intractable). Penultimately, we are taken into a mysteriously impermeable, even mystical, region of meaning as we try to attach some specific sense to prayer 'as' the milky way, bird of paradise or land of spices; even with the footnoted help of seventeenth-century astronomers, ornithologists and cartographers, Dr Andrews confesses, gladly, to a definite impenetrability in these closing images – which he then claims as reinforcing his insistence that the closing phrase 'something understood' is an even more bafflingly opaque conclusion.

His point is, perversely, that in attempting to 'understand' these preceding images the reader is brought to an awareness of the weirdness, the slippery difficulty, the peculiar oddness of that very process we call 'understanding': are we *sure* that we have 'understood' even one of these phrases fully, adequately, appropriately? Even more, do we know (and if so *how* do we know?) that we have 'understood' what is constituted by this total combination of compact images? At the end of our analysis do we any better 'understand' what 'prayer' *is*? At this point Dr Andrews' analytical screw tightens: to understand the poem fully we would finally have to understand the final phrase 'something understood' and to do what we would have to understand what understanding is. And, as Dr Andrews legitimately, but a shade maliciously, reminds us in an extended footnote to this chapter, *that* task preoccupied and, arguably, defeated seventeenth-century philosophers from Descartes – whose *Discourse on Method* was published only four years after Herbert's *Temple* – to Locke, whose *Essay Concerning Human Understanding* closed the century on a note of common sense and therefore uncertain optimism.

So far, I find this critical exercise rather enchanting, though to some extent derivative, but Dr Andrews then takes a sharp step further, into the more rarified air of linguistic (or is it logical?) philosophy and offers us an exhausting analysis of the logical (or is it linguistic?) paradoxes of the term 'understanding'. I can only grope after him here, but he seems to conclude, first, that since *complete* understanding of anything involves understanding *everything*, only God (if s/he exists) could claim that 'something' was, for her/him, 'understood', so only God could be said truly to pray (an odd but also biblical conclusion: consider Romans VIII: 26); and secondly, or conversely, that if prayer *is* 'something understood' then to understand this poem would be to pray it, to read it 'as' a prayer. In my admittedly amateur response to this logicolinguistic disquisition, I must confess to thinking that Dr Andrews has actually *mis*understood his own conclusion here, as well as playing some rather shifty games with the word 'something' (which one can, in fact, understand quite well in the seventeenth-century sense of 'partial'). Albeit, he concludes that the serious reader of this poem is finally faced with a dilemma (he calls it a 'double-bind', utilising a term from Gregory Bateson): either the reader tries to understand the poem as a *definition* of prayer, but this involves the impossible or paradoxical task of understanding understanding and therefore the reader can never understand what prayer is, even though the poem ostensibly sets out to tell us what prayer is; or, the reader *gives up* trying to understand the poem and therefore, if he continues trying to read the poem at all, opts for trying to read it '*as*' a *prayer* – even though he has by now acknowledged that he doesn't understand what prayer is, in other words doesn't understand what it is he's attempting to do in 'praying'.

It is here that Dr Andrews finally locates, and pounces upon, what he calls the 'conversion tactic' of the poem. He sees the reader of the poem as having been brought to the point of jettisoning his 'understanding' in favour of a 'belief' (a belief which takes the form, however provisional, of attempting to 'pray'), and that 'belief' is, fundamentally, an acquiescence to an *authority*, the authority of the poem itself. By that he means – to put it over-concisely perhaps – that the title changes its significance for the reader: we took it to indicate that the poem offered a definition of prayer, now we accept it as indicating that this poem *is* itself a prayer; if we accept the title in that latter sense all we can do with the poem is attempt to pray it, not even understanding what it is we are doing but, to pun mildly, simply accepting Herbert's word for it.

Of course, the trap doesn't quite close on us: we needn't read the poem at all, or we could (try to) read it 'simply as a poem'. Rather curiously for a literary critic, the stern Dr Andrews rejects this latter option as a weak-minded 'liberal' position, a gesture typical of twentieth-century indifferentism (he clearly has Dante's antechamber in mind). Instead he urges upon us the 'radical' response of demolishing the poem (he calls it, in a quaintly faded idiom, 'deconstructing'), by analysing the 'ideologic' underpinning the very possibility of prayer in order to conclude (predictably) that 'prayer' (both the poem and the act) *can't* finally be 'understood' at all, since its intelligibility rests upon the ultimately *unintelligible* premise of there being a God to pray (to) in the first place.

This rejection of the so-called 'liberal' literary critic's approach is far too off-hand, in my view, and I will return to it, but at least this first chapter has effected part of its aim: I now admit that Herbert's poem does have a twist in its tail that I hadn't previously been fully alert to, though it may gladden Dr Andrews' rather cold heart to know that I don't fully understand that twist even now. Looking back at the poem again, for example, I recognise that in all my previous readings that marvellous phrase 'Angels age' had been registered by me as an ambiguous paradox, with perhaps three possible meanings – but I am unable to decide which meaning I actually 'understand' *as* I read the poem. In practice, I leave all three hovering, if only because I know that I don't really understand the notion of 'angel', let alone the problem of how angels can have time in their lives – even if praying is, for them, having the time of their lives. . . .

SOURCE: extract from *The Literary Labyrinth: Contemporary Critical Discourses* (Brighton, 1984), pp. 35–8.

3. DRAMA

Jacques Lacan   On *Hamlet*   (1959)

. . . The tragedy *Hamlet* is the tragedy of desire. But . . . it is time to notice what one always takes note of last, i.e., what is most obvious. I know of no commentator who has ever taken the trouble to make this remark, however hard it is to overlook once it has been formulated: from one end of *Hamlet* to the other, all anyone talks about is mourning.

Mourning is what makes the marriage of Hamlet's mother so scandalous. In her eagerness to know the cause of her beloved son's 'distemper', she herself says: 'I doubt it is no other but the main, / His father's death and our o'erhasty marriage.' And there's no need to remind you of what Hamlet says about the leftovers from 'the funeral baked meats' turning up on 'the marriage tables': 'Thrift, thrift, Horatio.' . . .

Nor can we fail to be struck by the fact that in all the instances of mourning in *Hamlet*, one element is always present: the rites have been cut short and performed in secret.

For political reasons, Polonius is buried secretly, without ceremony, posthaste. And you remember the whole business of Ophelia's burial. There is the discussion of how it is that Ophelia, having most probably committed suicide – this is at least the common belief – still is buried on Christian ground. The gravediggers have no doubt that if she had not been of such high social standing she would have been treated differently. Nor is the priest in favor of giving her Christian burial ('She should in ground unsanctified have lodged / Till the last trumpet. For charitable prayers, / Shards, flints, and pebbles should be thrown on her' [v i]) and the rites to which he has consented are themselves abbreviated.

We cannot fail to take all these things into account, and there are many others as well.

The ghost of Hamlet's father has an inexpiable grievance. He was, he says, eternally wronged, having been taken unawares – and this is not one of the lesser mysteries as to the meaning of this tragedy – 'in the blossoms of [his] sin'. He had no time before his death to summon up the composure or whatever that would have prepared him to go before the throne of judgement.

Here we have a number of 'clues', as they say in English, which converge in a most significant way – and where do they point? To the relationship of the drama of desire to mourning and its demands.

This is the point I would like to focus on today, in an attempt to delve into the question of the object such as we encounter it in psychoanalysis – the object of desire.

There is first of all a simple relationship that the subject has to the object of desire, a relationship that I have expressed in terms of an appointment. But you will not have failed to notice that we are approaching the question of the object from quite a different angle when we speak of the object such as the subject identifies himself with it in mourning – the subject, it is said, can reintegrate the object into his ego. What does that mean? Aren't we dealing here with two phases which are not reconciled in psychoanalytic theory? Doesn't this call for an attempt to get deeper into the problem?

What I have just said about mourning in *Hamlet* must not obscure the fact that at the bottom of this mourning, in *Hamlet* as in *Oedipus*, there is a crime. Up to a certain point, the whole rapid succession, one instance of mourning after another, can be seen as consequences of the initial crime. It is in this sense that *Hamlet* is an Oedipal drama, one that we can read as a second *Oedipus Rex* and locate at the same functional level in the genealogy of tragedy. This is also what put Freud, and his disciples after him, onto the importance of *Hamlet*. . . .

It is not without interest to take note of the dissymmetries between the tragedy of Oedipus and the tragedy of Hamlet. It would be too elaborate an exercise to list them in detail, but I shall nevertheless give you a few indications.

In *Oedipus*, the crime takes place at the level of the hero's own generation; in *Hamlet*, it has already taken place at the level of the preceding generation. In *Oedipus*, the hero, not knowing what he's doing, is in some way guided by fate; in *Hamlet*, the crime is carried out deliberately.

The crime in *Hamlet* is the result of betrayal. Hamlet's father is taken by surprise in his sleep, in a way that is utterly foreign to the current of his waking thoughts. 'I was cut off', he says, 'even in the blossoms of my sin.' He is struck by a blow from a sector from which he does not expect it, a true intrusion of the real, a break in the thread of destiny. He dies, as Shakespeare's text tells us, on a bed of flowers, which the play-scene will go so far as to reproduce in the opening pantomime.

The sudden intrusion of the crime is somehow, paradoxically, compensated for by the fact that in this case the subject *knows*. This is not one of the less puzzling aspects of the play. The drama of Hamlet, unlike that of Oedipus, does not start off with the question 'What's going on?', 'Where is the crime?', 'Where is the criminal?' It begins with the denunciation of the crime, with the crime as it is brought to light in the ear of the subject. . . .

. . . Hamlet's father is barred not only from the world of the living but also from his just retribution. He has entered the kingdom of hell with this crime, this debt that he has not been able to pay, an inexpiable debt, he says. And indeed, this is for his son the most frightening implication of his revelation.

Oedipus paid. He represents the man whose heroic lot is to carry the burden of requited debt. On the contrary, Hamlet's father must complain for all eternity that he was interrupted, taken by surprise, cut off in midstream – that to him the possibility of response, of retribution, is forever sealed off.

You see that our investigation, as it moves along, leads us to ask questions about retribution and punishment. . . .

Freud himself indicated, perhaps in a somewhat *fin de siècle* way, that for some reason when we lived out the Oedipal drama, it was destined to be in a warped form, and there's surely an echo of that in *Hamlet*.

Consider one of Hamlet's first exclamations at the end of the first act: 'The time is out of joint. O cursèd spite / That ever I was born to set it right!' 'O cursèd . . .' – the word 'spite', which appears throughout Shakespeare's sonnets, can only be translated '*dépit*', grudge, vexation – 'he did it out of pure spite'. But let's be careful here. To understand the Elizabethans one must first turn certain words around on their hinges so as to give them a meaning somewhere between the subjective one and the objective one. Today the word 'spite' – as in 'he did it out of pure spite' – has a subjective meaning, whereas in 'O cursèd spite' it's somewhere in between, between the experience of the subject and the injustice in the world. We seem to have lost the sense of this reference to the world order. 'O cursèd spite' is what Hamlet feels spiteful toward and also the way that the time is injust to him. Perhaps you recognise here in passing, transcended by Shakespeare's vocabulary, the delusion of the *schöne Seele*,[1] from which we have not escaped, far from it, all our efforts notwithstanding. . . .

SOURCE: extracts from Lacan's essay 'On *Hamlet*', reproduced in Shoshana Felman (ed.), *Literature and Psychoanalysis* (Baltimore, 1982), excerpted from pp. 39–45. The French text is edited by Jacques Alain Miller from transcripts of Lacan's seminar, and translated by James Hulbert.

NOTE

1. Allusion to Hegel's dialectic of the withdrawn, contemplative 'beautiful soul' which . . . denounces the perceived disorder of the world around him without recognising that this disorder is a reflection of his own inner state.

Lisa Jardine *The Duchess of Malfi*: A Case Study in the Literary Representation of Women (1983)

The Jacobean drama has regularly attracted the attention of critics for its lively representation of women as strong, manipulative, self-willed, passionate and controlling of dramatic action. This 'masculine strength' wins the acclaim of the critic for its authenticity, and for its real insight into woman's character. It is the mark of the superior vision of the Jacobean dramatist: he sees beyond the contemporary stereotypes of meek and grieving womanhood to the 'true nature of woman' – to a full-bloodedly warrior-like femaleness to which the Renaissance for the first time gave a voice. . . . The suggestion that the Duchess is a faithful portrait of possible womanhood in the early seventeenth-century, or even dramatic projections of a kind of female outlook lurking beneath the calm surface of the Jacobean world, is puzzling, and in my view misleading. The rapidly growing body of information we can gather from non-literary sources, both of woman's actual position in early modern society and of contemporary attitudes towards her, is striking for the consistent picture it gives of the *absence* of emancipation of women, both at a theoretical and at a practical level.[1] Where, then, do the strong female characters who wheel-and-deal their way through the drama come from? . . .

In this essay I shall be looking at the impression of strength in the Jacobean female hero in one play, John Webster's *The Duchess of Malfi*, and offering tentative answers to these questions.[2] I shall be suggesting that the 'psychological insight' of the Jacobean dramatists' representations of women is related to actual seventeenth-century women and their roles in an unexpected way, and one which must give us pause for thought in our wider exploration of the literary representation of women. This is, if you like, a cautionary tale, and a direct challenge to those who suggest that the vision of the well-intentioned dramatist (be he Shakespeare or Webster or Middleton) can transcend the limits of his time and sex in the representation of women.

Let us begin by trying to identify some of the features of female characterisation which lead the critics to refer to them as 'strong' in the first place, and as admirable in that strength. Passion, sensuality, courage, intelligence, cunning, ambition – All these qualities are at various times shown by the Duchess. They add up to such forcefulness and spirited independence that generations of audiences have been seduced into accepting them as part of a consistent and believable female heroic persona. . . .

The female hero moves in an exclusively masculine stage-world, in which it is the task of the male characters to 'read' her. Is she what she appears? 'Look to't: be not cunning: / For they whose faces do belie their hearts / Are witches, ere they arrive at twenty years – / Ay: and give the devil suck' [I i 308–11]. Shakespeare's 'strong' women find themselves in a similarly male world: Gertrude in *Hamlet* (and her reflection in Ophelia), Desdemona in *Othello* (more manipulated than manipulating), Cleopatra in *Antony and Cleopatra*.

So when the critic tells us that the Jacobean dramatist shows peculiar insight into female character, and even into female psychology, what he or she means is that a convincing portrayal is given *from a distinctively male viewpoint* (even if this is not made explicit by the critic). . . . The strength of the female protagonist is seen through male eyes.

It is seen through male eyes, and as such it is dramatically compelling. But the female character traits to which the critics give this enthusiastic support are on inspection morally dubious: cunning, duplicity, sexual rapaciousness, 'changeableness', being other than they seem, untrustworthiness and general secretiveness. In *The Duchess of Malfi*, the first entrance of the Duchess is in an atmosphere fraught with explicitly offensive sexual innuendo, in which she is implicated, and which controls our assessment of her character:

> FERD.:   You are a widow:
>   You know already what man is, and therefore
>   Let not youth, high promotion, eloquence –
> CARD.:   No, nor anything without the addition, honour,
>   Sway your high blood.
> FERD.:   Marry! they are most luxurious [lust-
>   Will wed twice.   ful]
>   . . .

DUCH: Will you hear me?
   I'll never marry: –
CARD.:   So most widows say:
   But commonly that motion lasts no longer
   Than the turning of an hour-glass – the funeral sermon
   And it, end both together.   [1 i 293–304]

A handful of speeches later the sexual innuendo comes to a climax, and the Duchess reveals the accuracy of her brothers' predictions (confirming their dark travesty of female lasciviousness and 'doubleness') simultaneously:

FERD.:   You are my sister –
   This was my father's poinard: do you see?
   I'd be loth to see't rusty, 'cause 'twas his: –
   A visor and a mask are whispering-rooms
   That were ne'er built for goodness: fare ye well –
   And women like that part which, like the lamprey,
   Hath ne'er a bone in't.
DUCH.:   Fie sir!
FERD.:   Nay,
   I mean the tongue: variety of courtship
   . . .
   What cannot a neat knave with a smooth tale
   Make a woman believe? Farewell lusty widow.   [*Exit*]
DUCH.:   Shall this move me? If all my royal kindred
   Lay in my way unto this marriage,
   I'd make them my low footsteps   [1 i 330–43]

The picture of stereotyped female virtue painted in advance of her appearance by the Duchess's infatuated servant (and subsequent husband) Antonio cannot compensate for the impact of this initial encounter: 'I'll case the picture up. . . . / All her particular worth grows to this sum: / She stains the time past, lights the time to come' [1 i 207–9]. The Duchess's 'luxuriousness' (lustfulness) drives her powerfully into secret marriage and flouting of her brothers' wishes, just as Gertrude's sexuality, in *Hamlet*, drives her into her dead husband's brother's bed. Lower in her sexual drive than 'a beast that wants discourse of reason', the Duchess of Malfi steps out of the path of duty and marries for lust. Thereafter she remains heroically determined to follow through the consequences of her initial base action, until her resoluteness is gradually commuted into the splendour of resigned passive acceptance of inevitable downfall:

FERD.:   How doth our sister duchess bear herself
In her imprisonment?
BOSO.:   Nobly; I'll describe her:
She's sad, as one long us'd to't; and she seems
Rather to welcome the end of misery
Than shun it; – a behaviour so noble
As gives a majesty to adversity;
You may discern the shape of loveliness
More perfect in her tears, than in her smiles.   [IV i 1–8]

'Majesty' in the female hero is here at its most reassuring and admirable when associated with patient suffering: Griselda, the Virgin Mary, Hecuba prostrate with grief. A 'convincing' representation of the developing psychology of the female hero is apparently the transformation of lascivious waywardness into emblematic chaste resignation.[3] . . .

In the dramatic version of *The Duchess of Malfi*, active sexuality codes for female breach of decorum. In the moment of disobeying her brothers and remarrying (remarrying a social inferior, to emphasise that this is 'lust' not 'duty'), the Duchess of Malfi asserts her sexual self. In so doing she is metamorphosed from ideal mirror of virtue ('Let all sweet ladies break their flatt'ring glasses / And dress themselves in her' [I i 203–4]) into lascivious whore. It is not simply that her brothers view her as such; the dominant strain in the subsequent representation of her *is* such. And we have to ask ourselves what it is about that knowing step she takes which is sufficient to rock the social system and warrant such ritualised condemnation. From the moment of her assertion of sexual independence, the Duchess moves with dignity but inexorably towards a ritual chastisement worthy of a flagrant breach of public order. Thereafter her strength lies in her fortitude in the face of a doom she has brought upon herself.

Yet the initial stand taken by the Duchess retains its dramatic power, despite the fact that success is apparently never a real possibility, the threat to patriarchal order never an actual one. I want now to suggest that there was an early modern social order in which *apparently*, although not actually, women had become frighteningly strong and independent, and one which maps plausibly on to the dominant preoccupations of the drama. This is the idea of property inheritance and Land Law.

The sixteenth century in England was a period of major and far-reaching change in inheritance practice. Unfortunately, these changes are masked from the student of literature by blanket references, whenever some comment on customary inheritance is called for, to a ubiquitous law of primogeniture (inheritance of the entire estate by the eldest male heir). Immediately he has introduced his bastard son, Edmund, to Kent, in *King Lear*, Gloucester specifies his family position:

But I have a son, sir, by order of law, some year elder than this, who yet is no dearer in my account: though this knave came something saucily to the world before he was sent for, yet was his mother fair.   [I i 17–20]

This we are told is to establish that Edgar is Gloucester's legitimate *heir* as well as his legitimate son, since either way he is *older* than Edmund. Lear himself, meanwhile, divides his kingdom by 'partible' inheritance (equal division) among his daughters, in the absence of a male heir. Certainly by the sixteenth century this was considered to be the ideal state of affairs, as codified in English Land Law, but as recent historians and historians of the Land Law themselves are quick to point out, inheritance *practice* never conformed with the ideal, and consisted in modifying and evading the most stringent requirements of lineal inheritance as codified, because of disastrous consequences this could in practice have in fragmenting individual estates.[4]

During the sixteenth and seventeenth centuries, great landowners, under direct threat from wealthy status-seeking burghers, tinkered energetically with legislation and precedent in a determined effort to keep their dwindling estates together. The issue, inevitably, came down to a head-on conflict between land (the nobleman's asset) and cash (the increasingly powerful asset of the expanding mercantile class). And at the heart of every 'tinkering' to be found in the meticulously drawn up wills of the nobility and gentry of the period, one is almost certain to find a woman.[5] . . .

The prominent position occupied by·female heirs in all this discussion of the complex tactical manoeuvres surrounding inheritance is in striking contrast to their enforced submissiveness elsewhere within the Elizabethan and Jacobean social systems. This fact is, of course, somewhat ironic. It was not the intention of lawyers and landowners preoccupied with patrilinear succession to involve their women as other than means to a patriarchal end. But it remains true that female nobles and gentry do obtrude during this period in their capacity as carriers of inheritance.

Not that this gave them any *actual* power, and this is really the point at issue. They are technically strong (or strong enough to cause patriarchal anxiety), but actually in thrall. . . .

The Duchess acts out her remarriage and its consequences *as if* her forcefulness as royal heir, dowager of the Dukedom of Amalfi, carrier of a substantial dowry in movable goods (which she and Antonio take legitimately with them when they flee together), gave her *real* power. . . .

Proved pathetically wrong in her belief in emancipation through hereditary strength, the Duchess is reduced to the safe composite stereotype of penitent whore, Virgin majestic in grief, serving mother, and patient and true turtle dove mourning her one love. The Duchess acts out on stage her inheritance power which in real life was no power at all for the individual woman. . . . In Webster's play, the spectre of real female strength implicit in the inheritance structure is ritually exorcised. Headstrong, emancipated female love is chastened into figurative submission.

SOURCE: extracts from Jardine's essay on *The Duchess of Malfi*, in Susanne Kappeler & Norman Bryson (eds), *Teaching the Text* (London, 1983), excerpted from pp. 203–16.

NOTES

[Reorganised and renumbered from the original – Ed.]

1. For a full documentation on this and all other historical material used in this essay, see L. Jardine, *Still Harping on Daughters: Women and Drama in the Age of Shakespeare* (Brighton, 1983).

2. All references to *The Duchess of Malfi* are to the Revels Plays edition, edited by J. R. Brown (London, 1964).

3. On emblematic chastity, see Marina Warner, *Alone of All Her Sex: The Myth and the Cult of the Virgin Mary* (London, 1978), pp. 81–120.

4. For a lucid account of the history of the English Land Law and its modifications in practice, see A. W. B. Simpson, *An Introduction to the History of the Land Law* (Oxford, 1961). I am grateful to Professor Glanville Williams and Mr Peter Glazebrook for their advice on the history of the Land Law.

5. See J. P. Cooper, 'Patterns of Inheritance and Settlement by Great Landowners from the Fifteenth to the Eighteenth Centuries', in J. Goody, J. Thirsk & E. P. Thompson (eds), *Family and Inheritance* (Cambridge, 1976), pp. 192–305. I am extremely grateful to Diane Owen Hughes for referring me to this article.

SELECT BIBLIOGRAPHY

The following works are recommended for further reading on the topics indicated. They have been specially selected as suitable introductory material.

STUDIES EXPRESSING SCEPTICISM ABOUT THE NEW THEORIES

Helen Gardner, *In Defence of the Imagination* (Oxford, 1982).
James Gribble, *Literary Education: A Revaluation* (Cambridge, 1983).
Laurence Lerner (ed.), *Reconstructing Literature* (Oxford, 1983).

STUDIES ON THE NEW THEORIES IN GENERAL

Terry Eagleton, *Literary Theory: An Introduction* (Oxford, 1983).
John Peck & Martin Coyle, *Literary Terms and Criticism: A Student's Guide* (London, 1984).
Ray Selden, *A Reader's Guide to Contemporary Literary Theory* (Brighton, 1985).

STUCTURALISM

David Robey (ed.), *Structuralism: an Introduction* (Oxford, 1973).
Robert Scholes, *Structuralism in Literature: An Introduction* (New Haven, Conn., 1974).
John Sturrock, *Structuralism* (London, 1986).

STYLISTICS

Roger Fowler, *Linguistic Criticism* (Oxford, 1986).
Ronald Carter (ed.), *Language and Literature: An Introductory Reader in Stylistics* (London, 1982).

DECONSTRUCTION AND POST-STRUCTURALISM

Christopher Norris, *Deconstruction: Theory and Practice* (London, 1982).

READER-RESPONSE CRITICISM

Robert C. Holub, *Reception Theory: A Critical Introduction* (London, 1984).
Steven Mailloux, *Interpretive Conventions: The Reader in the Study of American Fiction* (Ithaca, N.Y., 1982).

FEMINIST CRITICISM

Mary Eagleton (ed.), *Feminist Literary Theory: A Reader* (Oxford, 1986).
K. K. Ruthven, *Feminist Literary Studies* (Cambridge, 1984).
Elaine Showalter (ed.), *The New Feminist Criticism* (London, 1986).

PSYCHOLOGICAL CRITICISM

Elizabeth Wright, *Psychoanalytic Criticism: Theory in Practice* (London, 1984).

MARXIST CRITICISM

Terry Eagleton, *Marxism and Literary Criticism* (London, 1976).

THE NEW THEORIES IN PRACTICE

John Drakakis (ed.), *Alternative Shakespeares* (London, 1985).
David Lodge, *Working With Structuralism* (London, 1981).
Douglas Tallack (ed.) *Literary Theory at Work: Three Texts* (London, 1987)

The series 'Rereading Literature', published by Basil Blackwell (Oxford), intends to apply the new theories to the most widely studied writers. The first batch of titles (1985) includes *Charles Dickens* by Steven Connor. The 'New Readings' series from Harvester Press (Brighton) has the same brief; early titles (1985) include *George Eliot* by Simon Dentith and *T. S. Eliot* by Angus Calder. Harvester also publish a 'Feminist Readings' series which includes *Henry James* by Vivien Jones and *D. H. Lawrence* by Hilary Simpson. Macmillan's series 'Women Writers' offers 'a serious reassessment of women's writing, on its own terms'. Early titles include *Emily Brontë* by Lyn Pykett and *Jane Austen* by Meenakshi Mukherjee.

NOTES ON CONTRIBUTORS

MIKHAIL BAKHTIN (1895–1975): influential Russian critic whose works were only widely published in the 1960s and 70s; a selection of his essays was published in English in 1981 under the title *The Dialogic Imagination.*

ROLAND BARTHES (1915–1980): major French structuralist critic, appointed Professor of Literary Semiology at the Collège de France in 1976. His books include *Mythologies* (Paris, 1957; London 1972), *The Pleasure of the Text* (Paris, 1973; London, 1976) and *Roland Barthes by Roland Barthes* (Paris, 1975; London and Basingstoke, 1977.)

PENNY BOUMELHA: Lecturer in English at the University of Western Australia; *Thomas Hardy and Women* is her first book.

RACHEL M. BROWNSTEIN: Lecturer in English at Brooklyn College; *Becoming a Heroine* is her first book.

JONATHAN CULLER: Professor of English and Comparative Literature at Cornell University; his publications include *Structuralist Poetics* (1975) and *On Deconstruction* (1983).

JONATHAN DOLLIMORE: Lecturer in English at Sussex University. *Radical Tragedy* is his first book.

DENIS DONOGHUE: Irish literary critic; Henry James Professor of Letters at New York University. His publications include studies of Swift and Yeats, and *Ferocious Alphabets* (1981).

T. S. ELIOT (1888–1965): poet, dramatist and literary critic.

LUCETTE FINAS: teaches French Literature at the University of Paris VII. She is the author of three novels and three volumes of critical essays and contributes to *Poésie*, the *Quizaine Littéraire* and the *Nouvelle Revue Française*.

STANLEY FISH: Arts and Sciences Distinguished Professor of English and Law at Duke University, North Carolina. His books include *Self-Consuming Artifacts* (1972) and *Is There a Text in This Class?* (1980)

ROGER FOWLER. Professor of English and Linguistics at the University of East Anglia; his numerous publications include *Languages of Literature* (1971), *Style and Structure in Literature* (1975) and *Understanding Language: Introduction to Linguistics* (1974).

WOLFGANG ISER: German literary critic and a founder of reader-response criticism. Professor of English at the University of Konstanz, his best-known books are *The Implied Reader* (1974) and *The Act of Reading* (1978).

LISA JARDINE: Fellow of Jesus College, Cambridge; her feminist study of renaissance drama, *Still on Harping Daughters* was published in 1983.

L. C. KNIGHTS: Shakespearean critic who has held professorships at Sheffield, Bristol and Cambridge universities. His many publications include *Some Shakespearean Themes* (1959), *Public Voices: Literature and Politics* (1971), *Explorations* (1946), *Further Explorations* (1965) and *Explorations 3* (1976).

JACQUES LACAN (1901–1981): influential French psychologist and post-structuralist theorist, formerly President of the 'Champ Freudien' department, University of Vincennes; *Écrits: a Selection* (1977) is an English translation of his major work.

F. R. LEAVIS (1895–1978): eminent literary critic and educationist.

A. D. NUTTALL: Professor of English at Sussex University; his books include *Overheard by God* (1980) and *A New Mimesis* (1983).

ROBERT SCHOLES: teaches at Brown University; his books include *Structuralism in Literature* (1974) and *Semiotics and Interpretation* (1982).

BERNARD SHARRATT: lecturer in English in the University of Kent at Canterbury; his publications include *Reading Relations* (1982) and *The Literary Labyrinth* (1984).

NICOLAS TREDELL: Associate Editor of the journal *PN Review* and a contributor to the *TLS* and *THES*.

GEORGE WATSON: Fellow of St John's College, Cambridge and University Lecturer in English; books include *The Literary Critics* (1962) and *The Discipline of English* (1978).

VILLIERS DE L'ISLE ADAM, Comte de (1838–89): French poet, novelist and dramatist.

ANNWYL WILLIAMS: Freelance writer, translator and teacher. Currently preparing a book-length collection of critical writings by Lucette Finas.

ACKNOWLEDGEMENTS

The editor and publishers wish to thank the following for permission to use copyright material: Mikhail H. Bakhatin, extracts from essay on *Little Dorrit* from *The Dialogic Imagination: Four Essays*, translated by Caryl Emerson and Michael Holquist, by permission of the University of Texas Press. Copyright ©1981 by the University of Texas Press; Roland Barthes, extract from 'The Death of the Author', *Manteia V*, (1968), by permission of Basil Blackwell Ltd; Penny Boumelha, extracts from *Thomas Hardy and Women: Sexual Ideology and Narrative Form* (1982), by permission of Harvester Press Ltd; Rachel M. Brownstein, extracts from *Becoming a Heroine: Reading about Women in Novels* (1984), by permission of Penguin Books. Copyright © 1982 by Rachel M. Brownstein; Jonathan Culler, extracts from essay 'Jacques Derrida' from *Structuralism and Since*, edited by John Sturrock (1979), by permission of Oxford University Press; Jonathan Dollimore, extracts from *Radical Tragedy* (1984), by permission of Harvester Press Ltd; Denis Donoghue, extracts from *Ferocious Alphabets* (1981) Faber and Faber Ltd (1981), by permission of A. D. Peters on behalf of the author; Terry Eagleton, extract from *Literary Theory: An Introduction* (1983), by permission of Basil Blackwell Ltd; T. S. Eliot, extracts from 'Tradition and the Individual Talent' in *Selected Essays* (1951) by permission of Faber and Faber Ltd; Lucette Finas, essay on 'Les Brigands' from *Le Bruit d'Iris*, translated by Anwyl Williams (1986); Stanley Fish, extracts from 'What is Stylistics and Why are They Saying Such Terrible Things About It? in *Approaches to Poetics*, edited by Seymour Chapman (1973), by permission of Columbia University Press; Roger Fowler, article 'Studying Literature as Language', *Dutch Quarterly Review of Anglo-American Literature* (1984), by permission of the Dutch Quarterly Review; Wolfgang Iser, extracts from 'The Reading Process: A Phenomenological Approach' in his *The Implied Reader: Patterns in Communication in Prose Fiction from Bunyan to Beckett* (1974), by permission of Johns Hopkins University Press; Lisa Jardine, extracts from essay on 'The Duchess of Malfi' in *Teaching the Text*, edited by S. Kappeler and N. Bryson (1983), by permission of Routledge & Kegan Paul plc; L. C. Knights, extracts from essay 'How Many Children Had Lady Macbeth?: An Essay in the Theory and Practice of Shakespeare Criticism' (1933), reprinted in *'Hamlet' and Other*

Shakespearean Essays (1979), by permission of Cambridge University Press; Jacques Lacan, extracts from essay 'On Hamlet', translated by James Hulbert (1959), included in *Literature and Psychoanalysis*, edited by Shoshana Felman (1982), by permission of Johns Hopkins University Press; F. R. Leavis, extracts from 'Literary Criticism and Philosophy: A Reply' in *Scrutiny*, VI (June 1937) and an extract from 'The Responsible Critic' in *Scrutiny*, XIX (1953), by permission of Cambridge University Press; Villiers de L'Isle-Adam, short story *The Brigands* (1883), translated by Hamish Miles in *Sardonic Tales* (1927), by permission of Alfred Knopf Inc; A. D. Nuttall, extract from *A New Mimesis* (1983), Methuen, by permission of Associated Book Publishers Ltd; Robert Scholes, extract from *Semiotics and Interpretation* (1982), by permission of Yale University Press; Bernard Sharratt, extract from *The Literary Labyrinth: Contemporary Critical Discourses* (1984) by permission of Harvester Press Ltd; Nicholas Tredell, unpublished essay 'Euphoria Ltd: The Limitations of Post-Structuralism and Deconstruction'; George Watson, extracts from *The Discipline of English* (1978), Macmillan Publishers Ltd; H. G. Widdowson, essay on 'The Conditional Presence of Mr Bleaney' in *Language and Literature: An Introductory Reading in Stylistics*, edited by Ronald Carter (1982), by permission of Unwin Hyman Ltd; W. K. Wimsatt and Monroe C. Beardsley, extracts from 'The Intentional Fallacy' (1946) reproduced in *The Verbal Icon: Studies in the Meaning of Poetry*, edited by W. K. Wimsatt (1970), Methuen, by permission of Associated Book Publishers Ltd.

Every effort has been made to trace all the copyright holders but if any have been inadvertently overlooked the publishers will be pleased to make the necessary arrangement at the first opportunity.

INDEX

Page numbers in **bold type** denote essays or extracts in this Casebook.